Journey Westward
Joyce, *Dubliners* and the Literary Revival

T0313403

Journey Westward

Joyce, *Dubliners* and the Literary Revival

FRANK SHOVLIN

LIVERPOOL UNIVERSITY PRESS

First published 2012 by
Liverpool University Press
4 Cambridge Street
Liverpool L69 7ZU

This paperback version published 2014

British Library Cataloguing-in-Publication data
A British Library CIP record is available

ISBN 978-1-84631-823-8 *cased*
ISBN 978-1-78138-002-4 *paperback*

Typeset in Calluna by Koinonia, Manchester
Printed and bound by CPI Group (UK) Ltd, Croydon CR0 4YY

For Maura,
from Connacht

Contents

Acknowledgements

I wish to acknowledge the impact of Paul Muldoon's 1998 Clarendon Lectures at the University of Oxford, my attendance at which prompted me to rethink completely the ways in which I read James Joyce and led directly to the writing of this book. For the generous support, without which completion of this book would have proved immeasurably more difficult, I thank the Arts and Humanities Research Council (UK), the British Academy and the University of Liverpool. St John's College, Oxford provided me with a welcome scholarly haven in the summer of 2005. I wish to warmly acknowledge the support of the President and Fellows of the college, with John and Christine Kelly in particular proving most gracious hosts. The Cora Maud Oneal Research Fellowship awarded to me by the Harry Ransom Center, University of Texas at Austin, allowed me to peruse Joyce's Trieste library on a research trip there in the spring of 2010. This book was conceived and went through a long gestation in the great city of Liverpool, and so I am very pleased that it is now being published by Liverpool University Press; I want, in particular, to acknowledge the help of my editor, Anthony Cond. Some versions of what I argue in this book first appeared in the *Joyce Studies Annual* and the *James Joyce Quarterly*.

My students at the Institute of Irish Studies, University of Liverpool, have been the key inspiration for this study. They put up patiently with my doubtless sometimes incoherent reveries on *Dubliners*, and I hope this book goes some way towards crystallizing many impromptu thoughts on Joyce's achievement. I was fortunate to be working closely with a cohort of talented graduate students during the composition of this study and would especially like to mention Niall Carson, Brian Chamberlain, Cathy Davies, Tony Halpen, Ciarán O'Neill, Anna Pilz, Ray Southern, Whitney Standlee and Kieron Winterson. My colleagues at the Institute have always been supportive, and their expert knowledge of differing aspects of Irishness has been a great help to me in thinking about Joyce. Helen Carey, formerly of the *Centre Culturel Irlandais*, Paris, provided me with an important opportunity to present my thoughts on Joyce and Jacobitism on Bloomsday 2006. Similar invitations to speak from the W. B. Yeats and the Merriman summer schools, and from the University of Strathclyde, the University of Manchester, the University of Texas at Austin and the National University of Ireland, Galway prompted me to revise earlier thoughts on Joyce's complex relationship with the Revival and with Irish history.

Tom Paulin read the entire manuscript and his comments were, as always, most judicious. Marianne Elliott, Mike Griffin and John Kenny kindly read sections for me – each strengthened the book. Keith Duggan and George Watson were this project's earliest and most enthusiastic supporters. George's death before its completion remains a source of profound sadness to me. Mark Kennedy walked the battlefield of Aughrim in my company; Enda Leaney argued passionately, and disingenuously, that Joyce was overrated; Patrick O'Sullivan and Seumas Gildea taught me to take whiskey seriously. Others who in various important ways helped to bring my work to fruition and who I wish to thank here are the Curoes of San Antonio, Maria-Daniella Dick, Martin Dyar, David Goldie, John Grant, Gregg McClymont MP, Paddy McDonagh, Robbie McLaughlin, Bob Nelson, Andrew Noble, the late Vera Ryhajlo and Brendan Shalvey. My son, Francis Xavier, who was born on Ivy Day 2009, helped keep everything in perspective. My greatest debt is recorded in the book's dedication.

Abbreviations

When quoting from Joyce's major works I follow the practice of placing page numbers in parentheses after each quotation. In the case of *Finnegans Wake* I also supply line numbers. The editions I use are as follows:

D *Dubliners* ed. Terence Brown (Harmondsworth: Penguin Books, 1992)
FW *Finnegans Wake* (Harmondsworth: Penguin Books, 1976)
P *A Portrait of the Artist as a Young Man* (Harmondsworth: Penguin Books, 1971)
SH *Stephen Hero: Part of the First Draft of 'A Portrait of the Artist as a Young Man'*, ed. Theodore Spencer; rev. edn with additional material John J. Slocum and Herbert Cahoon (London: Paladin, 1991)
U *Ulysses*, annotated student edition, ed. Declan Kiberd (Harmondsworth: Penguin Books, 2000)

Introduction:
'The journey westward'

I'd love to see Galway again.
— Gretta Conroy, 'The Dead'

Where was James Joyce from? If there is one question that even the most novice of initiates to the study of Irish literature could answer correctly, it is surely this one. Joyce's burning obsession with the city of his birth has provided Dublin a permanent place in literary history; his loving recreation of its streets, shops, statues, brothels and pubs stands as a valuable historical document as well as a magnificent and enduring artifice. Yet one of the earliest critical mentions of Joyce wishes to connect him not so much with Dublin but with the west. *Ireland in Fiction* (1916), a still-useful bibliographic guide by the Jesuit priest Stephen J. Brown, provides the following entry for the author of *Dubliners*:

> Joyce, James A., B. of Galway parentage about thirty years ago. Was a student of Clongowes Wood College and of University Coll., Dublin. Published some years ago a small book of verse that has been much admired, entitled Chamber Music. Is at present in Trieste.[1]

Joyce soon became aware of the book, and was keen to correct the error and provide a slightly fuller account of his background, as is clear from a letter of 1918 to his London agent:

> I shall be glad if you can send a note to the Reverend Stephen Browne [*sic*], S.J., Clongowes Wood College, Sallins, Kildare, Ireland thanking him in my name for the inclusion of me in his work Ireland in Fiction and, as he invites corrections for the second edition now in the press, informing him that I was born in 1882 (2 February), that my father's family came from Cork not from the west of Ireland. My father is from Cork city, his father from Fermoy, county Cork. The family comes, of course, from the west of

---

1 Stephen J. Brown, SJ, *Ireland in Fiction: A Guide to Irish Novels, Tales, Romances, and Folk-lore* (Dublin and London: Maunsel, 1916), 123.

I

Ireland (Joyce's country) but mine is a southern offshoot of the tribe. My
wife is from Galway city.[2]

That 'of course' is telling. Though keen to clarify the facts of his lineage,
Joyce was always pleased to think of himself as connected with Galway, his
surname that of one of the city's storied fourteen tribes.

Visiting Galway in the summer of 1912 – the second and last of two
such visits he would make in his lifetime – Joyce went to some efforts to
see places he associated with his composition of 'The Dead', that story in
which Gretta Conroy's memories of her native city play such a central role.
In particular, Joyce wanted to visit the graveyard where lay Michael Furey,
the tragic young man who had loved the young Gretta. Though Sonny
Bodkin, the Galway man on whom Furey is partly modelled, lies in the city
cemetery of Rahoon, Joyce thinks of Furey as being buried further west. 'I
cycled to Oughterard on Sunday', he writes to Stanislaus on 7 August, 'and
visited the graveyard of "The Dead"'. It is exactly as I imagined it and one
of the headstones was to J. Joyce.'[3] Here was one of those coincidences in
which this most superstitious of writers put such great store, and which
allowed him to further indulge an abiding fascination with the west of
Ireland.

James Hardiman's 1820 history of Galway, with which Joyce was
familiar, carries a venerable description of the Joyces and their provenance:

> This old Galway family is of ancient and honourable English descent, and
> was allied to the Welch and British princes. Thomas Joyes, the first of the
> name that came to Ireland, sailed from Wales in the reign of Edward I.
> [...] [H]e directed his course to the western part of Connaught, where he
> acquired considerable tracts of territory, which his posterity still inhabit.
> While on the voyage, his wife was delivered of a son, whom he named
> *Mac Mara, son of the sea*, he extended his father's acquisitions, and from
> him descended the sept of the Joyces, a race of men remarkable for their
> extraordinary stature, who, for centuries past inhabited the mountainous
> district, in Iar Connaught, called, from them, *Duthaidh Sheodhoigh*, or *Joyce
> country*, now forming the barony of Ross, in the County of Galway.[4]

2 James Joyce to James B. Pinker (29 July 1918), in James Joyce, *Letters*, ed. Stuart Gilbert
  (London: Faber and Faber, 1957), 115.
3 James Joyce to Stanislaus Joyce (7 August 1912), in James Joyce, *Letters*, vol. II, ed. Richard
  Ellmann (London: Faber and Faber, 1966), 300.
4 Quoted in James Hardiman, *The History of the Town and County of the Town of Galway,
  from the earliest period to the present time, Embellished with several Engravings. To which is
  added, a copious appendix, containing the principal charters and other original documents*
  (Dublin: W. Folds and Sons, 1820), 14–15.

James's father, John, owned an engraving bearing the coat of arms of the Joyces – dominated by the double-headed Hapsburg eagle – and carefully guarded it during the many moves from house to house in Dublin as the family fortunes declined.[5] In addition to these historic associations of the name 'Joyce' with Galway, James was very pleased that Nora was a native: unlike Gabriel Conroy he would never feel it necessary to blush at his wife's Connacht origins. Nora's knowledge of the west, her Galway accent and ways, 'completed or, at least, massively enhanced', writes one commentator, 'the private Joycean encyclopaedia'.[6]

The west, it goes without saying, was the revivalists' Utopia, location of Yeats's Innisfree, Synge's Aran and Lady Gregory's Kiltartan. One of the things this study will stress is that Joyce, too, was interested in what lay beyond the Shannon, but for rather more historically grounded, and sometimes more personal, reasons than those romantic, mythological considerations so close to Yeats's heart. Gabriel Conroy is suspicious of Molly Ivors' motivations in wishing to visit the Aran Islands; he is chary of her narrow gaelicism, her Celtic brooch, her eagerness to reject all that which is not Irish. But her whispered name-calling to him – 'West Briton!' – as they finish dancing wounds him more than he would like to admit, and by the story's end and the revelation of his wife's passionate Galway past he can shut out the west and its 'dark mutinous' border no more.

Armed with the knowledge of Joyce's Galway connections, the time has come for us to set out, like Gabriel, on a journey westward and, over the coming chapters, focus will shift repeatedly to the Irish west, both of fact and of fiction, in an effort to come to some better understanding of Joyce's motivations in writing *Dubliners* in the manner that he did. From the Nuns' Island of Michael Furey's last visit to Gretta, to the Aughrim of Jacobite Ireland's last stand, to the Killala of the last invasion of the country, this study finds itself drawn to the west in pursuit of answers to Joyce's historical questions. Suggesting that Joyce's stories are more complicated than has hitherto generally been understood, *Journey Westward*, via a series of close readings of often overlooked moments, tries to locate *Dubliners* in its appropriate cultural and historical contexts.

Each of the three chapters takes a different central theme or trope to help build towards a broader reconsideration of Joyce's attitude towards the history and culture of his homeland. Chapter One considers the ways in which Joyce critiques Protestant power in Ireland via a subtle series of prompts towards distillation and the production of whiskey in the late

5 See Richard Ellmann, *James Joyce* (Oxford: Oxford University Press, rev. edn, 1982), 11.
6 Andrew Gibson, *James Joyce* (London: Reaktion Books, 2006), 58.

nineteenth and early twentieth centuries. Chapter Two then opens out
this examination of Ireland's changing power structures by looking at an
array of Joyce's engagements with the past, with a particular emphasis on
the seismic historical shift brought about by the fall of Irish Jacobitism
in 1691. Finally, Chapter Three focuses on Joyce's allusive technique
employed while writing *Dubliners*, points to a number of previously
unconsidered texts that lie submerged in the stories, and considers what
these moments might tell us about Joycean attitudes to both the Literary
Revival and to Ireland's tragic history. Each chapter is divided into closely
argued subsections that merge to offer an overall sense of *Dubliners*
not just as the singular work of art it has long been considered, but as a
complex and intriguing book that still has much to reveal about itself to
the alert reader.

This study represents, of course, by no means the first attempt to suggest
that there is a great deal more going on in *Dubliners* than first meets the
eye. As early as 1929 one of Joyce's Parisian companions sought to question
any over-comfortable reception of the book. In his essay 'Before Ulysses –
and after', collected as part of a series of commentaries on Joyce's 'Work
in Progress', Robert Sage pointed to a central error on the part of readers
when approaching this new and difficult work:

> The general bafflement caused by those portions of James Joyce's *Work in
> Progress* which have appeared in *transition* seems to me an indication that
> most readers have failed to realize that Joyce's writings, from *Dubliners* to
> the present book, form an indivisible whole.[7]

Though, as the title of this book suggests, the bulk of *Journey Westward*
will concentrate on *Dubliners*, it frequently finds itself in mind of Sage's
caveat and looks to Joyce's greater oeuvre to help explain and expand upon
individual observations about the earlier work.

One scholar who has done more than almost any other to open up
Dubliners to multiple interpretations is Don Gifford, who, in the preface to
his very useful second edition of *Joyce Annotated: Notes for 'Dubliners' and 'A
Portrait of the Artist as a Young Man'* (1982), offers an apology for the 'disturb-
ingly clear' shortcomings of his original 1967 edition. While accepting that
some of these shortcomings may have resulted from his own 'insufficient
saturation in Dublin detail', Gifford then, strangely, blames James Joyce for
being too difficult, too opaque:

---

7 Robert Sage, 'Before Ulysses – and after', in Samuel Beckett et al., *Our Exagmination
  round his Factification for Incamination of Work in Progress* (1929) (London: Faber and
  Faber, 1972), 149.

I came to realize that I was missing 'occasions' not only because I lacked information or awareness, but also because in the earlier fictions Joyce was being too offhand and too subtle. He was not consistently attentive to how much a reader might miss, to how much the suggestive potential of cryptic allusion and 'mere detail' depended on the writer's ability to alert the reader, to provide frames of reference, markers, and clues which indicate how the text is to be read, how the trivial and the cryptic could be made to resonate.[8]

This seems an odd charge to make. If you, the reader, miss one of Joyce's allusions or fail to crack his code, it is not your fault but the author's. Joyce, the writer who famously boasted that his work would keep the professors guessing for centuries, would, doubtless, have been most amused at Gifford's uncomfortable apology and explanation.

The critical methodology preferred in this book is what, in a very different context, Saul Bellow once described, dismissively, as 'deep reading'. It is an approach that, he argued more than forty years ago, had 'become dangerous to literature':

Things are not what they seem. And anyway, unless they represent something large and worthy, writers will not bother with them. Any deep reader can tell you that picking up a bus transfer is the *reisemotif* (journey motif) when it happens in a novel. A travel folder signifies Death. Coal holes represent the Underworld. Soda crackers are the Host. Three bottles of beer are – it's obvious. The busy mind can hardly miss at this game, and every player is a winner.[9]

Bellow is right to be wary of over-zealous symbol hunting but, more often than not, Joyce, more than any other writer, really does mean everything to be read in multiple ways. As one small but not insignificant example, a beer bottle stuck in the sand on Sandymount beach as Stephen walks across it in the third chapter of *Ulysses* is not just a piece of litter, it is a symbol of Ireland's unhealthy addiction to alcohol, an addiction that will be considered in my opening chapter. Cóilín Owens' brilliantly illuminating account of 'A Painful Case' has recently shown us just how far the reader might begin to venture in a close reading of just one story in *Dubliners* – his sleuthing ought to convince scholars more than ever that critical analysis of the book must be considered still in its infancy.[10]

---

8 Don Gifford, *Joyce Annotated: Notes for 'Dubliners' and 'A Portrait of the Artist as a Young Man'* (Berkeley, CA: University of California Press, 2nd edn, 1982), vii.

9 Saul Bellow, 'Deep Readers of the World, Beware', in *Opinions and Perspectives from the New York Times Book Review*, ed. Francis Brown (Boston: Houghton Mifflin, 1964), 25.

10 See Cóilín Owens, *James Joyce's Painful Case* (Gainesville, FL: University Press of Florida, 2008).

But Bellow is certainly not on his own. For several scholars, the approach adopted here to reading *Dubliners* would be anathema. There is a critical school that wishes to see the book as primarily – sometimes even exclusively – a work of realist fiction. For such scholars, any effort to read *Dubliners* symbolically, allusively, or as part of some grand mythical schema, *à la Ulysses*, is misplaced, wrongheaded and diminishes the aesthetic impact of the collection. The critic most notably hostile to the search for symbols is Warren Beck, whose *Joyce's 'Dubliners'* (1969) opens with a thorough-going dismissal of such an approach and seeks, in particular, to discredit the attempt by Richard Levin and Charles Shattuck to uncover Homeric parallels in *Dubliners* similar, if not more pointed still, to those of *Ulysses*. 'In *Dubliners* the stimulations to insights', argues Beck, 'far from depending on analogy, take the serious vein of an implicatively presentational narra-tive art, such as has been refined in modern times to become the middle way of much significant thematic-organic fiction.' To prompt any move away from reading the book in this primarily naturalistic vein is, for Beck, a scholarly error:

> Obscuring this primary aesthetic aspect, and ungratefully suggesting that without something like their strained exegesis *Dubliners* would seem only 'a pleasant readable minor effusion, a collection of discrete sketches', the Richard Levin and Charles Shattuck operation lapsed into presupposi-tional criticism's frequent offense, actually violating some of the stories as entities. [...] Is it not time the long-lingering influence of such analogical-archetypal vaporings as the Levin-Shattuck piece and any later mutations of its methodology be aired out of the cubicles of Joyce criticism?[11]

As it happens, while disagreeing with Beck on much, this study agrees with him on his dismissal of the Levin–Shattuck theory, which strains too far to prove a spurious set of parallels. The theory caused a brief stir in Joyce studies when first published but did not take root. This and other symbol-hunting theories will be further examined in the final chapter. Beck's strident prose makes clear, however, that it is not just one particular theory that he finds troubling but a whole critical methodology.

More recently, Terence Brown, in his introduction to the Penguin edition of *Dubliners*, takes a similar, though considerably less confronta-tional and more nuanced stance to that of Beck in his suspicion of overly determined symbolic readings:

---

11 Warren Beck, *Joyce's 'Dubliners': Substance, Vision, and Art* (Durham, NC: Duke University Press, 1969), 7.

Dubliners has therefore endured a considerable amount of rather mechan-
ical symbol hunting as if the surface of the text, with its realistic detail
and subtleties of dialogue and socio/cultural allusion, can be disregarded
in pursuit of some definitive interpretation rooted in a symbology which
the ingenious critic has identified. It is as damage done to those finely
woven textures that constitute the work's finesse, that these exercises in
misguided scholarly acumen give most offence. For it is not that *Dubliners*
does not possess a complex structure and a detailed symbolism, for all the
realism it also achieves, but that such readings direct attention away from
a full encounter with the individual story itself to a reductive account of
some altogether simpler narrative which is a poor substitute for the true
Joycean experience.[12]

Brown seems conflicted. He confesses that there are grounds for symbolic
readings but suggests that such readings should not take place. The 'ingenious' critic is a bad critic and there is one 'true' Joycean experience, a way
of reading that must eschew symbol hunting and embrace realism. Brown's
often very useful notes that accompany the text of the stories stick rigidly
to this realist methodology. Under this schema then, 'Usher's Island', the
location for the Christmas party in 'The Dead', is explained thus: 'The
Misses Morkan live in a house which fronted on a quay named Usher's
Island, on the south bank of the river to the west of central Dublin.' That
is useful knowledge for the reader to have but the lack of contextualiza-
tion leaves it as a bald fact rather than as a key to further meaning, as
Joyce meant it to be. There are at least two notable ways in which the gloss
on Usher's Island might have been expanded. First, we know, via Richard
Ellmann's sleuthing, that Joyce had relatives who lived on Usher's Island
and on whom the Misses Morkan are clearly modelled.[13] Or, secondly,
we might consider the significance and resonance of Usher's Island as
a location in the rich tapestry of Dublin's history, as Kevin Whelan has
recently done. 'The scale of his achievement', argues Whelan's essay, 'is
to weave this complex historical understanding and narrative imagination into what seems at first reading a standard naturalist text.'[14] Focusing
mainly on the place of Usher's Island in the 1798 rebellion, Whelan writes
persuasively of Joyce's historiographical savvy and the ways in which this is
deployed in 'The Dead' – Chapter Two returns to these ideas when considering the significance of Jacobitism for Joyce's imagination and for the
composition of *Dubliners*.

12 Terence Brown, 'Introduction', in James Joyce, *Dubliners* (Harmondsworth: Penguin,
    1992), xxxii–xxxiii.
13 See Ellmann, *James Joyce*, 245.
14 Kevin Whelan, 'The Memories of "The Dead"', *Yale Journal of Criticism*, 15.1 (2002), 87.

To take one other example from 'The Dead' of the differences between what one might call the 'surface' approach and the 'allusive' approach, Brown offers a gloss on Lily's mispronunciation of Gabriel Conroy's surname at the beginning of the story. We are told by Joyce that Gabriel 'smiled at the three syllables she had given his surname' (*D* 177), and Brown comments thus: 'Gabriel is patronizing her because of her "flat" Dublin accent in which his name would be pronounced Con-er-oy'.[15] Again, that's a useful reading of a particular moment and gives us, without ever having to leave the imaginative world contained in the words on the page, an insight into Gabriel's class consciousness, which is an important aspect of the story. A radically different reading of Lily's three syllables was offered in 1965 by John V. Kelleher in his groundbreaking and, still for many, controversial essay 'Irish History and Mythology in James Joyce's "The Dead"'.[16] Kelleher's thesis, briefly, was that Joyce was inviting the alert reader to associate Conroy with 'Conaire', the gaelic, three-syllable form of the name. King Conaire is the central protagonist of a mythical Irish tale, *Togail Bruidne Da Derga*, or 'The Taking of Da Derga's Hostel', in which Conaire breaks various taboos, or 'geasa', such as that which forbids him to hunt birds, and, as a result, falls foul of the cosmic order. Similarly, if not so dramatically, Gabriel Conroy falls out of favour with the world over the course of 'The Dead', breaking taboos, such as that concerning the hunting of birds, in a fashion reminiscent of Conaire: 'Here I am, Aunt Kate! Cried Gabriel, with sudden animation, ready to carve a flock of geese, if necessary' (*D* 197).

It is not possible to say definitely that Kelleher's theory is correct whereas it is possible to fully agree with Brown, who rarely has to leave the confines of the text or a Dublin street map to provide a useful and illuminating note. But, when it comes to critical methodologies, it should not be a question of either/or. It was not Joyce's intention to have his work read or interpreted according to only one set of critical orthodoxies. And while some of the more over-determined symbolical readings of *Dubliners* border on the incredible and unhelpful, the reader ought never be afraid to examine closely what may seem trivial details in order to arrive at some broader conclusion. Joyce was very keen on utilizing 'trivial' things, seeing the word's etymology as a point where three ways meet. In *Stephen Hero*, Stephen shows a similar proclivity. 'As often as not', we are told, 'he would decide to follow some trivial indication of city life instead of entering the

---

15 Brown, 'Notes', in *Dubliners*, 307.
16 See John V. Kelleher, 'Irish History and Mythology in James Joyce's "The Dead"', in Charles Fanning (ed.), *Selected Writings of John V. Kelleher on Ireland and Irish America* (Carbondale, IL: Southern Illinois University Press, 2002), 40–56.

oppressive life of the college' (*SH* 42). It is in the spirit of chasing the apparently trivial that Chapter One pursues the significance of Joyce's interest in whiskey, and helps to demonstrate an important facet of Joyce's political sensibility. With Joyce we are, after all, as Seamus Heaney puts it, dealing with a writer, 'who could invest the very names of punctuation marks with historical riddles'.[17]

Trying to define just where Joyce stood politically, and how he felt about the centuries-old struggle between the island of his birth and her larger, more powerful neighbour, has generated intense critical debate. In the spring following the devastating hunger strikes by republican prisoners in the Maze prison during the summer of 1981, a debate took place in the letters page of *An Phoblacht/Republican News* around the question of Joyce's patriotic *bona fides*. One correspondent was certain that Joyce was undeserving of nationalist respect. 'I suggest', he wrote, 'that republicans and those concerned with our national culture have little reason to cherish the memory of a man whose confused intellectual fantasising caused him to reject his native land.'[18] Such a position unconsciously reflects the views of one of Joyce's earliest supporters and critics, the American modernist Ezra Pound. Pound's view of Joyce as a contented Irish exile exercised much early influence. In an essay titled 'The Non-Existence of Ireland' he wrote that Joyce had 'fled to Trieste and into the modern world'.[19] But, right from the start, there were also critics keen to stress the centrality of Ireland to the formation of the Joycean imagination. Herbert Gorman, writing one of the first books on Joyce, was conscious of two poles – international and national – behind his subject's work:

> He proudly lifts himself beyond nationalistic considerations if not above them and because this is so his cosmos extends farther than a single island. It embraces all Europe. Yet he is entirely Irish, the product of Irish culture and religion and instincts. This can never be doubted. Any attempt to cut him off from Irish letters will be foredoomed to failure.[20]

Literary criticism did not always heed Gorman's warning and the first fifty or so years of critical comment tended to side with Pound and pay too little attention to the Irish context. But the old comfortable verities that saw

17 Seamus Heaney, 'Place and Displacement', in Heaney, *Finders Keepers: Selected Prose 1971–2001* (London: Faber and Faber, 2002), 126.
18 Colla Ó Muirí, letter to the editor, *An Phoblacht/Republican News*, 11 February 1982. I am grateful to Kevin Bean for drawing my attention to this debate.
19 Quoted in Eric Bulson, *The Cambridge Introduction to James Joyce* (Cambridge: Cambridge University Press, 2006), 109.
20 Herbert S. Gorman, *James Joyce: His First Forty Years* (London: Geoffrey Bles, 1926), 6.

Joyce as a relieved cosmopolitan, happy to wave goodbye to Ireland and to damn its backward, defeated populace – its 'gratefully oppressed' – are now long gone, and have been replaced in some quarters with the image of Joyce as an angry patriot intent on avenging himself against British imperialism. Andrew Gibson is currently doing more than any other critic to demonstrate this latter aspect of Joyce's worldview in books such as *James Joyce* (2006) and *Joyce's Revenge* (2002). As such he does much to align Joyce's thinking with that of one of his most enduring creations, Stephen Daedalus, who from the beginning of his life as a thinker and writer 'became a poet with malice aforethought' (*SH* 32).

There is still, naturally and inevitably, considerable disagreement, even among those keen to stress Joyce's Irishness, about just where on the nationalist scale his work ought to be located. Joyce's friends Padraic and Mary Colum thought his politics rather tepid, arguing that 'the post-Parnell Irish nationalism was only a noise in the street, a movement of the crowd of which he would never consider himself a part'.[21] G. J. Watson, one of the earliest critics to offer a sufficiently nuanced sense of Joyce's complicated loyalties, sees his subject as somewhat more committed though essentially temperate, arguing that 'he had little taste for extremism, believed devoutly in his betrayal theory of Irish history, and always hated physical force'.[22] In subsequent years, the depth of Joyce's nationalism has been further emphasized by critics such as Seamus Deane in *Celtic Revivals* (1985) and Emer Nolan in her seminal *James Joyce and Nationalism* (1995). More recently, Andrew Gibson has sought to move Joyce closer to a militant, Fenian Irish nationalism, and sees the Anglo-Irish problem as the key informing issue at the core of Joyce's work: 'Joyce's task was to transform if not reverse a historical structure that had conferred immense power and significance on one of two adjacent cultures, at the massive expense of the other.'[23]

While perhaps not quite so sure of Joyce's nationalist sympathies, this study finds itself in agreement with Gibson on the vengeful and aggrieved nature of the Joycean sensibility, and sees the desire for revenge seeded throughout *Dubliners*, most prominently in 'The Dead'. Thinking of Joyce's later great novel, W. B. Yeats, on reading *Ulysses*, remarked memorably to Olivia Shakespear that Joyce had 'A cruel playful mind like a great soft tiger cat'.[24] Terence Brown considers Joyce's sometimes inexplicable

---

21 Mary and Padraic Colum, *Our Friend James Joyce* (London: Gollancz, 1959), 44.
22 G. J. Watson, *Irish Identity and the Literary Revival: Synge, Yeats, Joyce and O'Casey* (Washington, DC: Catholic University of America Press, 2nd edn, 1994), 158.
23 Gibson, *James Joyce*, 171.
24 W. B. Yeats, *The Letters*, ed. Allan Wade (London: Rupert Hart-Davis, 1954), 679.

preoccupation with ideas of treachery and points to 'his lifelong fascination with the theme of betrayal [...] springs of grievance and resentment which were less than fully rational'.[25] Rational or not, Joyce's sense of disgruntlement is often personal: he resented the concrete help he received from Lady Gregory and felt outside of the mainstream of Irish writing and, in particular, of the Protestant-led Literary Revival. On other occasions the resentment has deeper roots in Irish history: Chapter Two draws attention to the ways in which Joyce remembers Catholic defeat; Chapter Three considers, among a host of other allusions, Joyce's use in 'The Dead' of a ballad commemorating a hero of 1798. But this is Joyce and nothing is straightforward. However, the cumulative effect of the repeated backward glances to moments of Irish catastrophe – 1691, 1798, 1845 – is to stress a deeply felt sense of loss in Joyce's mind. 'If a victorious country tyrannizes over another', Joyce told a Trieste crowd in April 1907, 'it cannot logically take it amiss if the latter reacts.'[26]

Journey Westward, then, aims to demonstrate how *Dubliners*, through a series of subtle historical and literary allusions, goes about reacting to the conqueror. Despite all his misgivings about Ireland's long national struggle, both political and cultural, Joyce retains a deep-seated desire to commemorate the defeated Irish dead. In the end, as is perhaps inevitable with Joyce, I am, like Leopold Bloom in his study of Shakespeare, left with more questions than answers, yet the years spent thinking closely about this haunting book have only served to increase my admiration. I can only hope that the reader will agree that to hunt and dig and rummage through the rooms of *Dubliners* is not to do Joyce a disservice but to reignite old fires and shine light in darkened corners so that the book glows anew.

25 Brown, 'Introduction', in Joyce, *Dubliners*, xii.
26 James Joyce, 'Ireland: Island of Saints and Sages', in Joyce, *Occasional, Critical, and Political Writing*, ed. Kevin Barry (Oxford: Oxford University Press, 2000), 116.

1

'Endless stories about the distillery':
Joyce and Whiskey

With fell design, England suppressed our commerce, our factories, our
mines, our industries, and left us only the distillery.
— Father Michael Kelly (temperance crusader)

When we knew him first he used to be rather interesting, talking of faints
and worms; but I soon grew tired of him and his endless stories about the
distillery.
— James Joyce, 'The Sisters'

Flann O'Brien, the much-loved Irish comic writer, lived uncomfort-
ably in the shadow of James Joyce. An admirer of the great Dubliner's
achievements and one of the first to formally celebrate Bloomsday, O'Brien
was also deeply frustrated by his own inability to escape comparison with
the author of *Ulysses*. This anxiety is brought to the surface for comic
effect in O'Brien's late novel *The Dalkey Archive* (1964) where his central
character, the civil servant Mick O'Shaughnessy, finds Joyce alive and well
and working as a barman in the north County Dublin seaside resort of
Skerries. Shy of public recognition and adulation, Joyce tells Mick, 'I've had
things imputed to me which – ah – I've had nothing to do with.'[1] He goes
on to claim that he has in fact authored only one book, *Dubliners*, a collection that was co-written with Oliver St John Gogarty. Mick, astounded by
his discovery, feels compelled to introduce Joyce to the only other genius
he knows, the philosopher, inventor and distiller De Selby, in the hope that
a meeting of these two great minds might lead to riches:

> If in fact after a second interview with Joyce an arrangement was made
> for him to meet De Selby, Mick would have by that time the way made
> ready. Two elderly men, of giant intellectual potential, who had run wild
> somewhat in their minds might, in coming together, find a community
> of endeavour and unsuspected common loyalties. Both certainly knew

1 Flann O'Brien, *The Dalkey Archive* (London: Macgibbon and Kee, 1964), 145.

12

what whiskey was. Mick wondered whether in the absence of his deadly container De Selby would continue to produce perfectly mature whiskey which was only seven days old? Could one look forward to the founding of the firm of De Selby, Joyce & Co., distillers, maltsters and warehousemen, to market those high-grade spirits all over the world and make a fortune?[2]

It is hard to say if O'Brien knew just how close to the mark he was here in his association of Joyce with whiskey, but it was a linkage he had made first more than ten years previously in the pages of the literary magazine *Envoy*.

In 1951 *Envoy*'s editor, John Ryan, put together a Joyce special of the journal and thus became an important early champion of his fellow Dubliner's work in an Ireland that had officially largely ignored its greatest writer. Flann O'Brien, writing under his given English-language name of Brian Nolan, contributed a singularly bizarre and brilliant essay titled 'A Bash in the Tunnel'.[3] The essay describes a conversation had by O'Brien with a stranger in The Bailey bar, Dublin, in which the stranger tells him of a scheme whereby major but solitary drinking sprees are to be had by hiding in the lavatories of certain railway carriages. O'Brien is struck by the similarity between the image of this lone drinker and the condition of the Irish artist:

> But surely there you have the Irish artist? Sitting fully dressed, innerly locked in the toilet of a locked coach where he has no right to be, resentfully drinking somebody else's whiskey, being whisked hither and thither by anonymous shunters, keeping fastidiously the while on the outer face of his door the simple word ENGAGED!
>
> I think the image fits Joyce; but particularly in his manifestation of a most Irish characteristic – the transgressor's resentment with the nongressor.[4]

This last description of Joyce is marvellously accurate, and this chapter will attempt to demonstrate another way in which Joyce manages, often unfairly and unreasonably, to feel disgruntled with the Ireland of his times via the mechanism of distillation and its most potent product, whiskey.

Distillation and *Dubliners*

Readers have, since the initial publication of *Dubliners* in 1914, pondered the significance of three words in the opening paragraph of the collection's

---

2 O'Brien, *The Dalkey Archive*, 154.
3 It is very difficult to track the multiplicity of Flann O'Brien's pseudonyms. In this case he drops the 'O' from his more usual Brian O'Nolan.
4 Brian Nolan, 'A Bash in the Tunnel', in John Ryan (ed.), *A Bash in the Tunnel: James Joyce by the Irish* (Brighton: Clifton Books, 1970), 18.

first story, 'The Sisters', in order to gain a more profound understanding of the tales that follow. Those puzzling words – 'paralysis', 'gnomon' and 'simony' – which the unnamed boy narrator of the story tells us 'sounded strangely in my ears' (D 1), impact to greater or lesser degree on all the subsequent stories in the book. I do not intend to rehearse here the great many interpretations applied to this odd collection of words but would like to suggest, instead, that the inevitable intensity of the critical spotlight shone on that opening paragraph moves attention away from a seemingly innocuous word a couple of paragraphs later, a word that, as with all Joycean words, is chosen with great care and scrupulousness and reverberates throughout the collection in the same way as the more celebrated trio. That word is 'distillery'.[5] Why does James Joyce, that great master of words, that most meticulous of all artists, have Old Cotter, the 'Tiresome old fool' (D 1) of 'The Sisters' working in a distillery? Why does the pallid Mr Duffy of 'A Painful Case' live in a house from which 'he could look into the disused distillery' (D 103)? Why is the sour-faced office manager of 'Counterparts' named after a former distillery manager whom Joyce believed to have swindled his father? Why does the tragic Michael Furey of 'The Dead' sing his last to Gretta in a street synonymous with distillation? Why is Mr Browne of the same story the only member of the party to drink whiskey?[6] The attempt to provide answers to these questions will yield up a great deal about Joyce's motivations and desires in writing *Dubliners*.

The critic Michael Brian has come closest to understanding the significance of whiskey as a motif within *Dubliners*. Brian, prompted by Joyce's choice of trade for the tiresome Old Cotter, sees the circling and coiled nature of distillation as being of a piece with that of writing: 'not only do the stories form a circular repetition – a pattern repeated throughout Joyce's work – but the dominant image of distillation is endless, for it is itself a circulatory process'.[7] The notion of the artist's final choice of words

---

5 'Distillery' comes on the second page of text of the Grant Richards first edition of *Dubliners* but on the first page in most subsequent reproductions.

6 Joyce always spells the word as what we now know as the Scottish 'whisky' rather than the Irish 'whiskey'. This fact should not, however, be taken to mean that Joyce wished us to believe that Mr Browne was drinking Scotch. Dublin distilleries adopted the 'e' in the nineteenth century to distinguish themselves from provincial brands such as Persse's Galway Whisky. Cork-based Paddy Whiskey did not adopt the 'e' until 1979. See John Clement Ryan, *Irish Whiskey* (Dublin: Eason and Son, 1992), n.p. [22]. When writing about Irish whiskey I will follow current spelling conventions.

7 Michael Brian, '"A Very Fine Piece of Writing": An Etymological, Dantean, and Gnostic Reading of Joyce's "Ivy Day in the Committee Room"', in Rosa M. Bollettieri Bosinelli and Harold F. Mosher (eds), *ReJoycing: New Readings of Dubliners* (Lexington, KY: University Press of Kentucky, 1998), 223. John Gordon has also considered the idea of distillation as

to be placed on the page as a type of distillate is a common enough one, and distillation as a purifying, perfecting process appears across a wide range of literature. Cyril Connolly captures the idea nicely when seeing poetry as a purer, more refined product than prose. 'Poetry, to stand out', writes Connolly, 'must be a double distillation of life that goes deeper than prose. It must be brandy as compared to wine.'[8] We know that, from early in his writing life, Joyce enjoyed the image of whiskey and beer production as representative of a purifying process with potential for broader application. In *Stephen Hero*, for instance, the eponymous hero has come to think of his companion Cranly's friends as a yet-imperfect drink. 'Cranly's chosen companions', writes Joyce, 'represented the rabblement in a stage of partial fermentation when it is midway between vat and flagon and Cranly seemed to please himself in the spectacle of this caricature of his own unreadiness' (*SH* 127). Following Cyril Connolly's lead, perhaps Joyce's oeuvre, like Jameson, his favoured Irish whiskey, ought to be thought of in its purity and perfection as a triple distilled product.

While comparing literature with distillation may be a popular and even worthwhile way of thinking about the writing process generally, in the case of Joyce to leave it at that, as Brian has done, is to miss the very real historical and biographical significance of whiskey for the author. Joyce does not just idly place whiskey in a scene in the interests of realist verisimilitude: when he writes about the spirit he does so with exactitude and with intent. Hence the boy narrator of 'The Sisters' is familiar with the minutiae of the distilling process as we see via his reference to 'faints and worms' (*D* 1). Similarly, in one of those infrequent appearances of straightforward English in *Finnegans Wake*, Joyce, while telling the tale of Buckley and the Russian general, makes time for an aside on a vital piece of the distiller's kit:

> in the course of their tussle the toller man, who had opened his bully bowl to beg, said to the miner who was carrying the worm (a handy term for the portable distillery which consisted of three vats, two jars and several bottles though we purposely say nothing of the stiff, both parties having an interest in the spirits): Let me go, Pautheen! (82.4–9)

It was not only Buckley and the General who had an interest in spirits. Old Cotter, James Duffy, Mr Alleyne, Mr Browne: they are all of or at the distillery, all associated with negativity, death and loss, and all used by

---

analogous to Joyce's artistic process in his book, *Joyce and Reality: The Empirical Strikes Back* (Syracuse, NY: Syracuse University Press, 2004), 33–54.

8 Cyril Connolly, *Enemies of Promise* (1948) (London: André Deutsch, rev. edn, 1973), 144.

Joyce in his never-ending grudge with the world that saw his father and his family reduced from the happy days of yachting in Dublin bay or picnicking at the strawberry beds of Chapelizod to the horrors of the besotted household so memorably described by his brother Stanislaus in the months after their mother's death, a house in which drunken brothers fought each other while being upbraided by a drunken father. 'Another, perhaps,' wrote the abstemious Stanislaus, 'might have been able to distil low comedy out of a situation in which a drunken father rails at two drunken sons for being drunk, but I fancy to do so one must know the situation only at second hand.'[9] Stanislaus's choice of verb to describe the work of the vulgar comedian is not, perhaps, so throwaway as might at first seem.

Geography and Galway

The search for answers to the significance of whiskey in *Dubliners* begins in Nora Barnacle's hometown of Galway, or, more precisely, in the Nuns' Island of Gretta Conroy's final meeting with her young love, Michael Furey. The lead headline in the *Galway Advertiser* of 11 August 2005 declared that a bottle of Galway-distilled whiskey, long thought extinct, had made an appearance in a specialist whiskey shop in Swindon. Kenneth Thomas, the proprietor of the shop, valued the bottle at £100,000, making it the most highly priced bottle of whiskey in history.[10] The bottle, corked and with seal intact, had made its way to Mr Thomas via a circuitous route:

> This particular bottle has an interesting history. The son of the Persse family, who owned the distillery, decided that his future in life was not in the family business but in racehorse training. He moved to Lambourne, England (not far from this shop) and became a racehorse trainer. He kept one bottle from the distillery which was passed on to a lady friend when he passed away, with the view that it will be worth something one day.[11]

The whiskey in question was a bottle of Persse's Nuns' Island from the Persse distillery located at Nuns' Island, Galway.[12] This business thrived

---

9 Stanislaus Joyce, *My Brother's Keeper: James Joyce's Early Years*, ed. Richard Ellmann (1958) (Cambridge, MA: Da Capo Press, 2003), 250.
10 This valuation was quickly questioned as overly optimistic by the proprietor of a specialist whiskey store in Dublin who considered it not worth more than €5,000. See Paul Cullen, 'Last of Nun's Island whiskey for €146,000', *Irish Times*, 13 August 2005, 6. A second bottle subsequently turned up in Galway.
11 Quoted in Jennifer Hough, 'Bottle of rare Galway whiskey to reach €145,000: Historic Nuns' Island bottle turns up in UK whiskey shop', *Galway Advertiser*, 11 August 2005, 1.
12 'Nuns' Island' is the spelling preferred by Joyce in 'The Dead'. It is logically the correct

over the second half of the nineteenth century, eventually ceasing production in 1915.[13] Within thirty years of its passing, Persse's was being described by one connoisseur as 'the finest whiskey in the world'.[14] The central argument of this chapter is that an understanding and appreciation of this rare spirit's provenance holds a key to our reinterpretation of *Dubliners*.

Those readers who hold even a passing acquaintance with *Dubliners* will recall that it is in a rain-soaked garden in Nuns' Island that Michael Furey meets Gretta Conroy for the last time. Gretta has been living there with her grandmother, and is shortly to go and work in a Dublin convent. In the dark quiet of their Gresham Hotel room, Gretta recounts to her husband Gabriel that last fatal encounter:

> — Then the night before I left I was in my grandmother's house in Nuns' Island, packing up, and I heard gravel thrown up against the window. The window was so wet I couldn't see so I ran downstairs as I was and slipped out the back into the garden and there was the poor fellow at the end of the garden, shivering.
> — And did you not tell him to go back? asked Gabriel.
> — I implored of him to go home at once and told him he would get his death in the rain. But he said he did not want to live. I can see his eyes as well as well! He was standing at the end of the wall where there was a tree.
> — And did he go home? asked Gabriel.
> — Yes, he went home. And when I was only a week in the convent he died and was buried in Oughterard where his people came from. O, the day I heard that, that he was dead!
> She stopped, choking with sobs, and, overcome by emotion, flung herself face downward on the bed, sobbing in the quilt. Gabriel held her hand for a moment longer, irresolutely, and then, shy of intruding on her grief, let it fall gently and walked quietly to the window. (*D* 223)

Gabriel has, in a sense, been cuckolded by a ghost. His married life has been a charade, an empty bourgeois arrangement that cannot hope to compete with the grand passion of Gretta's Galway past and her love affair with a

---

spelling of this street name and I will be using it throughout. However, it is frequently spelt 'Nun's Island', both in the case of the street signage itself and by many critics. Thus, when quoting, I will not correct original spelling, nor point out the misspelling.

13   There is considerable confusion surrounding the Persse distillery's date of closure. The *Irish Times*, in its piece on the rare bottle, above, gives the date as 1908; the *Galway Advertiser* as 1913; whereas the whiskey writer and expert Brian Townsend provides a date of 1915. See Brian Townsend, *The Lost Distilleries of Ireland* (Glasgow: Neil Wilson Publishing, 1997), 98. The company was certainly in receivership in 1908, though the whiskey was still being advertised for sale in Galway up to 1915. See the *Irish Independent*, 23 July 1908, 8; and the *Connacht Tribune*, 30 January 1915, 6.

14   Maurice Walsh, 'Whiskey', *The Bell*, 2.5 (August 1941), 24.

boy who would rather die than live without her. This realization represents the central epiphany of the story and leads to Gabriel's examination of conscience that makes up the closing pages, culminating in the famous lyrical description of snow falling across the land, 'upon all the living and the dead' (*D* 225).

The story, and most especially its dénouement, has been much picked over by critics and I will provide some new thoughts on its conclusion in later chapters, but for now I would like to focus attention on the trigger mechanism that Nuns' Island represents. It has been a critical commonplace for some time to read significance beyond the merely geographical into Joyce's street names, addresses and walking routes. 'I am afraid I am more interested', Joyce once told Cyril Connolly, 'in Dublin street names than in the riddle of the Universe.'[15] That fascination is most obviously manifest in *Ulysses* but it is there, too, in *Dubliners*. Sometimes Joyce makes codebreaking easy for us. For example, in *Dubliners*' opening story, 'The Sisters', we are told that Father Flynn, the paralysed priest who is the story's object of fascination, was born in Irishtown and died on Great Britain Street. The most obvious interpretation of this information would be that Ireland represents health and life and that Britain represents paralysis and death. Ireland, as well as being paralysed by the Catholic Church, is under the yoke of British imperialism, a common theme in Joyce. It would be naive to imagine that Joyce chose the birth- and death-place at random, that, say, Rathmines and Stafford Street would have suited just as well. In fact, in this instance we know that Joyce took special care to make it clear for us. The first published version of 'The Sisters' as it appeared in the AE-edited *Irish Homestead* in August 1904 made no mention of Father Flynn's birthplace. When the story appeared as the opening one of *Dubliners* in 1914, Joyce, by mentioning Irishtown, had decided to make the Anglo-Irish struggle a stronger theme. Other revisions to the story made this new focus clearer still, of which more in the next chapter.

There are myriad examples from throughout Joyce of his fascination with place names and Nuns' Island is no exception. Padraic O'Laoi, a Galway local historian and Nora Barnacle's first biographer, was puzzled by Joyce's use of the street at such a crucial juncture in 'The Dead' and wondered where Joyce – at the time of the writing of his last story still not having visited Galway – had got the name. He concluded, naturally, that Nora must have been the source and that it held special romantic significance for her. 'I suggest', he writes, 'that Nun's Island was the trysting

---

15 Quoted in Cyril Connolly, *Previous Convictions* (London: Hamish Hamilton, 1963), 271.

place of Nora and Sonny Bodkin and later of Nora and Willie Mulvagh. Here, sheltered by the high walls that surrounded the former jail, Nora was safe to walk with her lovers, safe from the eyes of the gossipers and her uncle and guardian Thomas Healy.'[16] Beyond O'Laoi, surprisingly little critical attention has been brought to bear on this small Galway street, and many of those Joycean scholars who have stopped to wonder at its significance have been woefully wide of the mark. The first question one needs to ask when Joyce mentions a place or street name is, where is that? This should be followed by, why is it so called? Joyce enjoyed the notion that one might be in a position to draw a map of Dublin from the details provided in *Ulysses* and many critics have, inevitably, found Dublin street maps a significant aid in the study of that novel.[17] One might expect, then, that similar care would be taken with his short but not insignificant detour into Galway. Surprisingly, however, the location of Nuns' Island, that dark little street between the Catholic cathedral and the Garda barracks, has remained flatly elusive to a range of Joycean scholars.

James Joyce's 'Dubliners': Critical Essays (1969), in its appendix on place names in 'The Dead', provides the following bizarre entry: 'Nuns' Island: off the western coast, in the county of West Meath.'[18] This description could not be more wrong: Nuns' Island is both a street name and a piece of land surrounded by the fresh water of the river Corrib in the middle of Galway City, strictly speaking an island but only in a rather pedantic sense. It is not off any coast nor is it anywhere near County Westmeath, an entirely landlocked county in the province of Leinster. Besides the hopelessly inaccurate information on the location of Nuns' Island, the book goes on to make a further, less comical, but more important error in claiming that Nora Barnacle went to live with her grandmother on Nuns' Island at the age of five. The error is an instance of trying to shoehorn art into an imitation of life. Gretta tells Gabriel that she was living with her grandmother on Nuns' Island, but there is no proof that the same was true of Nora, who lived with her grandmother in the somewhat less poetically named street across the city, Whitehall.

The notion that Nora lived on Nuns' Island is an understandable mistake

---

16 Padraic O'Laoi, *Nora Barnacle Joyce: A Portrait* (Galway: Kennys Bookshops and Art Galleries, 1982), 33.

17 Don Gifford, for instance, in his invaluable study of *Ulysses*, provides maps for each of the chapters. See Gifford with Robert J. Seidman, *'Ulysses' Annotated: Notes for James Joyce's Ulysses* (Berkeley, CA: University of California Press, 2nd edn, revised and enlarged, 1989).

18 Clive Hart (ed.), *James Joyce's 'Dubliners': Critical Essays* (London: Faber and Faber, 1969), 178.

and stems from an interview with her eldest sister, Mary, in 1953. In the course of this interview, Mary said that her grandmother lived on Nuns' Island and this information was taken at face value by Joyce's biographer, Richard Ellmann. 'When Nora was five', he writes, 'her mother, surrounded by small children and pregnant once more, sent her to stay with a grand-mother on Nun's Island. She was to return after the birth, but when the grandmother offered to keep her, the arrangement continued.'[19] But, as Padraic O'Laoi points out, 'it was not to Nun's Island but to St. Augustine Street that James Joyce, on the 26th August 1909 "went to where you (Nora) lived with your grandmother".'[20] St Augustine Street leads into the cul-de-sac of Whitehall, home of Kate Healy, Nora's maternal grandmother, and, in the estimation of another of Nora's biographers, her 'first exile and the one which most shaped her personality'.[21]

Though not correct on the precise location, Ellmann is right in thinking that Nora was sent to live with her grandmother and did not, for much of her Galway childhood, live in the family home. The Barnacle family moved around Galway a great deal in the early years of the marriage and of Nora's youth, eventually settling in a little street across the Corrib from Nuns' Island named Bowling Green. Nora's mother, who spent much of the marriage separated from her husband, lived there from roughly 1896 to her death in 1939. By 1901, her maternal grandmother now dead, Nora was back living with her mother at 4 Bowling Green. It was in this house that Joyce, on visiting Galway in 1909, heard Nora's mother sing 'The Lass of Aughrim'. In his original draft of 'The Dead', Joyce had stuck to the addresses he knew Nora to have lived at, and decided to be strictly accurate in making Gretta a facsimile version of Nora. Thus he placed Gretta living with her grandmother in Bowling Green, but by 1910 he had decided to change this to Nun's Island, a spelling retained in the proofs for the 1914 edition of *Dubliners* but finally, and correctly, becoming 'Nuns' Island' in the first edition and in all subsequent editions.[22] The point is that Joyce knew that Nora had connections with St Augustine Street, Whitehall and Bowling Green, and had not lived with her grandmother on Nuns' Island,

---

19 Richard Ellmann, *James Joyce* (Oxford: Oxford University Press, rev. edn, 1982), 157.

20 O'Laoi, *Nora Barnacle Joyce*, 13.

21 Brenda Maddox, *Nora: A Biography of Nora Joyce* (1988) (Harmondsworth: Penguin Books, 2000), 20.

22 See James Joyce, *Dubliners: A Facsimile of Drafts and Manuscripts*, ed. Hans Walter Gabler (New York and London: Garland, 1978), 556; and James Joyce, *Dubliners: A Facsimile of Proofs for the 1914 Edition*, ed. Michael Groden (New York and London: Garland, 1977), 275.

yet when publishing 'The Dead', he chose to have Gretta live there. As with O'Laoi, I too have been puzzled by this seeming anomaly and would like to suggest some possible reasons for it beyond those romantic ones posited by Nora's biographer.[23]

Why Nuns' Island?

Joyce's decision to mention Nuns' Island has, naturally enough, prompted several critics to a consideration of Christian symbolism. Marjorie Howes, for instance, sees it as a kind of opposite to the Aran Islands to which the Gaelic enthusiast Miss Ivors invites Gabriel in 'The Dead'. As such, Nuns' Island becomes 'a Catholic alternative to supposedly pagan, primitive Aran'.[24] The choice of street name has also powerfully exercised the mind of Donald T. Torchiana in his intriguing collection of essays *Backgrounds for Joyce's 'Dubliners'* (1986). He correctly points out that Nuns' Island is so called because of the location there of a Poor Clare convent. He goes on, somewhat more tendentiously, to suggest a more intimate Joycean link with the convent in the shape of an early eighteenth-century behest:

> For the early chalice still preserved by the community is inscribed with the date 1701 and the words 'Pray for the soule of John Joyes and his wife Agnes Joyes who made this challis for the use of the convent of St. Clare in Galway, 1701.' A successful Galway goldsmith, Joyce ultimately bought the estate of Rahoon from a Colonel Whaly, a former officer in Cromwell's forces – and Rahoon is one of a number of possible sites for Sonny Bodkin's grave.[25]

Joyce would certainly have been fascinated by the name John Joyes – the same name as his father – but Torchiana offers no evidence that Joyce had ever seen this chalice or was familiar with it by hearsay.[26] While much of the world known intimately to Joyce no longer stands, the convent of the Poor

23 Interestingly and coincidentally, Nora's address for correspondence when visiting Galway for the last time in April 1922 was c/o Miss Casey, 5 Nun's Island. Miss Casey ran a boarding house at that address. See James Joyce, *Letters*, vol. III, ed. Richard Ellmann (London: Faber and Faber, 1966), 64; and O'Laoi, *Nora Barnacle Joyce*, 99.

24 Marjorie Howes, '"Goodbye Ireland I'm going to Gort": geography, scale, and narrating the nation', in Derek Attridge and Marjorie Howes (eds), *Semicolonial Joyce* (Cambridge: Cambridge University Press, 2000), 68.

25 Donald T. Torchiana, *Backgrounds to Joyce's 'Dubliners'* (Boston: Allen and Unwin, 1986), 246.

26 Towards the end of his life Joyce became intrigued by an advertising flyer for a ship named the 'John Joyce'. See letter to Frank Budgen (28 August 1937), in Joyce, *Letters*, vol. III, 404.

Clares and its grounds remains one of the last untouched sites in a rapidly expanding Galway and is still home to a small community of nuns.[27]

Though the Poor Clares had had a presence in Galway since the sixteenth century, associated as they were with the long-established Franciscans, they did not have an independent convent building at their disposal until 1649 when, under the leadership of Abbess Mary Bonaventura Browne, they were given a grant of land by the Galway Corporation. In their petition for the land, they had asked for 'sufficient roome for building a monasterie and rooms convenient thereunto, a garden and orchard in the next island, adjoining to the bridge of Illananntenagh'.[28] The area of 'Illananntenagh', as it is called in the petition, or Oileán Altanach, as it is more properly rendered in Irish, is the name by which the street of Nuns' Island is known today on bilingual street signs.[29] The nuns were not to enjoy their gains for very long, as in 1652 Galway fell to Cromwellian forces under General Coote and they were forced into exile, many of them to Spain. Those who survived this period abroad returned to Galway in 1686 when, after the Stuart restoration, conditions were more favourable for Roman Catholic religious orders. After Williamite successes in the 1690s the order was again persecuted when on 1 May 1698 troops ransacked the city's churches and the nuns were obliged to go into hiding. Again in 1712 and in 1731 official efforts were made to suppress the order in Galway. For much of the eighteenth century the Poor Clares were associated with a house on Market Street where they remained until 1825 when they returned to what their chronicler calls 'their old place on Island Altanagh'.[30] This return to the island was made possible by a successful royal petition in the mid-eighteenth century, as outlined by Hardiman in his history of Galway:

27 In another twist to the rather bizarre failure of writers to locate Nuns' Island, even the presence of the convent has remained elusive to some. Brian Townsend, for instance, in a study of Ireland's distilleries, writes that, 'One is tempted to assume that a convent or other religious edifice stood on the island, but none of the sources I consulted could confirm this.' Townsend, *Lost Distilleries of Ireland*, 98.

28 Quoted in James Hardiman, *The History of the Town and County of the Town of Galway, from the earliest period to the present time, Embellished with several Engravings. To which is added, a copious appendix, containing the principal charters and other original documents* (Dublin: W. Folds and Sons, 1820), 274.

29 Peadar O'Dowd writes that, technically, Oileán Altanach is the strip of land between the river Corrib and the Gaol or Cathedral river on which now stands Galway's Catholic cathedral and beyond which is the Poor Clare convent. See O'Dowd, *Old and New Galway* (Galway: Connacht Tribune and the Archaeological, Historical & Folklore Society, Regional Technical College, Galway, 1985), 71.

30 Mrs Thomas Concannon, *The Poor Clares in Ireland (a.d. 1629–a.d.1929)* (Dublin: M. H. Gill and Son, 1929), 69.

In 1740, the ladies of this house petitioned queen Caroline of England, stating the various hardships which they had suffered by repeated persecutions, and the entire deprivation of their property, and humbly besought her majesty to compassionate the situation of distressed and defenceless females, retired from the world, by ordering them to be restored to that part of their ancient property situate in Island-altenagh, or the 'Nuns Island'.[31]

Joyce was familiar with Hardiman's history of Galway and it was an important source for the small amount of journalism he wrote on the city and environs. Indeed, Kevin Barry has argued that Joyce's use of the book borders on plagiarism, his account of Galway in 'The City of the Tribes: Italian Memories in an Irish Port' (1912) being 'almost wholly lifted from James Hardiman's history of the city'.[32] With his voracious appetite for history and, by the time of composing 'The Dead', his increasingly sharpened sense of nationalist resentment, the sorry tale of the persecuted Poor Clares and their eventual return to Galway is likely to have captured Joyce's imagination. And yet the location of the historic convent on Nuns' Island is not Joyce's only, nor indeed his primary, reason for using it as a key pivot in his greatest story.

There are three other buildings associated with Nuns' Island which may have exercised Joyce's imagination. Two of these – the 'Bish' school and the old gaol – I will discuss briefly; the third, Persse's distillery, is Joyce's most important focus and will be considered in some detail. On 5 December 1862 St Joseph's secondary school, popularly known as the 'Bish' because of its first patron, Bishop McEvilly of Galway, was established on Nuns' Island by the Patrician Brothers.[33] The school's primary objectives were to provide affordable secondary education for Catholic boys and to 'counteract the proselytising influences of the Model Schools in Newcastle Road'.[34] Despite such proselytization, Galway was then, and has remained, overwhelmingly Catholic. Nora's maternal uncle, Michael Healy, having proved himself a good student at the Patrician Brothers' primary school, known colloquially as 'the Mon', went on to study at the secondary school on Nuns' Island. Again, if but as an echo, the theme of religious and political conflict is evident.

More clearly, this struggle is represented in the shape of Galway gaol. This large building stood on the site of what is now Galway's Catholic

31 Hardiman, *History*, 276, note e.
32 Kevin Barry, 'Introduction', in James Joyce, *Occasional, Critical, and Political Writing* (Oxford: Oxford University Press, 2000), xxi.
33 See O'Dowd, *Old and New Galway*, 106–7.
34 O'Laoi, *Nora Barnacle Joyce*, 6.

cathedral and adjoining car park and was operational from 1810 to 1939. As well as being a major Galway landmark and symbol of British dominion through Nora's youth and at the time of Joyce's visits to the city, Joyce would also have been familiar with the building via a Lady Gregory play first staged at the Abbey Theatre in October 1906, titled *The Gaol Gate*. This short, one-act drama deals with a visit to Galway gaol by Mary Cahel and Mary Cushin, the mother and wife respectively of a prisoner, Denis Cahel. They have walked through the night from the Slieve Echtge mountains of north Clare and south Galway – countryside adjacent to Lady Gregory's Coole – to visit Denis, having received a letter from prison authorities which they are unable to read. 'Isn't it a great pity', says the older woman, 'for the two of us to be without learning at all?'[35] The women assume, because of the prattle of neighbours, that Denis has turned informer on two neighbours, Pat Ruane and Terry Fury (a source, perhaps, for Michael Furey of 'The Dead'), jailed with him over a shooting incident. However, on showing the letter to the gatekeeper of the gaol, he tells them that the letter was sent to inform them of Denis's imminent execution by hanging. They have come a day too late and Denis lies buried in the prison yard. The play ends with the women keening, proud of Denis's heroism but heartbroken by a death brought about by his refusal to betray his guilty friends.

The injustice is, in some ways, reminiscent of an infamous and all-too-real miscarriage of justice that occurred in the Joyce country district of County Galway in 1882. The so-called Maamtrasna murders, in which a family named Joyce were massacred in an isolated region of Gaelic-speaking Connemara, led to the arrest and execution of three neighbours in Galway gaol. The oldest of the hanged men, Myles Joyce, was widely believed to be innocent, and the trial of the condemned men was compromised by the gap in understanding between an English-speaking court and Gaelic-speaking accused. James Joyce, always interested in those bearing his name and increasingly fascinated at this time by the injustices brought about by British rule in his home country, chose to write about the case for the Triestine newspaper *Il Piccolo della Sera* in September 1907 as an example of the misunderstandings inherent between the Irish and the English and the tragic consequences that such confusion can bring about. Writing of Myles Joyce, he says, 'The figure of this bewildered old man, left over from a culture which is not ours, a deaf-mute before his judge, is a symbol of the

---

35 Lady Gregory, *The Gaol Gate*, in *Selected Writings*, ed. Lucy McDiarmid and Maureen Waters (Harmondsworth: Penguin Books, 1995), 357.

Irish nation at the bar of public opinion.'[36] Myles Joyce, then, like the two Marys of *The Gaol Gate*, falls victim to an ignorance of language and to the harshness of the British penal system as it was being operated in Galway.

Galway gaol was again used by Lady Gregory the following year as a setting for one of her most popular plays, *The Rising of the Moon*, first staged at the Abbey in March 1907, in which a rebel prisoner escapes via the harbour. In subsequent notes for the play she recalls the impact this forbidding building had on her as a young girl:

> When I was a child and came with my elders to Galway for their salmon fishing in the river that rushes past the gaol, I used to look with awe at the window where men were hung, and the dark, closed gate. I used to wonder if ever a prisoner might by some means climb the high, buttressed wall and slip away in the darkness by the canal to the quays and find friends to hide him under a load of kelp in a fishing boat, as happens to my ballad-singing man.[37]

While we can say with some confidence that Joyce, while living in Trieste and Rome in the 1906–7 period, was keeping sufficiently abreast of events in Ireland to know of *The Gaol Gate*, we cannot know whether he means us to make any association between the Nuns' Island of 'The Dead' and the unmentioned Nuns' Island of Lady Gregory's play. However, it is tempting to make the connection as Lady Gregory plays a significant role throughout the story that Joyce wrote around the same time as his interest in, and account of, the murders in Maamtrasna.

Persse's Nuns Island Whisky

The last Nuns' Island building to be discussed here is Persse's distillery, home of the fabulously expensive spirit discussed above and a place very clearly linked with the author of *The Gaol Gate*. Lady Gregory was born Isabella Augusta Persse at Roxborough, south County Galway, on 15 March 1852. Roxborough was the large estate that was home to one branch of the wealthy and landed Persse family. The family had first come to Ireland in 1610, the year that saw the arrival of clergyman Reverend Robert Persse, who prospered as England strengthened her grip on Ireland in the aftermath of victory in the Nine Years War of 1594–1603. Robert subsequently lost much of his land in the 1641 rebellion and it fell to his clergyman nephew Dudley

36 James Joyce, 'Ireland at the Bar', trans. Conor Deane, in Joyce, *Occasional, Critical, and Political Writing*, 146.
37 Lady Gregory, *Selected Writings*, 540.

– a family name and later the name of Lady Gregory's father – to press home the Persse family's claims in the years after the rebellion. Dudley's first living in Ireland was in the ancient Dublin parish of St Michan's, well known to Joyce and directly across the river Liffey from the location of the Morkans' Christmas party in 'The Dead' (the church tower is clearly visible from the upper windows of the house on Usher's Island). Coincidentally, St Michan's church is adjacent to the massive Jameson distillery, which was built in the late eighteenth century. Dudley, having established himself in St Michan's in 1661, went on to expand his livings across Ireland and was the first of the Persses to acquire land in Galway, eventually becoming archdeacon of Tuam and dean of Kilmacduagh. The Persses remained, throughout their history in Ireland, strongly devoted to Protestantism and hostile to Catholicism. The last of the Galway Persses, Burton Walter (d. 1935), 'specifically voided his bequests to anyone mentioned in his last will and testament who may have been foolish enough to convert to Catholicism, a condition he equated with death (he may have had his housekeeper or day laborer in mind)'.[38]

In the latter half of the nineteenth century the Persses became synonymous with good whiskey. Besides the Roxborough branch, the other most prominent wing of the Persses lived at nearby Moyode House near Athenry; it was this branch that became more closely associated with whiskey distillation. Augusta's father, Dudley, as master of Roxborough, continued to derive his primary income from rents. Nevertheless, for Galwegians and whiskey drinkers everywhere such subtleties would have meant little. 'Persse' was the name on the bottle and it is for superior whiskey rather than for the grand houses of Roxborough, Moyode and elsewhere that the name is now remembered, if it is remembered at all. Little trace is left of the name in contemporary Ireland though two of present-day Galway's most popular hostelries, The King's Head and The Quays, boast wonderful antique mirrors advertising 'Persse's Nuns Island Whisky', from a distillery founded, the mirrors tell us, in 1815, and proud to be official suppliers to the House of Commons.[39] Lady Gregory makes a brief reference to the whiskey-producing branch of her family in her 1906 one-act comedy *Hyacinth Halvey*, when the roguish Fardy encourages the hapless Hyacinth to break into Cloon's Protestant church via an open window. There will be

38 James Charles Roy, *The Fields of Athenry: A Journey Through Irish History* (Boulder, CO: Westview Press, 2001), 198–201.

39 In addition to Persse's association with the House of Commons, the bottle recently discovered in the Swindon wine shop indicated on its label that the whiskey was supplied to King Edward VII, thus underlining that it was aimed at the upper end of the market.

easy access, Fardy tells him, 'where they are putting coloured glass in it for the distiller'.[40]

As part of the Protestant ascendancy of the Irish eighteenth and nineteenth centuries, the Persses lived a life of remarkable privilege. A visitor to a Moyode banquet in 1877 described the scene for the *Galway Express*. The house was 'magnificently furnished and decorated, reminding one of the ancestral halls of some Italian prince, with the heavy marble mantles, the splendid carved mahogany and rosewood furniture, the exceedingly large windows with deep gilt moldings before you; and behind, the huge covered tables, all odorous with spice and wine'.[41] This was a lifestyle that inevitably created an almost unbridgeable void between planter and planted, as one recent commentator has remarked: 'As the Persse family road [*sic*] to hounds and entertained their fellow gentry with lavish house parties and horse races (for 'the Moyode Cup'), interspersed with jaunts into Galway, where various of their number maintained townhouses, the Catholic peasantry buried themselves in toil, debt, and heroic memories.'[42] This gap in lifestyles between landlord and tenant, victor and vanquished, was one that Augusta Persse knew only too well and that, while wishing to retain it in some measure, she did much to narrow through her activities as a writer and collector of folklore. It was, equally, a gap of which James Joyce, thirty years Augusta's junior, was bitterly conscious and one that he, as a member of Ireland's losing class, would seek to attack, diminish and narrow through his skill as a writer and satirist.

The Persse distillery did not begin life on Nuns' Island but on nearby Earl's Island, as the pub mirror tells us, in 1815. E. B. McGuire's history of Irish whiskey informs us that by the 1820s Burton Persse owned two separate distilleries in Galway, one in Newcastle, the other at Newtowns-myth. There were, in addition to these, two other distilleries in Galway at the time, one owned by Richard Lynch and another by Patrick Joyce of Nuns' Island, whose plant had, by 1833, reached an output of 100,000 proof gallons. For whatever reason, the Joyces' success did not last long and their distillery was, for a few years in the 1840s, converted into a woollen mill. This period was the high point of whiskey distilling in Galway, encouraged by a government keen to stamp out illegal poteen stills in the west of Ireland. The Persses eventually came out on top in the battle for whiskey supremacy in the west. 'By 1846', McGuire writes, 'the Newcastle distillery was being run by Thomas Moore Persse and Company,

40 Lady Gregory, *Selected Writings*, 348.
41 Quoted in Roy, *Fields of Athenry*, 228.
42 Roy, *Fields of Athenry*, 221.

but shortly afterwards the Newcastle lease expired and Persse restored the old Joyce distillery which became known as Nun's Island distillery.'[43] It was not until 1847, as Connacht suffered the most dreadful privations as a result of famine, that the Persse plant moved to the location that gave the best-known expression of the whiskey its name, though there remained a bonded warehouse on Earl's Island for some time after that date. The bonded store was eventually converted to a military barracks in which the 17th Lancers were billeted and is now part of the National University of Ireland's Galway campus.[44] The nearby Distillery Road, which takes its name from the Persse enterprise, now forms one of the main entrances to the University.

The Nuns' Island distillery was synonymous from the outset with Henry Stratford Persse, younger brother of Dudley, Augusta's father, and H. S. Persse continued to be the name on the bottle up to the distillery's closure in much the same way as the original 'Arthur Guinness' is memorialized on all subsequent bottlings of his stout.[45] The Ireland that saw the emergence of Persse's Nuns Island distillery as a major Galway industry was then a world leader in the production of whiskey. 'In Ireland', enthused one commentator in 1838,

> where distillation is carried on to a greater extent than in any other portion
> of the world of equal magnitude, and where it forms a branch of such great
> commercial importance and enterprise, the speculative mind is naturally
> led to enquire into the causes which have produced such wonderful efforts
> in this branch of trade.[46]

By the late nineteenth and early twentieth centuries Scottish whisky had taken the mantle of world leader as a result of its move away from single malt to blended and, while huge operations like the Dublin-based John Jameson and Sons could adapt and compete, many smaller distilleries, Persse's among them, closed. 'The Scots got lucky', writes one connoisseur,

---

43 E. B. McGuire, *Irish Whiskey: A History of Distilling, the Spirit Trade and Excise Controls in Ireland* (Dublin: Gill and Macmillan; New York: Barnes and Noble Books, 1973), 359–60.
44 See O'Dowd, *Old and New Galway*, 59 and 31.
45 H. S. Persse died in 1899 after which his family emigrated from Galway to England. See 'Daughter of Old Galway Distiller Visits Her Home', *Connacht Tribune*, 15 June 1963, 28.
46 Samuel Morewood, *A Philosophical and Statistical History of the Inventions and Customs of Ancient and Modern Nations in the manufacture and use of Inebriating Liquors; with the Present Practice of Distillation in all its varieties: together with an extensive illustration of the consumption and effects of opium, and other stimulants used in the east, as substitutes for wine and spirits* (Dublin: William Curry, Jun., and William Carson; London: Longman, Orme, Brown, Green, and Longmans; Edinburgh: Fraser, 1838), 583.

'the Irish jumped the wrong way in refusing to blend.'[47]

Although it was such a successful business and a landmark on the Galway map for the best part of a hundred years, surprisingly little information survives on the Nuns' Island distillery in the way of folk memory or historical record. We owe our best description of the place and its produce to the nineteenth-century English whiskey-lover Alfred Barnard. Barnard, like Leopold Bloom a one-time advertising agent, wrote a series of articles for *Harper's Weekly Gazette* – the London-published organ of the wholesale wine and spirit trades – in the 1880s on the great array of distilleries in the kingdom. These articles were brought together to form *The Whisky Distilleries of the United Kingdom* (1887), a lively and entertaining travelogue which is not just a fascinating contemporary account of life in some of the more far-flung corners of the kingdom as it then was, but is arguably still the most important book devoted to the study of whiskey and its producers in Britain and Ireland. At the time of writing these articles and putting together the prefatory remarks for the ensuing book, Barnard, while admitting his status as an enthusiastic amateur, could point to the very great importance of distillation as an industry 'which brings the largest revenue to the Imperial Exchequer of any industry in the Kingdom'.[48]

At the time of Barnard's two-year-long excursion, most of which was given over to the 129 distilleries in Scotland, there were just 28 such plants in Ireland, although Irish whiskey still accounted for a significantly higher proportion of total output within the kingdom than these figures might suggest, with Scotland at 17,982,338 gallons per annum and Ireland at 10,620,584 in the period 1885–6.[49] Of the 28 Irish distilleries, only one, Persse's, was still in production west of the Shannon, and Barnard in his book makes the journey westward after his examination of the Dublin distilleries and onward through distilleries at Monasterevan, County Kildare; Tullamore, County Offaly (then King's County); and Kilbeggan, County Westmeath. Historically, it was a time of great unrest in the country with the heady mix of land agitation and Home Rule coming to the boil. Barnard shows himself well aware of these factors and is sympathetic to the smallholders' cause, as is evident in this description of a demonstration witnessed in Tullamore:

> A procession, headed by a band of music, came in sight, followed by a rickety jaunting car, drawn by a venerable horse, rather groggy on his legs.

47 Richard Joynson, 'Introduction', in Alfred Barnard, *The Whisky Distilleries of the United Kingdom* (1887) (Edinburgh: Birlinn, 2003), vi.
48 Barnard, *Whisky Distilleries*, v.
49 See Barnard, *Whisky Distilleries*, v.

The animal's harness was decorated with sprigs of evergreen, while on the car, under an arbour of the same, sat a middle-aged lady, with a pleasant air of jollity on her face, who, we were informed, was an evicted martyr, just released from prison. She was followed by hundreds of nondescript vehicles, and a great crowd of sympathisers. Whilst the first band was playing 'Wearin' o' the Green,' the second, which brought up the rear, gave us 'God bless Ould Ireland,' and although we hailed from the land of the Saxon, 'We were not afraid.' Indeed we enjoyed the fun immensely, and got mixed up with the crowd, feeling quite content for the time being to quaff Daly's Whisky, so freely offered us, and were almost induced to join their ranks.[50]

There is more than a touch here of the Victorian tourist and there are tremors too of that breed of Arnoldian Celticism that has the Celt an impractical opponent of fact. But that is not the whole story. Barnard appears to have a genuine sympathy for the cause of Irish nationalism and refers in later sections of the book – as I will show in the following chapter – to English treachery being at the root of Irish troubles. Of the peasantry on his journey towards Galway he says, 'it is well known that they are passionately fond of their home and country'. And he continues to describe ruefully the conditions in which these peasants live: 'As we passed along, we could not help noticing that their dwellings and little farm buildings were dreadfully out of repair and fast falling into decay, and it was quite evident that they were not let out on repairing leases.'[51] The west of Ireland's impoverished, rebellious and exceptional nature continued to be stressed by travel-writers, journalists and historians throughout much of Joyce's writing life. The year in which he writes 'The Dead' sees his local Triestine newspaper report on the subject in memorable terms: 'For two or three months, that is since the Dublin Convention decided not to support the Irish Council Bill and so declared war against the Government, all of the region west of the Shannon has been in a genuine state of war.'[52] To say that Connacht in 1907 was at war is a journalistic exaggeration but nonetheless the description adds strength to Joyce's piercing adjective in his famous description of Ireland's great river: 'the dark mutinous Shannon' (D 225).

As with Joyce some twenty-five years after Barnard's travels into the west, it would seem that Hardiman's *History of Galway* informs Barnard's view of the city, and as with Joyce in his later newspaper article for *Il Piccolo*, Galway becomes the 'City of the Tribes'. One suspects the hand

50 Barnard, *Whisky Distilleries*, 387.
51 Barnard, *Whisky Distilleries*, 395.
52 *Il Piccolo della Sera*, 6 August 1907. Quoted in John McCourt, *The Years of Bloom: James Joyce in Trieste 1904–1920* (Dublin: Lilliput Press, 2000), 113.

of Hardiman behind Barnard's descriptions of Galway as 'arranged on the plan of a Spanish town'; his insistence that, during the reign of Henry VIII, 'Galway supplied nearly the whole of the Kingdom with wine'; and his retelling of the infamous story of Judge Lynch and his actions in having his own son hanged for the murder of a Spanish wine merchant.[53] But on the Persse family's involvement with the whiskey industry Barnard has, not surprisingly, a good deal more to say than Hardiman, for whom the Persses were just starting out as a family of industrial significance in Galway City. For Hardiman, writing prior to 1820, Persse is a name more immediately associated with beer than with whiskey:

> A public brewery, on an extensive scale, has been for some years past established at Newcastle, near the town, the property of Mr. Persse, of Roxboro', and another at Madeira island, beyond the west bridge. The porter made here, but particularly in the former, has been much esteemed, and had for some time a good deal superseded the use of ardent spirits among the lower orders. This, however, interfered but little with Mr. Joyce's extensive distillery at Newtown Smith, in which superior spirits have, for many years past, been distilled under the superintendence of Mr. Finn.[54]

Thus, it would seem that, in addition to their Nuns' Island plant, the Joyces also distilled on the other bank of the Corrib. It is difficult to come to any definite conclusion as to who owned what distillery and where, but it is clear, nonetheless, that Joyce and Persse were, by 1840, the two key players in the industry. It is likely that James Joyce would have known about his namesake's rise and fall via Hardiman and Nora. Nora's family home in Bowling Green was, after all, just across the river from Nuns' Island and adjacent to Newtownsmyth, and she worked for several years in the Presentation convent at one end of Nuns' Island at a time when the Persse plant was still flourishing.

By the time Barnard came to write about Galway's drinks industry, the Persses had moved decisively from brewing to distilling. Crucially, as Barnard tells us, this change was at the expense of the Joyces:

> The Nun's Island Distillery was established at the beginning of the century, and is the only Distillery in Connaught. It was purchased from the Encumbered Estates Court in the year 1840, by the father of the present proprietor, who considerably enlarged and improved it. Prior to that date, from 1815 to the period mentioned, it belonged to the Joyce family.[55]

53 See Barnard, *Whisky Distilleries*, 397.
54 Hardiman, *History*, 299.
55 Barnard, *Whisky Distilleries*, 397. Though Barnard is correct about the passing of the

At the time of Barnard's visit the distillery's proprietor is still listed as H. S. Persse and it was producing a massive 400,000 gallons of whiskey per annum thanks to the fast-flowing waters of the Corrib, described by Barnard as 'a foaming torrent, that would turn all the mills in Manchester'.[56]

Did James Joyce read Barnard's *Whisky Distilleries of the United Kingdom* in either periodical or book format? It is not possible to provide a certain answer to this question though it seems highly probable that, given the preoccupations and past glories of his father, John Stanislaus, James was familiar with Barnard. For John, himself, had been intimately involved in the distilling industry and it was a period in his life that he frequently recalled and, as was his wont, misremembered to his benefit. Through much of his later life, John's chosen reading material was the periodical literature of the drinks trade, a leading example of which was *Harper's Weekly Gazette*.[57] The drinks trade ran on both sides of James Joyce's family but his father had a particular intimacy with whiskey production having owned a large number of shares in, and having been secretary of, the Dublin and Chapelizod distillery, which had been incorporated in 1874 and had operated in Chapelizod through the later 1870s. By the time of Barnard's tour it had changed hands and become known as the Phoenix Park distillery.[58] It is a place that, for once, is remembered directly by Joyce in *Dubliners* as the location of the home of Mr James Duffy, the intellectual loner of 'A Painful Case': 'He lived in an old sombre house and from his windows he could look into the disused distillery or upwards along the shallow river on which Dublin is built' (*D* 103). In addition to this being a clear-eyed nod to his father's happy past and an echo of one of the few books owned by John Stanislaus, Sheridan Le Fanu's gothic novel *The House by the Churchyard*, set in and around the Liffey valley, there is also here, in the memories of Chapelizod and the Liffey, the first stirrings of *Finnegans Wake*, a novel that from start to finish is fascinated by breweries, distilleries, Guinness, Jameson, publicans and all the paraphernalia associated with the drinks

_____

   distillery from Joyce to Persse, he cannot be correct on the subject of how this occurred, the Encumbered Estates Act not having been passed until 1849.

56 Barnard, *Whisky Distilleries*, 397.

57 One of James Joyce's many biographers tells us of John Joyce that 'In old age his only regular reading was the organ of the Licensed Vintners Association'. Peter Costello, *James Joyce: The Years of Growth 1882–1915* (London: Kyle Cathie, 1992), 45.

58 I am reliant for much of the information on John Joyce's time in the distillery on Stanislaus Joyce, *My Brother's Keeper*; Costello, *James Joyce: The Years of Growth*; and John Wyse Jackson and Peter Costello, *John Stanislaus Joyce: The Voluminous Life and Genius of James Joyce's Father* (London: Fourth Estate, 1998). On the Phoenix Park distillery, see Barnard, *Whisky Distilleries*, 378–81.

trade.[59] As I am a very long way from being Joyce's ideal insomniac reader, I do not intend to spend any great deal of time dissecting the *Wake* but there are a few moments in the book worth considering if we are to get to the bottom of Joyce's game with whiskey.

Drinking in the *Wake*

Joyce takes the title of his final book from the song of the same name, though with the expected possessive apostrophe excluded. In the song, 'Finnegan's Wake', whiskey plays a major part and, though it is not mentioned directly in the novel, Joyce hovers close to it with HCE's 'will you whoop for my deading is a? Wake? *Usqueadbaugham!* Anam muck an dhoul! Did ye drink me doornail?' (24.14–15). This is almost a direct quotation from the song in which Tim Finnegan is revived from his deathbed by whiskey, *uisce beatha*, the water of life:

> Then Micky Maloney raised his head
> When a noggin of whiskey flew at him,
> It missed and falling on the bed,
> The liquor scattered over Tim;
> Bedad he revives, see how he rises
> And Timothy rising from the bed,
> Says 'Whirl your liquor round like blazes,
> Thanam o'n dhoul, do ye think I'm dead?'[60]

Whiskey as a life-giver, an *uisce beatha*, would seem to work against the spirit's negative symbolic function in *Dubliners* but, as with everything in the *Wake*, this, too, is not straightforward, as we see in the penultimate chapter of the book. As this chapter draws to a close, HCE suffers a series of setbacks, the final and most calamitous being the destruction of his distillery: 'Till, ultimatehim, fell the crowning barleystraw, when an explosium of his distilleries deafadumped all his dry goods to his most favoured sinflute and dropped him, what remains of a heptarch, leareyed and letterish, weeping worrybound on his bankrump' (589.35–590.3). This

---

59 Most critics have failed to see the importance of Joyce's familial associations with Chapelizod, choosing instead to concentrate on the Tristram and Isolde myth. For example, see Martha Fodaski Black, 'Joyce on Location: Place Names in Joyce's Fiction', in Michael Begnal (ed.), *Joyce and the City: The Significance of Place* (Syracuse, NY: Syracuse University Press, 2002), 21–2; and Thomas E. Connolly, 'A Painful Case', in Hart (ed.), *James Joyce's 'Dubliners'*, 107–14.

60 Quoted in Roland McHugh, *Annotations to 'Finnegans Wake'* (Baltimore, MD: Johns Hopkins University Press, rev. edn, 1991), 24.

disastrous distillery explosion refers both to a real event, an accident at Roe's distillery, Dublin, in 1860 that is referred to at least twice elsewhere in the *Wake*, after which legend had it that whiskey flowed down the streets; and to the financial collapse of the Dublin and Chapelizod distillery in which Joyce's father was a major investor.[61] James Atherton, in *The Books at the Wake* (1959), has also suggested a way in which beer – particularly Guinness – comes to stand for genesis, and whiskey for apocalypse.

> It will be noticed that the word Genesis has been mutated to suggest Guinness's. This trope is repeated two pages later in, 'With a bockalips of finisky fore his feet. And a barrowload of guenesis hoer his head' (6.26). After this the two themes divide and go their separate ways. But when Finnegan is laid out the corpse begins – has its head – under Genesis with the barrow representing a funeral barrow. It ends – has its feet, or has 'finisky' – after the Apocalypse. This symbolizes the way in which the Bible is used in the Wake.[62]

Atherton goes on to describe 'Finisky' as 'a typical word in the Wake' in so far as it can be read to mean a wide range of things beyond just whiskey: 'Examined more closely it is finis, end, with the Russian suffix for "son of". It says "Finn is sky". It is "Phoenix" or Fionn Uisge – the self-resurrecting bird or a clear spring of water, but in either sense Dublin's great park. Finally it could mean, "The sky is ended".'[63] In Joyce's recurring use of Phoenix Park in *Finnegans Wake* he is inevitably thinking too of the Phoenix distillery that rose from the ashes of his father's ruined business.

Another way in which whiskey cannot go unnoticed in the *Wake* is that Joyce somehow found the name of Dublin's largest whiskey producers, John Jameson and Son, particularly musical, and he repeats it on several occasions and in several forms throughout the book. As with *Dubliners*, whiskey is there on the opening page, with Jameson making a veiled appearance as 'Rot a peck of pa's malt had Jhem or Shen brewed by arclight'

---

61 Interestingly, Roe's distillery owned the house on Usher's Island that Joyce uses as his setting for 'The Dead'. See Costello, *James Joyce: The Years of Growth*, 26. Joyce may also be conscious here of George Egerton's intriguing short story 'Mammy'. On the night of a raging distillery fire, Mammy, the matriarch of a brothel, is forced to carry a dying young prostitute through the streets of Dublin so that she can be administered the last rites by the priests who refuse to come to her. Dublin is rendered hellish by the whiskey that runs in rivers of flames through its streets. See George Egerton, 'Mammy', in *Flies in Amber* (London: Hutchinson, 1905). I am grateful to Whitney Standlee for drawing my attention to this story.

62 James Atherton, *The Books at the Wake: A Study of Literary Allusions in James Joyce's 'Finnegans Wake'* (London: Faber and Faber, 1959), 173.

63 Atherton, *Books at the Wake*, 173, fn. 1.

(3.12–13). Joyce's favourite whiskey then makes various other appearances over the course of his confusing narrative as 'Jhon Jhamieson and Song' (126.5), 'jammesons' (333.16), 'Jon Jacobsen' (424.27), 'Shamous Shamonous, Limited' (425.6), and on Shaun's departure we are told that he goes 'with half a glance of Irish frisky (a Juan Jaimesan hastaluego)' (470.32–3). The reason for Joyce's delight in the name Jameson is, I think, straightforwardly as a homonym of his own name: as his books might in some way be thought of as his children, 'James's sons', so too the whiskey. His grandfather and great-grandfather had also run a business in Cork called 'James Joyce and Son' which went bankrupt in 1852.[64]

In one of his more forlorn periods of composition when he began to think of the possibility of handing over responsibility for finishing *Finnegans Wake*, he thought of the Dublin writer James Stephens, as much for reasons of artistic integrity as because of his devotion to the Jameson's whiskey trademark, as he outlines to Harriet Shaw Weaver in a letter of May 1927:

> As regards that book itself and its future completion I have asked Miss Beach to get into closer relations with James Stephens. [...] He is a poet and Dublin born. Of course he would never take a fraction of the time or pains I take but so much the better for him and me and possibly for the book itself. If he consented to maintain three or four points which I consider essential and I showed him the threads he could finish the design. JJ and S (the colloquial Irish for John Jameson and Son's Dublin whisky) would be a nice lettering under the title.[65]

Of course Joyce knew only too well that the book would not be finished if he did not do the job himself – the notion of Stephens, or anyone else, being able to pick up where Joyce left off was preposterous, hence the puckish aside about Jameson's.

Besides Jameson, several other brands of whiskey are named in the *Wake*. Power's (the only big Irish distiller in the control of a Catholic family) gets in on a few occasions both under its own name and under its trademark of 'three swallows'. Also mentioned are Johnny Walker, Bushmills, Roe's distillery and, of course, Persse's. There may well be others concealed in the text that I am not seeing but the name Persse is, unusually for *Finnegans Wake*, right out in the open in the form of Hosty's scurrilous rhyme about the ever-mutating innkeeper and central character of the novel H.

64 Jackson and Costello, *John Stanislaus Joyce*, 26.
65 James Joyce to Harriet Shaw Weaver (20 May 1927), in James Joyce, *Letters*, ed. Stuart Gilbert (London: Faber and Faber, 1957), 253–4. Note Joyce's spelling of 'whisky'.

C. Earwicker, of whom, Hosty insists, 'I parse him Persse O'Reilly else he's called no name at all' (44.13–14). Most critics – typically Roland McHugh in his indispensable *Annotations to 'Finnegans Wake'* – have interpreted 'Persse O'Reilly' as a version of the French for earwig, *perce-oreille*, and as a composite of two nationalist heroes of the 1916 Rising, Padraig Pearse and The O'Rahilly.[66] Of course, when addressing the complexities of *Finnegans Wake* multiple meanings are not just always possible but inevitable. In the case of Hosty's ballad, however, most critics have passed over or neglected the obvious allusion to Lady Gregory and her family's distillery in looking for a key to Joyce's code. One exception is William York Tindall, who, on the question of 'Persse', goes further than most exegetes, seeing earwigs, 1916 rebels, Lady Gregory and the Estonian word for arse.[67] With any other writer and with any other book we could dismiss such claims, but not with *Finnegans Wake*. As regards the Gregory allusion, other than the straightforward use of the name Persse, Joyce may be referencing Lady Gregory and her husband, Sir William Gregory, in the third verse of the ballad:

> He was fafafather of all schemes for to bother us
> Slow coaches and immaculate contraceptives for the populace,
> Mare's milk for the sick, seven dry Sundays a week,
> Openair love and religion's reform,
> (Chorus) And religious reform,
>   Hideous in form. (45.13–18)

While the subject of the rhyme is, on a surface level, HCE, if we are to act on the prompt of 'Persse' then we might read 'the father of all schemes to bother us' as a reference to Sir William Gregory and an amendment to the Poor Law Act that he proposed in 1847 and that became known as the Gregory Clause. The clause was an ill-conceived attempt at famine relief that, by insisting that small landholders abandon their holdings in order to get relief, helped landlords clear their estates and did a great deal more harm than good to the destitute of the Great Hunger of the 1840s. The puritanical 'religious reform, hideous in form' that enforces abstemiousness refers to Lady Gregory and the Persse family's reputation as proselytizers – a charge to which Lady Gregory was acutely sensitive, as we shall see in the next chapter.

---

66 See McHugh, *Annotations to 'Finnegans Wake'*, 44; and James Fairhall, *James Joyce and the Question of History* (Cambridge: Cambridge University Press, 1993), 231.
67 William York Tindall, *A Reader's Guide to 'Finnegans Wake'* (1969) (Syracuse, NY: Syracuse University Press, 1996), 6.

Whiskey, Chapelizod and the Joyces

As *Finnegans Wake* is set around a Chapelizod licensed premises, so too the root of Joyce's whiskey obsession must be sought in that pretty west Dublin suburb, and in John Joyce's misadventures there. John Stanislaus Joyce had been born into a comfortable, rentier background in Cork in 1849. His father died in 1866 and John stood to inherit a lucrative portfolio of property. He made a half-hearted attempt to study medicine at Queen's College, Cork, but was more interested in the usual attractions attendant upon undergraduate study. He was a fine oarsman and had a large repertory of songs, as is fondly recalled by his eldest son in the 'Sirens' episode of *Ulysses*. His widowed mother worried about this young rake's prospects in the world, and finally made up her mind to move the family to Dublin after John, with two college friends, made an abortive attempt to run off and join the French war effort against Prussia in 1870. Sympathy for France ran high in John's native city, and the Cork Distilleries Company was not untypical in making a subscription for the relief of the French wounded.[68] Mrs Joyce had political connections in Dublin that she hoped to use to her and her son's benefit. She was an O'Connell by birth, related to 'The Liberator', Daniel O'Connell, and to the then Lord Mayor of Dublin, Peter Paul McSwiney. Though John later became involved in both national and Dublin Corporation politics – experience later put to memorable use by James in 'Ivy Day in the Committee Room' – he was not successful in securing a sinecure on his initial arrival in the city. Instead, he invested the very large sum of £500, part of a coming-of-age gift from his grandfather, in a new business venture with a fellow Corkman, the wine merchant Henry Alleyn. This business was named the Dublin and Chapelizod distillery.

In later life, John recalled his years in Chapelizod with great fondness. For these memories, we are largely reliant on his son, Stanislaus, as he recounted them in *My Brother's Keeper* (1958), as well as on a disputed interview given by John, at the request of James, to an anonymous journalist in Dublin towards the end of his life. This interview was published by Maria Jolas in the *James Joyce Yearbook* in 1949.[69] The authenticity of the interview was subsequently called into question by a number of Joycean scholars, including John V. Kelleher and Hugh Kenner, while being defended by

68 See John Irvine, *Uisce Beatha: The Evolution & Archives of the Irish Whiskey Distilling Industry* (n. pl.: Irish Distillers, 1985), 12.

69 See Anonymous, 'Interview with Mr. John Stanislas [*sic*] Joyce (1849–1931)', in Maria Jolas (ed.), *A James Joyce Yearbook* (Paris: Transition Press, 1949), 159–69.

others.[70] One favoured theory of the sceptics was that the interview was an elaborate hoax set up by Brian O'Nolan. John Joyce's biographers have accepted the interview as authentic and, for the purposes of this study, I too accept the legitimacy of the interview: even for an inveterate and ingenious joker like Flann O'Brien, the details provided in the piece seem too involved, intimate and at times tedious for them to be forgeries. Quite simply, there is nothing comedic about the interview. Much of what John says chimes closely with the recollections of Stanislaus published some nine years later – nowhere is this truer than in his happy memories of his time in the distillery.

The job of distillery secretary allowed John to indulge in a great deal of what he did best – pressing the flesh, sweet-talking customers and charming workmen and colleagues alike. Chapelizod was home to a hotel owned by an Englishman, Robert Broadbent, which became a favourite watering hole of John's as he indulged in his then chosen pastime of bowls. A fictional version of this establishment plays a key role in *Finnegans Wake* where, as the Mullingar Hotel, it is the home of H. C. Earwicker. It was thanks to his work in the drinks trade that John met the nineteen-year-old May Murray, soon to be his wife and matriarch of the Joyce family. May's father, John Murray from Longford, was also indebted to alcohol for his living. Stanislaus remembers his grandfather as an agent for wines and spirits. In fact John Murray had a long pedigree in the industry having worked variously as the proprietor of a pub, The Eagle House, in Round-town, Dublin, and as a sales representative for one of the largest and most successful distillers in the country, John Power's, a firm that managed to weather the storm of Scottish whisky's rise in the late nineteenth and early twentieth centuries. And so James Joyce is intimately connected – immersed even – in whiskey on both sides of his family. John Murray was a customer of the Dublin and Chapelizod distillery and took a liking to the young and affable businessman, John Joyce. The cordial relations between future father-in-law and son-in-law did not last and John Joyce developed an irrational dislike of the Murrays, liking in later years to refer to his wife's father as 'a bottle-washer in a paper hat'.[71]

John Joyce's memories of the distillery are worth quoting at length in order to establish a clear picture of the significance the place played in his

70 For an assessment of the controversy around this interview, see Margaret Heckard, 'The Literary Reverberations of a Fake Interview with John Stanislaus Joyce', *James Joyce Quarterly*, 13.4 (Summer 1976), 468–71.

71 Jackson and Costello, *John Stanislaus Joyce*, 124.

subsequent sense of disgruntlement, a side of his personality inherited by his eldest son:

> I knew the place very well for I was Secretary to the Distillery there for 3 or 4 years. It was owned by the Dublin and Chapelizod Distilling Coy. You know that the premises were very historic. Formerly the place was used as a Convent, then Begor it became a soldiers' barracks and after that William Dargan got it and set up a Flax Factory. His monument is in Merrion Square. Eventually it became a distillery. It was owned by Corkmen, Henry Alleyn was the Chairman of it and John Dunbar, afterwards M.P. for New Ross, and a brother-in-law of Alleyns, was one of the directors. Alleyn knew my father very well. I applied for shares – I had money at that time – and I took £500 worth on condition that they appointed me secretary. At that particular time I had nothing particular to do, and after an interview by Henry Alleyn, Dunbar, George Delaney, another director and a Corkman too, I was appointed secretary. Delaney knew my friend John [recte Peter] Paul McSweeney who was a first cousin of my mother's – he was twice Lord Mayor of Dublin. John Daly who was a first cousin of mine and M.P. for Cork was also Mayor of that city.
>
> Anyway I was appointed Secretary with a salary of £300 and I stopped there for about three years. Chapelizod was a very quaint old spot. The Earl of Donoughmore's family are buried there in the old church; he lived in the house on the hill, which is now a lunatic asylum.

Several of John's – and subsequently James's – obsessions arise in this short memory: pride in family connections, a fascination with local history, famous old houses and families with aristocratic connections, and a keen interest in public statues – memorably pervasive in both 'The Dead' and throughout *Ulysses*. When asked about the quality of the water in the Liffey – a crucial production factor for any distillery – John replied that he knew 'Not a damn bit because I never drank it without whiskey in it.'[72]

John Joyce was secretary of the distillery for approximately three years, from 1875–8, at which point it ran into financial difficulties that led to closure and significant losses for John. This was the first of many financial blunders made by John over a life that would bring his family from the comfortable coastal surrounds of Bray to the penury of Cabra, a journey later recounted by James in *A Portrait of the Artist as a Young Man*. Not surprisingly, then, the collapse of the distillery left a lasting legacy and became a point of acute resentment for John, who vigorously sought a scapegoat in the shape of Henry Alleyn. It would seem, given Stanislaus's clear recall of this debacle, a crisis that occurred ten years before he was

72 Anonymous, 'Interview with Mr. John Stanislas Joyce', 159–60, 162.

even born, that the rise and fall of the Dublin and Chapelizod distillery weighed heavily on John Joyce's mind. Stanislaus takes his father at his word in his recollection of the case:

> The manager, whose name my brother has borrowed for the manager in 'Counterparts', had been a friend of my grandfather's in Cork. My father used to describe him as a kind of duodecimo Lord Chesterfield, a figure still remembered in Ireland. He drove out every morning to Chapelizod, where the distillery was, in a dog-cart with a tiger sitting behind him with folded arms. The workmen hated him, and once tried to kill him by dropping a heavy beam of timber on him from a gallery when he was going his rounds. My father was quick enough to pull him under a shed an instant before the beam crashed just where he had been standing. My father, instead, was a favourite with the men, with whom he used to play bowls. I do not know how long the secretaryship lasted, about three or four years it seems, until my father discovered that the manager was embezzling the money of the firm. After a very heated discussion and a torrent of abuse from the manager, which came to an end only when the young secretary was preparing to use violence, my father called a meeting of the shareholders. The manager decamped, and the firm was wound up. At the meeting the shareholders voted their thanks 'to the young man who had saved them from greater loss' and appointed him trustee. Whatever money was realized from the winding-up of the distillery was lodged in his name in the Bank of Ireland, and must still be there, I presume, unless the statute of limitations has provided for its disposal.[73]

This tale of a dashing and popular young hero who attempts to come to the rescue of a noble enterprise only to be defeated by the double dealing of an older, craftier businessman is just that, a tale. Richard Ellmann, when preparing *My Brother's Keeper* for publication, went to the trouble of looking for John Joyce's missing money in the Bank of Ireland, only to find that no such deposit existed. Forty years later, John Joyce's biographers dug deeper and cleared Henry Alleyn of any guilt in the unfortunate distillery's demise. Rather than fleeing as an embezzler, Alleyn 'retired in dignity' and eventually died quietly in retirement in 1880.[74] Joyce knew all too well what his father could be like in embroidering tales of his own past, as is clear from the following brief passage in *Stephen Hero*: 'Stephen's father was quite capable of talking himself into believing what he knew to be untrue. He knew that his own ruin had been his own handiwork but he had talked himself into believing that it was the handiwork of others' (*SH*

73 Stanislaus Joyce, *My Brother's Keeper*, 27–8.
74 See Jackson and Costello, *John Stanislaus Joyce*, 76–8.

115). For Joyce, this proclivity of his father's was always forgiven, even seen as charming.

Revenge in 'Counterparts'

Interestingly, Stanislaus, no admirer of his father in *My Brother's Keeper*, retells the old story of the embezzled money as fact, and it is clear that James was also familiar with the tale of the villainous Mr Alleyn and chose, as Stanislaus also reports, to exact a delicate measure of revenge through his story of office unhappiness and the violence attendant upon alcoholic overindulgence, 'Counterparts'. This story looks at a day in the life of its central protagonist, Farrington, as he longs to get away from his desk job at the firm of Crosbie & Alleyne, has a rather pathetic showdown with Mr Alleyne that he later retells as a victory (echoes of John Joyce's brush with another Mr Alleyn), goes on a drinking spree in which several small humiliations further blacken his mood, and returns home drunk where he beats his little son above the cries of the boy's protestations. The reader is left in little doubt that Farrington is a man going nowhere, that the frustrations inherent in his job are only likely to get worse, and that his family will continue to be on the receiving end of his drink-sodden temper.

David Lloyd has linked the alcoholic excess of the story to the despair of a conquered land, describing 'Counterparts' as being 'bitterly diagnostic of the paralysis of Irish men in colonial Ireland, of their alienation and anomie which, so often, is counterpointed by drinking'.[75] Farrington's defeat at the hands of an Englishman in an arm-wrestling contest certainly lends some credence to such an interpretation. But, while there is doubtless a political symbolic slant to Farrington's perambulations, there is also a more straightforwardly autobiographical root to the story. Joyce was to some degree drawing from personal experience. Certainly, if Stanislaus is to be believed, such heartbreaking scenes as conclude 'Counterparts' were not uncommon in the Joyce household as John Joyce slipped further into financial difficulties. It may be that James Joyce – who, let us remember, had a much better relationship with his father than did Stanislaus – intended Farrington as a counterpart of John Joyce, and it is certainly the case that Mr Alleyne of the story acts in that fashion for Mr Alleyn of the Dublin and Chapelizod distillery.[76]

75 David Lloyd, 'Counterparts: *Dubliners*, masculinity, and temperance nationalism', in Attridge and Howes (eds), *Semicolonial Joyce*, 129.
76 Don Gifford, and after him Terence Brown, disagree with this loaded reading of 'Alleyne'. Both point to a C. W. Alleyne, a solicitor with offices on Dame Street, listed in *Thom's*

As in John Joyce's memory of Henry Alleyn, Mr Alleyne of 'Counterparts' is a harsh and unpopular boss. While the original Mr Alleyn was from Cork, 'Counterparts' has him as an Ulsterman with 'a piercing North of Ireland accent' (D 82). Farrington – or simply and coldly 'the man', as he is referred to throughout most of the story – has had poor relations with Alleyne from the outset, his boss having caught him impersonating his Ulster accent. Early in the story Alleyne has reason to upbraid Farrington for failing to get a contract copied and for a generally lackadaisical attitude to his work. Alleyne, as Farrington sees him in his office, is 'a little man wearing gold-rimmed glasses on a clean-shaven face', with a head 'so pink and hairless that it seemed like a large egg reposing on the papers' (D 82). Farrington, chastened by the dressing down, leaves the office for a quick glass of porter, fails to complete the copy requested by Alleyne, and is subsequently discovered to have left another file short of two copied letters. For this he gets a second, this time public, lecture about the unsatisfactory standard of his work, and manages some measure of revenge with a smart retort:

> — I know nothing about any other two letters, he said stupidly.
> — *You – know – nothing*. Of course you know nothing, said Mr Alleyne. Tell me, he added, glancing first for approval to the lady beside him, do you take me for a fool? Do you think me an utter fool?
> The man glanced from the lady's face to the little egg-shaped head and back again; and, almost before he was aware of it, his tongue had found a felicitous moment:
> — I don't think, sir, he said, that that's a fair question to put to me. (D 87)

This remark, not surprisingly, infuriates Alleyne, so that he becomes deeply flushed and 'his mouth twitched with a dwarf's passion' (D 87). Farrington is told in no uncertain terms that the remark will cost him his job if an apology is not forthcoming. Farrington recalls how Alleyne 'had hounded little Peake out of the office in order to make room for his own nephew' (D 88) and suspects his own life will be made intolerable if he stays. Unwilling to imagine this awful future, the solution to Farrington's problems lies, for now, in drink as he feels 'his great body again aching for the comfort of the public-house' (D 88).

Having pawned his watch in Terry Kelly's of Fleet Street, Farrington rehearses in his head the way he will retell the story of the put-down to his drinking pals. Nosey Flynn buys him a half-one of whiskey in Davy Byrne's,

---

Directory of 1904, p. 1468. See Don Gifford, *Joyce Annotated: Notes for 'Dubliners' and 'A Portrait of the Artist as a Young Man'* (Berkeley, CA: University of California Press, 2nd edn, 1982), 74; and Terence Brown, 'Notes', in Joyce, *Dubliners* (Harmondsworth: Penguin Books, 1992), 4.

saying 'it was as smart a thing as he ever heard' (D 89). Next Leonard and O'Halloran arrive, with O'Halloran also plumping for whiskey ('tailors of malt') as due reward after hearing the story. When Higgins, a work colleague of Farrington's, enters the pub, he is asked to give his version of the story, which he is only too happy to do 'for the sight of five small hot whiskies was very exhilarating' (D 89). But, from this lofty height, the night begins to deteriorate as that terrible moment for any true drinker arrives: 'When that round was over there was a pause' (D 90). After this uncomfortable point, in addition to Higgins and Nosey Flynn making a quick getaway, the whiskey becomes rather less exhilarating and begins to take on the negative tone to which it will later return in 'A Painful Case' and, more powerfully, 'The Dead'.

Over the course of one paragraph the remaining drinkers wander from Davy Byrne's to the Scotch House on Burgh Quay and from there onward to Mulligan's of Poolbeg Street. Through his use of the word 'Scotch' in the middle of this triumvirate, Joyce means to trigger once more the central image of whiskey, an image reinforced a few lines later by the requested drink of Weathers, an English associate of Leonard's 'who was performing at the Tivoli as an acrobat and knock-about *artiste*' (D 90). Weathers very clearly represents English domination in 'Counterparts' in one of the most direct allusions to Ireland's colonial condition that Joyce permits himself over the course of *Dubliners*. In addition to being defeated twice at arm-wrestling by Weathers, Farrington also feels himself snubbed by an Englishwoman in Mulligan's at whom he has been making eyes. As with Farrington and his friends, Weathers' drink of choice is whiskey, with the notable exception in his case that he is keen to stress a country of origin: 'Farrington stood a drink all round. Weathers said he would take a small Irish and Apollinaris. Farrington, who had definite notions of what was what, asked the boys would they have an Apollinaris too; but the boys told Tim to make theirs hot' (D 90). Apollinaris is a German mineral water, and the drink ordered by Weathers is both sophisticated (Farrington knowing 'what was what') and expensive (Farrington is later much relieved when Weathers switches to a glass of bitter in Mulligan's). It is notable, given the Joyce family's losses on Irish whiskey and the earlier use of the name Alleyn in the story, that Farrington is undermined and humiliated by an Englishman drinking Irish. And just to ensure that we have not missed the significance of the spirit's qualifying adjective, Joyce repeats it almost immediately: 'O'Halloran stood a round and then Farrington stood another round, Weathers protesting that the hospitality was too Irish' (D 90). The hot whiskeys preferred by 'the boys' would have been made with an inferior whiskey, most likely one of the cheaper Scotch blends then making inroads on the Irish market and closing small distilleries such as Persses and the Dublin and Chapelizod.

The Politics of Drink

The indirect association of social and economic superiority with whiskey in 'Counterparts' through the figure of the Ulsterman Alleyne, and the direct association of English domination with the spirit in the person of Weathers, re-emerges in the figure of Mr Browne in 'The Dead'. Browne is a neglected and, where considered at all, a frequently misinterpreted and misunderstood character within the story. Willard Potts reads him as 'the comic butt of "The Dead"'. This misreading in turn leads to a broader misconception regarding Joyce's feelings about the tension between Protestant and Catholic in the Dublin of his times. 'There is one Revival issue', argues Potts, 'that Joyce does not take, or at least does not treat, seriously in "The Dead": the relationship between the two cultures.'[77]

   John Kelleher, Paul Muldoon and Donald Torchiana take a radically different view of the character, all seeing Browne as a representative of death. 'Joyce uses Mr Browne', writes Torchiana, 'as might Holbein in his series of woodcuts, *The Dance of Death*.'[78] This darker vision of who or what Browne might represent is more convincing than that forwarded by Potts for a number of reasons, but in order to get to the bottom of Joyce's intentions in creating the character of Mr Browne, we ought to start with the two unique aspects of the man as he attends the Morkans' Christmas party: he is the only Protestant present and he is the only reveller to drink whiskey.

   Dubliners being a book written by a down-at-heel Catholic about lower- and lower-middle-class Dublin at the turn of the nineteenth century, it is not surprising that Protestants are scarce in its pages. While times were improving for Catholics and while not all Irish Protestants were of the ruling elite, Catholics could not, for the most part, aspire to the upper levels of mercantile, professional or political society. Joyce's contemporary at UCD, Arthur Clery, wrote of the almost complete separation of Catholic and Protestant in early twentieth-century Dublin. 'Perhaps the most surprising aspect of the religious question in Ireland, and yet the one least noticed,' he asserts,

---

77 Willard Potts, *Joyce and the Two Irelands* (Austin, TX: University of Texas Press, 2000), 86.
78 Torchiana, *Backgrounds for Joyce's 'Dubliners'*, 226.

is the way in which the Catholic and the Protestant live socially apart. This
exists quite as much in Dublin as in the North. [...] I have only once in my
life dined in a Protestant house. Though I am entering on middle life, and
my dancing days almost over, I have never yet been at a dance in a Protestant house.[79]

All of the stories in *Dubliners*, from the priest-centred opener 'The Sisters'
to the declining gentility of 'The Dead', are dominated by struggling Catholics. Joyce was in no doubt that Ireland was under the pernicious influence
of two imperial systems: that of its powerful island neighbour and that of
the Roman Church. Protestants, in such a world, are not significant for
their religious affiliation but for their perceived caste. For Joyce's Dubliners,
Protestantism was associated with wealth and power, and this centuries-
old gap between denominations led to the development of what Willard
Potts has called 'the Two Irelands'.[80] In such a society, the surprising thing
at a Christmas party such as the one held on Usher's Island in 'The Dead'
is not that there should be only one Protestant guest but that there should
be any at all. Indeed, Browne's presence becomes a little tricky at one point
when Mary Jane has to check Aunt Kate in her criticism of a papal decree
barring women from membership of church choirs: 'Now, Aunt Kate,
you're giving scandal to Mr Browne who is of the other persuasion' (*D* 195).
Browne, curious about Catholic practice, is not the slightest perturbed and
merely smiles at 'this allusion to his religion' (*D* 195).

Browne's Protestantism alone is an oddity that seems to work primarily
to suggest that, as many critics have pointed out, there is a certain 'West
Britishness' to the Usher's Island gathering. We are told early in the story
that among the artworks hanging in the Morkans' house are a picture of
the balcony scene in *Romeo and Juliet* and a picture of the two murdered
princes in the Tower of London. Both of these, one with its associations
with England's national bard and the other nodding towards royalist
sympathies, suggest, at the very least, a household largely uninterested
in the budding Irish nationalism of the day as represented by Miss Ivors,
the young Gaelic enthusiast who flirts with and then chastises Gabriel
as a 'West Briton'. As such, one might see the presence of a Protestant as
being of a piece with the pictures hanging on the drawing-room wall. But
if one considers Browne's other unique attribute, his whiskey drinking,
along with his religious affiliation, then another, more complex picture
emerges.

79 Arthur Clery, *Dublin Essays* (Dublin and London: Maunsel, 1919), 45.
80 See Potts, *Joyce and the Two Irelands*, *passim*.

Arthur Clery wrote of Joyce's Ireland that 'apart from Drink, which Protestants make and Catholics sell', all other Irish industries were Protestant controlled.[81] Protestant grandee families with names such as Guinness, Jameson and Persse had, from the late eighteenth century, made fortunes from the manufacture of alcohol, a product for which there was enormous demand both at home and abroad. And the association of ascendancy power with whiskey did not end with independence. When, after the foundation of the Free State, W. B. Yeats entered the Irish Senate, his chief mentor was the distiller and director of the Bank of Ireland, Andrew Jameson, a man, writes Roy Foster, who was the 'quintessential *ancien régime* Unionist'.[82] Foster goes on to describe the sealing of this friendship via Jameson's proposal of Yeats for membership of that most ascendancy of institutions, the Kildare Street Club – a place memorably used by Joyce as symbolic of colonial control in 'Two Gallants'. When the *Catholic Bulletin* of the 1920s wished to attack Yeats's Abbey Theatre they referred to it as the 'Persse–Pollexfen' theatre, recalling Protestant merchant wealth in the backgrounds of both Lady Gregory and Yeats.[83] Twenty years earlier D. P. Moran in *The Leader* was also keen to highlight the Persse and Pollexfen names in his attack on what he felt was the sectarianism of the Abbey Theatre. 'Why does not Lady Gregory (nee Persse) write funny plays about the proselytising Persses of Galway?' wrote Moran. 'Why does not Yeats write blank verse about his kinsfolk, the Pollexfens of Sligo? [...] It is a much too one-sided argument for our taste.'[84] In late July 1904, as Joyce began to write the stories that would become *Dubliners*, Moran castigated John Jameson (Andrew's cousin) for running an anonymous advertisement seeking to employ a Protestant carpenter. 'John does not stipulate', quipped Moran, 'that none but [the] "saved" should get drunk on whisky.'[85]

The rapid accumulation of wealth by those involved at all levels of the drinks trade fascinates Leopold Bloom as he wanders around Dublin in *Ulysses*. In the 'Calypso' episode as he walks past Larry O'Rourke's public house and wine merchants at the corner of Eccles Street and Dorset Street, he ponders enviously how the trade operates:

> Where do they get the money? Coming up redheaded curates from the county Leitrim, rinsing empties and old man in the cellar. Then, lo and

81 Clery, *Dublin Essays*, 46.
82 R. F. Foster, *W. B. Yeats: A Life, II: The Arch-Poet 1915–1939* (Oxford: Oxford University Press, 2003), 229.
83 See Foster, *W. B. Yeats: A Life, II*, 721, fn. 57.
84 Quoted in Potts, *Joyce and the Two Irelands*, 35–6.
85 Quoted in Potts, *Joyce and the Two Irelands*, 44.

behold, they blossom out as Adam Findlaters or Dan Tallons. Then think
of the competition. General thirst. Good puzzle would be cross Dublin
without passing a pub. (*U* 69)

And a short while later in the 'Lotus Eaters' chapter he does the sums on
the vast wealth of the Guinness family:

> Lord Iveagh once cashed a sevenfigure cheque for a million in the bank
> of Ireland. Shows you the money to be made out of porter. Still the other
> brother lord Ardilaun has to change his shirt four times a day, they say. Skin
> breeds lice or vermin. A million pounds, wait a moment. Twopence a pint,
> fourpence a quart, eightpence a gallon of porter, no, one and fourpence a
> gallon of porter. (*U* 97)

For all the money that is to be made out of beer, it is whiskey that does the
real damage to one's health, as Bloom acknowledges to himself on the way
to Paddy Dignam's burial: 'Blazing face: redhot. Too much John Barley-
corn. Cure for a red nose. Drink like the devil till it turns adelite. A lot of
money he spent colouring it' (*U* 119). 'Who distilled first?', wonders Bloom:
'Some chap in the blues. Dutch courage' (*U* 229).

One writer who was unstinting in his critique of Ireland's alcohol
producers was George Moore. Moore's *Parnell and His Island*, a scabrous
collection of musings on life in late nineteenth-century Ireland and a book
with which we know Joyce was conversant through his reference in 'The
Day of the Rabblement' to 'Mr Moore and his island', has, at its opening, an
image of the corrupt merchant who, as the landlord class declines, begins
to feed off Ireland's poor.[86] This merchant type, Moore tells us, lives in
the affluent suburb of Dalkey, a fact perhaps deliberately echoed by Joyce
in 'The Dead' when he observes that many of Mary Jane's music students
'belonged to better-class families on the Kingstown and Dalkey line' (*D*
176), and again recalled in the make-up of Stephen's class of private school-
boys in *Ulysses*: 'Welloff people, proud that their eldest son was in the navy.
Vico Road, Dalkey' (*U* 29). The argument that Joyce was sampling from
Parnell and His Island becomes more persuasive when one reads closely the
early sentences of the book's first chapter titled 'Dublin', which describes a
decaying and paralysed city. The trade of Moore's corrupt merchant should
come as no surprise:

> On the terrace by me stands a fat man, the type of commercial prosperity
> (he is a distiller); his family is about him, enjoying the delicate listless-
> ness of this summer afternoon. Now I hear the rushing rumble of a train,

86 James Joyce, 'The Day of the Rabblement', in Joyce, *Occasional, Critical, and Political
   Writing*, 51.

the strident whistle tears the air and is repeated high and far through the
sonorous distances of this strange mountain. [...]

No town in the world has more beautiful surroundings than Dublin.
Seeing Dalkey one dreams of Monte Carlo, or better still of the hanging
gardens of Babylon, of marble balustrades, of white fountains, of innumer-
able yachts, or courts of love, and of sumptuous pleasure palaces; but alas,
all that meets the eye are some broken-down villas! The white walls shine
in the sun and deceive you, but if you approach you will find a front-door
where the paint is peeling, and a ruined garden.

And in such ruin life languishes here! The inhabitants of the villas are,
for the most part, landlords whom circumstances have forced to shut up
their houses and to come here to economise; or, they may belong to the
second class of landlords: widows living on jointures paid by the eldest
sons, or mortgagees upon money placed by them or by their ancestors
upon the land. For in Ireland there is nothing but the land; with the exception of a few distillers and brewers in Dublin, who live upon the drunk-
enness of the people, there is no way in Ireland of getting money except
through the peasant.[87]

Coming together here we get several tremors of what is to come in 'The
Dead': the Dalkey and Kingstown line, a once magnificent and now
crumbling Dublin, a country ruined by empire and the corruption of the
distillery.

Moore, himself a member of the declining landlord class, was not the
only commentator to see in the drinks industry – and particularly in the
production of whiskey – a signal example of decay, decline and skuldug-
gery. In recent years, both James Fairhall and Willard Potts have given
some consideration to the political significance of alcohol and the drinks
trade in the Dublin of Joyce's youth. Fairhall notes that 'Dubliners reveals a
sharp awareness of the social damage caused by drinking. Drinking figures
prominently in several stories and peripherally in most of the others.'[88] He
goes on to demonstrate how manufacturers and sellers of alcohol in Dublin
had great political power, making up the largest single occupational block
on the Corporation. The industry had particular sway over the Irish Parliamentary Party, to the extent that Arthur Griffith saw the drinks trade, or,
as he termed it, the 'whiskey ring', as a serious threat to political progress,
and especially to the progress of his brand of nationalism. Similarly, James
Connolly felt that the power of the publicans to swing elections needed

---

87 George Moore, *Parnell and His Island* (1887) (Dublin: University College Dublin Press,
2004), 1–2.
88 Fairhall, *James Joyce and the Question of History* (Cambridge: Cambridge University Press,
1993), 99.

to be undermined as he made clear in a 1903 municipal election speech: 'There can never be [...] clean, healthy or honest politics in the City of Dublin, until the power of the drink sellers is absolutely broken.'[89]

Joyce bore in common with Griffith a hatred of the Irish Parliamentary Party. He could not forgive them for what he saw as their part in the fall and death of his idol, Charles Stewart Parnell, and 1907, the year in which he completed 'The Dead', also witnessed his most impassioned condemnation of the party as a group of traitors, opportunists and crooks. In May of that year his article 'Home Rule Comes of Age' – borrowing its title from an article that appeared the previous month in Griffith's *Sinn Féin* – appeared in *Il Piccolo della Sera*:

> the Irish Parliamentary Party is bankrupt. For twenty-seven years it has been agitating and talking. In that time it has drawn 35 million from its supporters, and the fruits of its agitation are that Irish taxes have increased by 88 million, while the Irish population has decreased by 1 million. The deputies themselves have improved their lot, apart from such small discomforts as a few months in prison or a few lengthy sittings. From being peasants' sons, street traders and clientless lawyers, they have become salaried administrators, factory and company bosses, newspaper owners and large land holders. Only in 1891 did they give proof of their altruism when they sold Parnell, their master, to the pharisaical conscience of the English non-conformists, without exacting the thirty pieces of silver.[90]

In addition to being merchants and landlords, Joyce might also have mentioned this *nouveau riche* clique of carpetbaggers as being brewers and publicans, as Griffith, Connolly, D. P. Moran and others were wont to do. As Patrick O'Farrell has ably demonstrated, the 'Irish parliamentary party remained unable to shed its image of involvement with the liquor interest – an image which did it great harm among the ascetical revivalists of religion and nationalism'.[91]

89 Quoted in Fairhall, *James Joyce and the Question of History*, 98–9. Fairhall points out that this election is the same one in which John and Stanislaus Joyce were involved as canvassers and that James uses as background for 'Ivy Day in the Committee Room', a story in which the canvassers are paid in beer. One critic has written cogently of this nexus that 'no more effective symbol of the relation between two of the main interests of Dubliners in the beginning of this century has ever been created'. See David Daiches, 'Dubliners', in Peter K. Garrett (ed.), *Twentieth-Century Interpretations of 'Dubliners'* (Englewood Cliffs, NJ: Prentice Hall, 1968), 31.

90 James Joyce, 'Home Rule Comes of Age', in Joyce, *Occasional, Critical, and Political Writing*, 144.

91 Patrick O'Farrell, *England's Irish Question: Anglo-Irish Relations 1534–1970* (London: Batsford, 1971), 226.

While Fairhall considers chiefly the journalism and pronouncements on drink of Arthur Griffith and James Connolly, Willard Potts takes a fruitful look at the ways in which D. P. Moran's Irish Irelandism, as espoused in *The Leader*, impacted on Joyce's worldview. Though it goes without saying that Joyce was no Irish Irelander himself, nor had he the virulent dislike of West Brits, Sourfaces and other assorted traitors to the Irish cause, he certainly drew from Moran's colourful vocabulary both in *Dubliners* and, later, in *Ulysses* to flavour the speech of his characters. Potts points out that one of Moran's favourite targets was the drinks industry – or, as he liked to call it, 'Bung' – and especially the manufacturers of alcohol, 'most, if not all, of whom were Protestants'.[92] 'The best known of these Protestant drink producers', continues Potts, 'were the owners of the Guinness Brewery, Lord Ardilaun and Lord Iveagh, who compounded their sins by owning the pro-English *Daily Express*, for which Gabriel Conroy wrote his reviews. Moran acknowledged their ownership of the paper by referring to it as the *Bung Express*.'[93]

The *Daily Express*, and Gabriel's reviews therein, form, along with the allusions via Nuns' Island to the Persses, another angle of attack by Joyce on Lady Gregory and her class, which I will discuss in greater detail in the next chapter. And Joyce's familiarity with Moran's anti-drink rhetoric appears directly in the 'Cyclops' chapter of *Ulysses* when Alf Bergan orders drink from the barman Terry O'Ryan in Barney Kiernan's pub:

> Terence O'Ryan heard him and straightway brought him a crystal cup full of foaming ebon ale which the noble twin brothers Bungiveagh and Bungardilaun brew ever in their divine alevats, cunning as the sons of deathless Leda. For they garner the succulent berries of the hop and mass and sift and bruise and brew them and they mix therewith sour juices and bring the must to the sacred fire and cease not night or day from their toil, those cunning brothers, lord of the vat. (*U* 386–7)

The reference to these mock-heroic brothers, though brewers rather than distillers, helps to illustrate Joyce's awareness of the fierce debate swirling around the uses and abuses of alcohol in turn-of-the-century Dublin. Earlier in the book, as Stephen idles on Sandymount strand, a beer bottle becomes emblematic of a cancer at the centre of Irish society: 'A porter-bottle stood up, stogged to its waist, in the cakey sand dough. A sentinel: isle of dreadful thirst' (*U* 50).

92 D. P. Moran's one published novel, a copy of which formed part of Joyce's Trieste library, exhibited strong antipathy to the Irish penchant for alcoholic excess. See D. P. Moran, *Tom O'Kelly* (Dublin: Cahill and Co./J. Duffy and Co., 1905).

93 Potts, *Joyce and the Two Irelands*, 37.

The political opposition to the drinks trade ought to be seen within the wider framework of several powerful waves of temperance campaigning in Ireland from the early nineteenth century onwards. Associated most strongly in its first years with the name of Father Theobald Mathew, and in the later decades of the century with Father James Cullen, the movement to bring sobriety to Ireland, while motivated by concerns for health and religious well-being, also took on a political hue. The tendency of the drive for temperance to be allied with nationalism is evident, for example, in the hugely popular ballad collection, *The Spirit of the Nation* (1845), in which the preface appeals for the use of the book's ballads as both patriotic motivation and temperance marching songs:

> Music is the first faculty of the Irish, and scarcely any thing has such power for good over them. The use of this faculty and this power, publicly and constantly, to keep up their spirits, refine their tastes, warm their courage, increase their union, and renew their zeal, is the duty of every patriot. [...] Will the temperance bands learn to play these airs, and the young men, ay, and the young women, of the temperance societies learn to sing our songs, and chorus them till village and valley ring?[94]

This is a classic instance of the temperance catch-call 'Ireland Sober is Ireland Free', which Joyce mocks in *Finnegans Wake* as 'Ireland sober is Ireland stiff' (214.18).

In Joyce's youth the temperance movement gained added momentum thanks to the work of Father Cullen and his journal *The Messenger of the Sacred Heart*. A temperance campaign launched by Cullen in 1889 had won over a quarter of a million abstinence pledges within two years. Cullen founded the Pioneer Total Abstinence Association in 1901, which made further dramatic inroads into Ireland's drinking culture.[95] Cullen's success was in part due to a mixing of temperance zeal with nationalist rhetoric, as is evident from a speech made at one of the disastrous battlefields of 1798, Vinegar Hill, just outside the Wexford town of Enniscorthy:

> Vinegar Hill, on which we stand, has its warnings for us. In these very fields your fathers fought and fell – fell not so much beneath the fire of the north Cork militia and the orange yeomanry as by the treachery of drink. Drink lost the battle at Ross, lost the battle at Wexford, and helped to the disaster of Vinegar Hill [...] Ireland lost all her fights through drink.[96]

94 Anonymous, 'Preface', in Charles Gavan Duffy et al., *The Spirit of the Nation* (1845) (Poole and Washington DC: Woodstock Books, 1998), vi.

95 Figures on the growth of the temperance movement in late nineteenth-century Ireland are taken from O'Farrell, *England's Irish Question*, 224–7.

96 Quoted in Elizabeth Malcolm, 'Temperance and Irish Nationalism', in F. S. L. Lyons and

While for the lachrymose balladeers at song in the Ormond Hotel of 'Sirens', then, the Croppy Boy is brought down by British treachery, for Father Cullen the thirst for strong drink is at the root, not just of defeat in 1798, but of all Irish historical collapse. The craze for abstinence and temperance becomes the target of the nameless narrator's ire in the 'Cyclops' episode of *Ulysses* when he describes a get-together at which he recalls 'a lot of colleen bawns going about with temperance beverages and selling medals and oranges and lemonade and a few old dry buns, gob, flahoolagh entertainment, don't be talking. Ireland sober is Ireland free' (*U* 402). And, of course, temperance is there much earlier, in 'The Dead', through the characters of Freddy Malins and his mother. Freddy is the likeable drunkard at the party whom the Morkan sisters fear will turn up 'screwed' and whose 'poor mother made him take the pledge on New Year's Eve' (*D* 185).

But James Joyce's distaste for distillers is not related to a distaste for whiskey. That is to say, Joyce was no temperance crusader, but he was conscious of distilling's reputation as it is portrayed in *Parnell and His Island* and in the journalism of Arthur Griffith, D. P. Moran and others. Whiskey and its production were associated with England, with the landlord caste and with imperial domination generally, as is demonstrated in a sermon made by the temperance priest Father Michael Kelly: 'With fell design England suppressed our commerce, our factories, our mines, our industries, and left us only the distillery.'[97] Given this contemporary view of whiskey, and taking into account the Joyce family's own misfortunes in the failed distillery at Chapelizod, it is not so surprising that Joyce blends the spirit into the mix of *Dubliners* as a consistently negative omen. And it is in this light that we must read the Protestant Mr Browne's quaffing of the liquor at the Morkans' Christmas party. Mr Browne, then, far from being the comic relief of 'The Dead', is, as Donald Torchiana asserted, death itself. If we are to understand what Joyce is trying to tell us about Ireland, Irish society and his relationship to it then we need to dwell for a moment on the neglected character of the whiskey-drinking Protestant.

Who is Mr Browne?

Before looking at who Joyce might have had in mind when creating the character of Mr Browne, a brief rehearsal of John V. Kelleher's famous,

R. A. J. Hawkins (eds), *Ireland under the Union: Varieties of Tension* (Oxford: Clarendon Press, 1980), III.

97 Quoted in O'Farrell, *England's Irish Question*, 225.

and much referenced, essay 'Irish History and Mythology in James Joyce's "The Dead"' (1965) is necessary. Kelleher argues for three new ways to look at 'The Dead': 'a symbolistic level on which Death is personified in Mr. Browne'; 'a level of reference to early nineteenth-century Catholic Dublin'; and 'a series of strong though incomplete references to the Old Irish saga *Togail Bruidhne Dá Derga*, "The Destruction of Da Derga's Hostel"'.[98] While Chapter Two will return to a consideration of Kelleher's second level, which interests itself in Irish history, I do not intend to re-examine his brilliant, and still controversial, thesis about Da Derga's Hostel for the simple reason that it is the most completely sealed of his arguments.[99]

The first level of what Kelleher calls 'reverberatory planes' in 'The Dead' is Mr Browne's deathliness and it is the level to which, despite its professed pervasiveness, he accords least attention:

> It is by far the most constant and complicated of the three. In any case, most of you are at least partly aware of it – the symbolistic meanings of the snow, of whiteness, of shadow and shade, of west and going west, of the discussion at the dinner table of dead singers and of old operas like Donizetti's *Lucrezia Borgia* and the Italian tenor who sang five encores to *Yes, Let Me Like a Soldier Fall*.[100]

Kelleher also points out that several characters in the story are ill, that Michael Furey died of consumption, and that the air in the house on Usher's Island is stale; even the hall-door bell in the story's opening paragraph is 'wheezy'. He goes on to mention the discussion at the party of the lives of monks in Mount Mellaray who, according to Mary Jane, sleep in coffins. Browne is fascinated by the idea of such a community, and Joyce uses the discussion as a point of conflict between the rational Protestant, Mr Browne, and the superstitious and unquestioning Catholics, Mary Jane, Aunt Kate and Freddy Malins. 'The coffin', says Mary Jane, tired of Browne's interrogation, 'is to remind them of their last end' (D 202). Finally, Kelleher cites the moment in the story when the very frail Aunt Julia – a woman

---

98 John V. Kelleher, 'Irish History and Mythology in James Joyce's "The Dead"', in Charles Fanning (ed.), *Selected Writings of John V. Kelleher on Ireland and Irish America* (Carbondale, IL: Southern Illinois University Press, 2002), 43–4.

99 Maria Tymoczko has taken Kelleher considerably further in her forensic examination of Irish myth in Joyce. See Tymoczko, *The Irish 'Ulysses'* (Berkeley, CA: University of California Press, 1994), *passim*; and Tymoczko, '"The Broken Lights of Irish Myth": Joyce's Knowledge of Early Irish Literature', *James Joyce Quarterly*, 29.4 (Summer 1992), 763–74. Paul Muldoon, in his exegesis of 'The Dead', relies heavily on Kelleher while at the same time expanding upon his 'Da Derga' thesis. See Muldoon, *To Ireland, I* (Oxford: Oxford University Press, 2000), 50–66.

100 Kelleher, 'Irish History and Mythology', 54.

clearly not far from death – enters to sing on Browne's arm. After she has sung 'Arrayed for the Bridal', Browne declares to the gathered audience, 'Miss Julia Morkan, my latest discovery!' (*D* 194).

While all of the moments cited are persuasive, the key passage quoted by Kelleher in defence of his idea that Browne is a representative of death comes as the partygoers prepare to leave and go off once more into the snowy night:

> The piercing morning air came into the hall where they were standing so that Aunt Kate said:
>   – Close the door, somebody. Mrs Malins will get her death of cold.
>   – Browne is out there, Aunt Kate, said Mary Jane.
>   – Browne is everywhere, said Aunt Kate, lowering her voice.
> Mary Jane laughed at her tone.
>   – Really, she said archly, he is very attentive.
>   – He has been laid on here like the gas, said Aunt Kate in the same tone,
> all during the Christmas. (*D* 207)

That linkage of cold air with death along with the image of Browne being everywhere makes it almost irresistible to see Joyce working away at his allusive and associative best. And then that very odd phrase about Browne being 'laid on like the gas' occurs and the attentive reader's alarm bells should ring. None have been more alert than Paul Muldoon in this regard as, drawing from and expanding on Kelleher, he makes some useful remarks about Joyce's use of the word 'gas' in 'The Dead', seeing in it a reference to the Irish word '*geasa*' or taboo.

As part of his reading of *Togail Bruidhne Da Derga*, Kelleher notes that King Conaire of the saga, represented by Gabriel Conroy of 'The Dead', breaks a series of taboos. Among the strictures that Conaire must not transgress are the hunting of birds and travelling to the right around Tara. Kelleher argues that Gabriel breaks both taboos by, first, carving the goose and, secondly, travelling to the party by a route that would have placed Tara Street on his right. What Kelleher fails to note is that in the original Irish the word for taboo is *geasa*. Muldoon, with a better knowledge of Irish, is awake to the significance of the word and sees in Joyce's repeated, and sometimes odd, use of the word 'gas' a word association, in fact an almost exact homonym, with *geasa*. This helps to explain why Mr Browne is described as being 'laid on like the gas', why the gas in the pantry makes the pale Lily 'look still paler' (*D* 177) and why the ghost who ultimately presides over the whole night is 'a boy in the gasworks' (*D* 221). Muldoon notices that Joyce uses the phrase about Michael Furey's workplace twice in consecutive sentences, thus 'drawing so much attention to it as to suggest that

Joyce himself is "in the geasworks", in the business of attending to those geasa'. In addition to Browne, like death, being omnipresent, Muldoon notes a possible source for his name: 'Browne, by the way, particularly in the Hiberno-Norman form, de Brun, would be a close approximation of the pronunciation of *Bruidne* in *Togail Bruidne Da Derga*'.[101]

Who, other than *Bruidne* or the grim reaper, might Mr Browne be? 'Names hold many clues', writes Clare Culleton in her helpful study of naming in Joyce, 'and they're a fascinating place to start, since they raise exciting issues and can help redesign our approach to Joyce, energizing our readings of his familiar texts.'[102] Among those to attempt an interpretation of Browne's name is Don Gifford, who thinks the likely source a sixteenth-century clergyman, George Browne, the first Protestant archbishop of Dublin who was 'politically shrewd enough to survive the accession of Mary I'.[103] Richard Ellmann, keen to read the gathering on Usher's Island as a close parallel of actual figures in the Joyce family circle, thinks the source to be most likely the Protestant husband of Joyce's mother's first cousin, a music teacher cum insurance agent named Mervyn Archdall Browne. 'Joyce', argues Ellmann, 'keeps him in "The Dead" under his own name.'[104] Mervyn Archdall Browne is listed in *Thom's Directory* as a teacher of pianoforte and singing. John Kelleher, while the foremost symbolist reader of Browne, is attracted to Ellmann's naturalistic reading and points to the re-emergence of the name in *Ulysses* when, at Paddy Dignam's funeral in Glasnevin, Leopold ponders the unhealthy nature of cemeteries: 'Must be an infernal lot of bad gas round the place. Butchers for instance: they get like raw beefsteak. Who was telling me? Mervyn Brown' (*U* 131). 'Browne would know', comments Kelleher, 'he is an expert.'[105] Though Muldoon does not mention this reference from *Ulysses*, doubtless he would be pleased at the reappearance of the *geas* in conjunction with death and decay.

Richard Ellmann tells us of a ghostly Browne to whose legend Joyce was attracted as a schoolboy in Clongowes – the Browne family having owned the building before it was turned into a school in the early nineteenth century – though he makes no attempt to link this phantom with the lone Protestant on Usher's Island:

101 Muldoon, *To Ireland, I*, 52
102 Claire A. Culleton, *Names and Naming in Joyce* (Madison, WI: University of Wisconsin Press, 1994), 5.
103 Gifford, *Joyce Annotated*, 115.
104 Ellmann, *James Joyce*, 246.
105 Kelleher, 'Irish History and Mythology', 55.

> One member of the Browne family was a marshal in the Austrian army, and
> in 1757 took part in the Battle of Prague. His ghost, wearing a bloodstained
> white uniform, ascended the stairs of the castle to the gallery, then walked
> along it to a room at the end. His sisters and his servants soon after discov-
> ered that the marshal had been killed at Prague at that very moment.[106]

The critical attraction of this dead soldier as a source for Mr Browne is
his status as one of that exiled group of eighteenth-century Irish soldiers
known as the Wild Geese who we know greatly exercised Joyce's mind.

Both Browne and Brown are commonly found as surnames in Ireland
among both Protestants and Catholics and, beyond those previously critically advanced, there are a range of possibilities for Joyce's choice of name
for the lone Protestant partygoer. The Brownes were, like the Joyces, one of
the fourteen tribes of old Galway and the two families shared very similar
coats of arms, featuring as centrepiece the Hapsburg eagle. Joyce, when
writing about Galway in 1912, uses the image of these eroded coats of arms
as signals of decay:

> The old Spanish homes are in ruins. The castles of the tribes have been
> demolished. Tufts of weeds grow in the windows and in the wide court-
> yards. Above the porticoes the heraldic arms cut into the black stone are
> fading: the wolf of the Capitol with the two twin brothers, the two-headed
> eagle of the Hapsburgs, the black bull of the Darcy family, descendants of
> Charlemagne. In the city of Galway, writes an ancient chronicler, reign the
> passions of pride and lust.[107]

Today, the tribes of Galway are remembered chiefly on hurling sweatshirts
and, less glamorously, in the names of the roundabouts that ring the city.
Several of the tribes' names, such as fFrench and Skerrett, have disappeared
altogether, while others such as Browne, Joyce and O'Flaherty continue to
thrive.

When Joyce, as a young man, was still considering the possibility of a
life as a singer he decided on Gordon Brown as a stage name after his great
philosophical hero Giordano Bruno.[108] As early as 1901 and 'The Day of the
Rabblement', Joyce delighted in leading his audience astray by referring
to Bruno as 'the Nolan', after the heretic's hometown of Nola. For an Irish
readership this usage would naturally have been misleading, as 'Nolan' is
a very common surname, and we have in the teenage Joyce's pamphlet an

---

106 Ellmann, *James Joyce*, 29.
107 James Joyce, 'The City of the Tribes', in Joyce, *Occasional, Critical, and Political Writing*,
     200.
108 See Richard Ellmann, *The Consciousness of Joyce* (London: Faber and Faber, 1977), 11.

example of his irresistible attraction to puns and wordplay.[109] This particular game re-emerges in *Finnegans Wake* with his repeated manipulation of
the name of the well-known Irish publishing company, Browne and Nolan.
However, and despite all the game playing, Bruno remained for Joyce a
figure of great reverence and so seems an unlikely source for our whiskey
drinker.

A more likely association and source can be found in the publishing
history of 'The Day of the Rabblement'. This essay, which attacks the
motivation and conduct of the Irish Literary Theatre, was written with
the intention of having it published in *St Stephen's*, the literary magazine
of University College Dublin. The essay was considered unsuitable by the
University's Father Harry Browne and was rejected because of its reference to Gabriele D'Annunzio's *Il Fuoco* (1900), a novel much admired by
Joyce but which had been placed on the Vatican Index of Prohibited Books.
Interestingly, if we wish, like Ellmann and Gifford, to stick to the idea of
Browne as a Protestant, Stanislaus tells us that this censorious Catholic
priest fits the bill as 'still another converted Protestant, rumoured to have
a wife and daughter somewhere in England'.[110] Having been rejected by *St
Stephen's*, Joyce published the essay at his own expense alongside Francis
Sheehy Skeffington's feminist piece, 'A Forgotten Aspect of the University
Question', in a pamphlet with a limited run of 85 copies. In this case, the
use of the death-dealing Mr Browne of 'The Dead' can be seen more clearly
as an act of vengeance against Joyce's first censor much as Mr Alleyne of
'Counterparts' had been introduced to traduce the name of John Joyce's
one-time boss.

The negative aura of Mr Browne is reinforced by considering perhaps
the most obvious allusion of all, that of colour. One scholar who has
made an entire book-length study of the question of colour in Joyce, J.
Colm O'Sullivan, has noticed the extraordinary repetition of 'Browne' or
'brown' in Joyce's final story. '"The Dead"', writes O'Sullivan, 'is by far the
most colourful story in *Dubliners*. It contains a real oddity in the recur-
rence of Mr. Browne's name no fewer than forty-five times. In addition
the word "brown" in its own right occurs eight times and the name of the
poet Browning three times.'[111] He then goes on to comment briefly on the
Giordano Bruno and Browne and Nolan connections in *Finneqans Wake*,

109 Stanislaus Joyce confirms that it was Joyce's intention to confuse his readership. See
Joyce, *My Brother's Keeper*, 146.
110 Stanislaus Joyce, *My Brother's Keeper*, 144.
111 J. Colm O'Sullivan, *Joyce's Use of Colors: Finnegans Wake and the Earlier Works* (Ann Arbor,
MI: UMI Research Press, 1987), 4.

the novel with which his study is most concerned. Mr Browne, of course, draws attention to the colourful allusions of his name in the following rather puzzling aside:

> The pudding was of Aunt Julia's making and she received praises for it from all quarters. She herself said that it was not quite brown enough.
> – Well, I hope, Miss Morkan, said Mr Browne, that I'm brown enough for you because, you know, I'm all brown. (*D* 201)

This is one of those odd moments that occur quite frequently in *Dubliners*, and especially in 'The Dead', when one finds a phrase or an emphasis that seems to make little sense or leaves one questioning how it works for its keep in this most self-avowedly scrupulous of books. Terence Brown takes a stab at an interpretation and upbraids a previous scholar for not sharing a joke:

> Possibly a familiar catchphrase or piece of advertising copy which allows Mr Browne to crack a rather forced joke. The critic Bernard Benstock has suggested that the words may even be 'an intentional echo of an off-colour joke involving a man named Browne (spelled with the same final "e"); it ends with a deflation of Browne's Anglo-Saxon chauvinism'. It's a pity Professor Benstock did not see fit to share this drollerie with his readers.[112]

We can only certainly say two things about this for now: first, when such an inexplicable moment occurs in Joyce it has been placed there very deliberately and is not some sort of carelessness on the writer's part and, secondly, Browne – and, therefore, Joyce – is keen to emphasize his 'brownness'.

So what is the significance of the colour brown in Joyce? Peter K. Garrett has argued convincingly that there is 'strong external evidence of Joyce's association of the color brown with the condition of paralysis'. In support of this claim, he points to 'those brown brick houses which seem the very incarnation of Irish paralysis' (*SH* 216) in *Stephen Hero* and to the houses in 'Araby's' opening paragraph which 'gazed at one another with brown imperturbable faces' (*D* 21). Joyce also uses the colour negatively earlier in *Stephen Hero* when contrasting earth and sky: 'The air was webbed with water vapours and all the flower-beds and walks confronted the grey of the sky with a truculent sodden brown' (*SH* 199). Garrett argues that the pervasiveness of Browne caught in Aunt Kate's phrase, 'Browne is everywhere', 'may seem to convey the same symbolic implication present in the

---

112 Brown, 'Notes', in James Joyce, *Dubliners*, 313. Brown is referring here to Benstock's notes in Hart (ed.), *James Joyce's 'Dubliners'*.

motif "snow was general all over Ireland": paralysis is pervasive'.[113] As with Garrett, Brewster Ghiselin sees the colour as a negative, 'associated with the limitations of life in Ireland', and points to Miss Ivors' brown eyes as evidence for the thesis.[114] Garrett, despite his attraction to a symbolic reading of 'brown' in 'The Dead', is quick to enter a naturalistic caveat:

> it is eminently arguable that Mr. Browne's realistic aspect remains more significant than these symbolic suggestions, that in his jovial, crude vitality he displays a human substantiality which resists being reduced to a simple, symbolic image. Interpretations of *Dubliners* will be affected considerably by the reader's view of the relationship between such symbolic and natural-istic elements, his sense of which determines meaning.[115]

But why should one have to choose? Clearly Joyce means us to read it both ways. Yes, Mr Browne is a crude, garrulous, whiskey-drinking party-goer, but he is also a representative of death and paralysis. *Dubliners* must always be read thus, slipping in and out of naturalism and symbolism, often stencilling one technique over the other.

The Still that was Mill

Whatever way you wish to interpret Mr Browne's character, it would be remiss to neglect the drink in his hand. The key intersection in the story, which ties it back into Nuns' Island and to the landed Persse family, is that of Protestantism with whiskey. Whiskey is, for Joyce, a complex and multi-layered device by which he can achieve several results: he can gain revenge for his wronged father; he can draw attention to the caste system of early twentieth-century Ireland; and he can attack Lady Gregory, the ascendancy nerve centre of the Literary Revival – a party to which, he feels, he has not been invited. Revenge and resentment, however unjusti-fied, bubble away under the surface of *Dubliners*, and it is to the distillate of whiskey that we must look for traces of how these feelings are worked out and controlled through the book. For Joyce there is always the return to thoughts of the distillery. In the early 1930s, as his first biographers began to collect material, Joyce instructed his friend and sometime secre-tary Paul Léon to assist Frank Budgen who was then preparing the book

113 Peter K. Garrett, 'Introduction', in Garrett (ed.), *Twentieth-Century Interpretations of 'Dubliners'*, 9.
114 Brewster Ghiselin, 'The Unity of Joyce's *Dubliners*', in Garrett (ed.), *Twentieth-Century Interpretations of 'Dubliners'*, 68.
115 Garrett, 'Introduction', in Garrett (ed.), *Twentieth-Century Interpretations of 'Dubliners'*, 9.

that would become *James Joyce and the Making of 'Ulysses'*. On St Patrick's Day 1933 Léon passed instructions for Budgen to Harriet Shaw Weaver. 'About Mr Budgen', he wrote, 'for completion of his book he must go to Dublin in order to paint Chapel Izod (I am not sure of my spelling) the source of the Liffey to illustrate his book.'[116] Budgen duly agreed and went to paint at the distillery; by 1939, when he had come to write about *Finnegans Wake*, John Joyce's first Dublin place of work was no more. 'Chapelizod is the scene', wrote Budgen, 'of Sheridan Lefanu's delightful novel, *The House by the Churchyard* [...] Joyce's father worked in the massive distillery, now redundant, derelict, and to let, formerly the barracks of Lefanu's artillerymen.'[117] We may never fully understand the significance of Chapelizod's 'still that was mill' (*FW* 265.1–2) for Joyce but he provides us with sufficient pointers across his oeuvre, and particularly in *Dubliners*, to see that his own 'endless stories about the distillery' reverberate and echo in ways that those of us who wish to understand him and his work should not ignore.

That there was a game being played by Joyce for which whiskey was at the root was guessed at by one of the *Wake*'s earliest reviewers. When, in 1939, 'Work in Progress' finally became *Finnegans Wake* after a seventeen-year gestation it was greeted with almost unanimous bafflement. As a book, wrote B. Ifor Evans in the *Manchester Guardian*, it 'does not admit review'. But, having admitted that, Evans, thinking of 'Finnegan's Wake', then went on in his article to try and make something of it: 'Who, it may be asked, was Finnegan? But I gather that there is an Irish story of a contractor who fell and was stretched out for dead. When his friends toasted him he rose at the word "whiskey" and drank with them.' He then concludes his review with a knowing prompt relating back to the story of the whiskey-loving contractor: 'In a book where all is considered, this legend, too, has its relevance.'[118] As to what that relevance was Evans did not hazard a guess, because he failed, quite understandably, to realize that the key to tracing the locus of whiskey's significance had been penned by Joyce some thirty-five years earlier in his first published story. As readers of the *Irish Homestead* for 13 August 1904 leafed through their paper, and read of 'the old distiller who owns the batch of prize setters', they were not to know that before them in this apparently unremarkable little story by the oddly named Stephen Daedalus lay the entry point to one of James Joyce's

116 From Paul Léon to Harriet Shaw Weaver (17 March 1933), in Joyce, *Letters*, vol. III.

117 Frank Budgen, *James Joyce and the Making of 'Ulysses' and other writings* (Oxford: Oxford University Press, 1972), 330.

118 B. Ifor Evans, 'Who, it may be asked, was Finnegan?', *Manchester Guardian*, 12 May 1939.

most complex and enduring labyrinths.[119] As Mick O'Shaughnessy of *The Dalkey Archive* notes, Joyce 'certainly knew what whiskey was'.

119 Stephen Daedalus [James Joyce], 'The Sisters', *Irish Homestead*, 13 August 1904, reproduced in Joyce, *Dubliners*, ed. John Kelly (New York: Alfred A. Knopf Everyman's Library, 1991), 266, fn. 1.

2

'Their friends, the French':
Joyce, Jacobitism and the Revival

> Was it for this the wild geese spread
> The grey wing upon every tide;
> For this that all that blood was shed?
> — W. B. Yeats, 'September 1913'

> Forget not the felled! For the lomondations of Oghrem!
> — James Joyce, *Finnegans Wake*

By the autumn of 1930 Joyce's artistic reputation was secure, *Ulysses* had catapulted him into the first rank of world writers, and his 'Work in Progress', which would eventually become *Finnegans Wake* in 1939, had begun to appear – albeit to puzzlement – in an array of literary journals. The portrait painters had started to eye posterity – the most recent to seek a sitting with Joyce was Augustus John, one of the great artistic chroniclers of the Irish Literary Revival. Joyce, as keen to layer his painted image as he was his several books, had mischief in mind. Writing to Mrs Herbert Gorman in London shortly before the sitting was to begin, we see him thinking about his wardrobe: 'Do you know a Scotch shop in London which sells plaid ties? If so I should like you to buy me one and send it. The plaid I prefer (I think it is the Murray) has a lot of red in it as a ground and of course blue and white and yellow all over it.'[1] The request, at first glance stressing a simple sartorial preference, had profounder intent, as Joyce made clear to Herbert Gorman a week later: 'A.J. started my portrait a few days ago with that highly treasonable Stuart royal tie.'[2] This awareness on Joyce's part of the deposed Stuart royal family should not come as a surprise given a series of clues left behind in his writings, and yet to come in *Finnegans Wake*. Indeed, the Ireland of Joyce's birth and early manhood was a country that had exhibited a lasting and peculiar attachment to the

---

1 James Joyce to Mrs Herbert Gorman (22 October 1930), in James Joyce, *Letters*, vol. III, ed. Richard Ellmann (London: Faber and Faber, 1966), 204–5.
2 James Joyce to Herbert Gorman (30 October 1930), in Joyce, *Letters*, vol. III, 206.

Stuart or Jacobite cause, a hangover inaugurated in the late seventeenth century on the battlefields of the Boyne and Aughrim, yet still both painful and inspirational over two hundred years later.

Joyce's interest in the lost cause of Jacobitism has been passed over by critics and general readers alike. This chapter will suggest that such failure to recognize a consistent strain in his work leads to misunderstandings and misinterpretations of Joyce's attitude to Irish nationalism and his engagement with Irish history and historiography. The most important (and most neglected) manifestation of the Jacobite hue to Joyce's work comes in *Dubliners*, particularly in 'The Sisters', 'After the Race' and 'The Dead', but it is also prominent in some of his more fugitive occasional pieces as well as arising in *Ulysses* and being consistently present throughout *Finnegans Wake*. Before looking at the key Jacobite echoes in *Dubliners*, let us consider some of Joyce's more overt nods in the direction of the fallen King James II and the fractured Stuart line.

The year 1912 sees this long-standing interest at its clearest with Joyce writing two very different pieces, both conscious of the Stuart kingship. The first of these, the pungent poem 'Gas from a Burner', is a satirical blast at Joyce's perceived enemies in Dublin written in the wake of his disastrous effort to have *Dubliners* published by Maunsel and Company. Joyce's chief tormentor in the affair, which dragged on for three years, was Maunsel's manager, George Roberts, and it is he who begins to narrate 'Gas from a Burner':

> Ladies and gents, you are here assembled
> To hear why earth and heaven trembled
> Because of the black and sinister arts
> Of an Irish writer in foreign parts.

The poem was written by Joyce on his way back to Trieste after the final failure, despite his willingness to make several key changes to the text, to have the book published. It was a low point for Joyce and, while 'Gas from a Burner' takes swipes at a range of contemporary Irish writers published by Maunsel, from George Moore to Joseph Campbell to Lady Gregory, the poem is remarkable for its comic flourishes at this dark time. While the narration of the piece changes repeatedly and without warning between Roberts and Joyce, it is Roberts who is the prime target. For Joyce, Roberts joins the long list of betrayers who form such an indispensable part of Irish life, as Roberts himself states early in the piece:

> But I owe a duty to Ireland:
> I hold her honour in my hand,

> This lovely land that always sent
> Her writers and artists to banishment
> And in a spirit of Irish fun
> Betrayed her own leaders, one by one.

Parnell is quickly wheeled before the reader as prime evidence of this Irish propensity. But Joyce is keen to point out that Roberts, an Ulsterman of Scottish descent, is also given to treachery. Thinking of the pretender Charles Stuart, the much-storied 'Bonnie Prince Charlie', Joyce writes:

> I pity the poor – that's why I took
> A red-headed Scotchman to keep my book.
> Poor sister Scotland! Her doom is fell;
> She cannot find any more Stuarts to sell.[3]

As Stuart Ireland died at Aughrim in 1691, so Stuart Scotland had fallen finally in 1745 at Culloden. For Joyce, jumping, as he was wont to do, through history, Charles Stewart Parnell and Bonnie Prince Charlie become representative cases of treachery in the neighbouring countries of Ireland and Scotland.

An earlier 1912 reference to the Stuarts comes at the opening to Joyce's lecture on Daniel Defoe delivered in March at the Università Popolare, Trieste. Defoe, in his attachment to the bric-à-brac of everyday life as the source material for great writing, was a hero of Joyce's.[4] He is, reckons Joyce, 'the father of the English novel' and 'the great precursor of the Realist movement'. Yet for all his advocacy of Defoe as a writer, Joyce's political sympathies are directly opposed to those of his artistic hero, as is made clear in the opening paragraph of the lecture. Defoe, in his support for the Duke of Monmouth's rebellion of 1685 and in his subsequent advocacy of William of Orange in the Glorious Revolution, was a lifelong opponent of the Stuart royal family and of their Jacobite supporters. Joyce, on the other hand, as an Irish Catholic for whom the person of King William III, both as historical figure and as Orange icon, stood as an emblem of defeat and repression, shows an unsurprising sympathy for the Stuarts:

> In the year of grace, 1660, the exiled, fugitive, and dispossessed Charles Stuart landed on English soil at Dover and, escorted by the fanfare and torches of a jubilant people, headed towards the capital to assume the

3 James Joyce, 'Gas from a Burner', in Joyce, *The Critical Writings*, ed. Ellsworth Mason and Richard Ellmann (1959) (Ithaca, NY: Cornell University Press, 1989), 242, 243, 245.
4 For some intriguing thoughts on Joyce's attachment to Defoe, including an argument for a possible allusion within 'The Dead' to *Robinson Crusoe*, see Tom Paulin, *Crusoe's Secret: The Aesthetics of Dissent* (London: Faber and Faber, 2005), 296–8.

crown that his father, the martyr king, had removed eleven years previously when he was executed on the gallows in Whitehall by order of the regicide generals. The corpses of Cromwell and Ireton were disinterred and dragged to Tyburn (the Golgotha, site of skulls, in English history) where they were hanged on the gibbets and then, putrefied as they were, beheaded by the executioner. Merriment returned to Merry England; the gracefulness, culture, pomp, and luxury of the Stuart courts returned. The young king flung open the doors of his palace to flatterers of both sexes. Holding his lapdog in his arms, he gave audience to his ministers. [...] But this triumph was misleading and, within a short time, the star of the Stuart dynasty had set forever, and Protestant succession, embodied by the person of William of Nassau, had become the cornerstone of the British constitution. Here, according to the textbooks, the chapter of ancient history comes to an end, and that of modern history begins. [...] His victory also signifies a crisis of race, an ethnic revenge. From the days of William the Conqueror onwards, no monarch of Germanic stock had wielded the English sceptre.

The picture of King Charles, lapdog in hand, is not altogether positive, but it is joyous and light and shows no sympathy for the Republican heroes Cromwell and Ireton who, for Irish Catholics, represented something akin to two of the four horsemen of the apocalypse. William III is 'an ethnic revenge', the coming of Germanic, Protestant rectitude to the English throne. For his Triestine audience the significance of that phrase may well have passed over, but to Irish ears the figure of William as a vengeful return would have been all too familiar. The 'Anglo-Saxon soul' as embodied by William is, writes Joyce, there too in Defoe's greatest creation, Robinson Crusoe, who, in his stoic conquest of his island under the most difficult of conditions, is the archetypical Englishman, possessed of 'virile independence, unthinking cruelty, persistence, slow yet effective intelligence, sexual apathy, practical and well-balanced religiosity, calculating dourness'. It is these qualities that have led the English to being masters of Ireland and of a great part of the world as Joyce writes in 1912, and in *Robinson Crusoe* Joyce sees a kind of blueprint and prediction of imperial expansion: 'Whoever re-reads this simple and moving book in the light of subsequent history cannot but be taken by its prophetic spell.'[5]

Joyce's isolation of the fall of the Stuarts and the rise of King William as the moment in which the 'unthinking cruelty' of Anglo-Saxon, Protestant domination takes hold in England results from his Irish, Catholic

5 James Joyce, 'Realism and Idealism in English Literature (Daniel Defoe – William Blake)', in Joyce, *Occasional, Critical, and Political Writing*, ed. Kevin Barry (Oxford: Oxford University Press, 2000), 164, 167, 163, 175, 175.

background and from the reinvigoration of a retrospective Jacobitism in late nineteenth- and early twentieth-century Ireland. This renewal of interest in the Stuart cause is especially evident in popular historiography, in ballad composition and in the writings of many of the Literary Revival's leading figures. While much has been written about the Revival's interest in the centenary of the United Irishmen's rebellion of 1798, few have noted an abiding interest on the part of figures as diverse as Lady Gregory, Charles Gavan Duffy, Douglas Hyde and W. B. Yeats in a historical epoch more than a hundred years before the events of Vinegar Hill, Castlebar and Ballinamuck. In Yeats's celebrated 'September 1913' the era of Jacobite and of United Irish resistance merge into one hagiography:

> Was it for this the wild geese spread
> The grey wing upon every tide;
> For this that all that blood was shed,
> For this Edward Fitzgerald died,
> And Robert Emmet and Wolfe Tone,
> All that delirium of the brave?[6]

The Wild Geese was the name given to those Jacobite Irish troops and their families who were given leave to exile themselves to the continent after the final settlement in Limerick of the Williamite War of 1689–91. They and their most charismatic officer, Patrick Sarsfield, Earl of Lucan, became popular nationalist heroes in the centuries that followed. Irish troops, both first generation and beyond, made up significant sections of an array of continental Catholic armies for decades and won greatest fame for their part in the French victory at the Battle of Fontenoy in 1745 – recalled in *Finnegans Wake* variously as 'fontannoy' (9.6–7) and 'Fountainoy' (212.14). Joyce would have enjoyed the fact that when he visited his father in 1909 the old man was living at 44 Fontenoy Street; several of Joyce's letters from that period use this as an address. Coincidentally, Joyce's great-aunt Ellen Callanan, model for one of the Morkan sisters of 'The Dead', died at 41 Aughrim Street, named after the calamitous battle that finished Jacobite hopes in 1691. In any event, Yeats's uncomplicated linkage of the heroes of the 1690s with those of 1798 and Emmet in 1803 is by no means unusual: it was a commonplace of Irish nationalist balladry in the late nineteenth and early twentieth centuries to yoke a number of generations of rebels, no matter how different in their motivations, under one flag.

---

6 W. B. Yeats, 'September 1913', in Yeats, *The Poems*, ed. Daniel Albright (London: Everyman, 1994), 159–60.

Ten years before Yeats's musings on the death of John O'Leary and the passing of Romantic Ireland, he had referred in a review of Lady Gregory's *Poets and Dreamers* (1903) to the defeated Jacobites of Aughrim. The review was titled 'The Plains of Galway' and appeared as the penultimate essay in the collection *Ideas of Good and Evil* (1903), published shortly after Lady Gregory's book of translations and essays appeared. Joyce was acquainted with 'The Plains of Galway' and had a personal interest in it as he had reviewed the same Lady Gregory title in the *Daily Express*.[7] Unlike Yeats's glowing endorsement, Joyce saw little merit in *Poets and Dreamers*. Though he finds something of value in Lady Gregory's work on the blind bard Raftery, Joyce for the most part sees *Poets and Dreamers* as an example of the romanticized poverty of expression encouraged by the Revival. His description of her interviews with elderly Galway neighbours is an early version of Stephen Dedalus's diary entry towards the conclusion of *A Portrait of the Artist as a Young Man* in which Mulrennan encounters the frightening old man on his tour of the west. Joyce's *Daily Express* review, titled 'The Soul of Ireland', is a source for this later fictional encounter: 'Half of her book is an account of old men and old women in the West of Ireland. These old people are full of stories about giants and witches, and dogs and black-handled knives, and they tell their stories one after another at great length and with many repetitions.'[8] The review did not impress Joyce's editor, E. V. Longworth, who took the unusual step of including the initials 'J. J.' at the end of the piece, thus exposing Joyce's identity to the woman who had got him the reviewing work in the first place, Lady Gregory. Joyce remembers this tactic of Longworth's in 'The Dead' when Gabriel Conroy is exposed to the nationalist Molly Ivors as a reviewer in the *Daily Express* as a result of the publication of his initials. For Gabriel to write in this newspaper of broadly unionist sympathies makes him, in Miss Ivors' eyes, a 'West Briton'.

The parallel of the initials is not Joyce's only nod to 'The Soul of Ireland' in 'The Dead'. Yeats's review, 'The Galway Plains', is also on his mind and is in part the spur for his decision to use the song 'The Lass of Aughrim' as the trigger mechanism behind Gretta's remembrance of Michael Furey and alienation from Gabriel. Yeats frames his review as a recollection of a day climbing the Slieve Aughty hills near Coole. He looks out over the plains of east Galway and thinks of Lady Gregory's fieldwork among the people of Galway and Clare:

7 Joyce had a copy of the 1905 Maunsel edition of *Ideas of Good and Evil* in his Trieste library.
8 James Joyce, 'The Soul of Ireland', in Joyce, *Occasional, Critical, and Political Writing*, 74.

> A great part of the poems and stories in Lady Gregory's book were made or gathered between Burren and Cruachmaa. It was here that Raftery, the wandering country poet of ninety years ago, praised and blamed, chanting fine verses, and playing badly on his fiddle. It is here the ballads of meeting and parting have been sung, and some whose lamentations for defeat are still remembered may have passed through this plain flying from the Battle of Aughrim.[9]

The plains and their people have become a repository of truth, a living history book in which ancient memories and understandings are still recoverable for those, like Lady Gregory, with the necessary tools. Yeats, unable to speak Irish, will never be able to access this storehouse and so, he regrets, will never write an epic.[10] Joyce was not convinced by any of this and would have been bemused by Yeats's insistence that the soul of a nation is only discoverable amid the peasantry. 'There is still in truth upon these great level plains', wrote Yeats, 'a people, a community bound together by imaginative possessions, by stories and poems which have grown out of its own life, and by a past of great passions which can still waken the heart to imaginative action.' The city dwellers, the Londoners, the Dubliners, are, for Yeats, a lost cause: 'England or any other country which takes its tune from the great cities and gets its taste from schools and not from old custom, may have a mob, but it cannot have a people.'[11] Joyce would have chuckled. In using 'The Lass of Aughrim' and, more obliquely, in his term 'the dark central plain' in the final paragraph of 'The Dead', Joyce is throwing back at Yeats and Lady Gregory what he feels is their over-romanticized, unrealistic vision of Ireland's west.

That small bit of mischief and vengefulness on Joyce's part is, however, only one layer of the many uses he finds for that most emotive of Irish history's words: 'Aughrim'. An aspect of Lady Gregory's *Poets and Dreamers* that Joyce does not discuss in his review is her interest in Jacobitism and in Jacobite poetry. For the people around the Coole and Kiltartan districts among whom Lady Gregory moved, observed and listened, Aughrim, the bloodiest battle in Ireland's history, was still an open wound, as she recalls from a visit to an old neighbour on the Clare border:

---

9   W. B. Yeats, *Ideas of Good and Evil* (Dublin: Maunsel, 2nd edn, 1905), 334–5.

10 Thomas Kinsella uses 'The Galway Plains' at the opening of his study of the dual nature of Irish literature's linguistic contours, *The Dual Tradition*, in order to criticize Yeats for linguistic disingenuousness. See Kinsella, *The Dual Tradition: An Essay on Poetry and Politics in Ireland* (Manchester: Carcanet, 1995), 1.

11 Yeats, *Ideas of Good and Evil*, 337.

And then he told me of the Battle of Aughrim, that is still such a terrible memory; and how the 'Danes' – the De Danaan – the mysterious divine race that were conquered by the Gael, and who still hold an invisible kingdom – 'were dancing in the raths around Aughrim the night after the battle. Their ancestors were driven out of Ireland before; and they were glad when they saw those that had put them out themselves, and every one of them skivered.'[12]

The slaughter at Aughrim and the resultant collapse of Catholic Ireland's last great hope for restoration of power, land and dignity had left a scar on the folk imagination like no other engagement in Irish history and it bubbles up again and again in Irish literature right up to the present.[13] For writers sympathetic to the Jacobite cause in the aftermath of the battle, there developed a new allegorical style of poetry known as the Aisling, a poetic tradition that reaches its height in eighteenth-century Ireland under such writers as Aodhagán Ó Rathaille and Eoghan Ruadh Ó Súilleabháin. In her essay 'Jacobite Ballads' Lady Gregory describes the form:

There is a common formula for most of these songs or 'Visions', Aislinghe, as they are called. Just as artists of to-day find no monotony in drawing Ireland over and over again with her harp, her wolf-dog, and her round tower, so the Munster poets found no monotony in representing her as a beautiful woman, white-skinned, with curling hair, with cheeks in which 'the lily and the rose were fighting for mastery'. The poet asks her if she is Venus, or Helen, or Deirdre, and describes her beauty in torrents of alliterative adjectives. Then she makes her complaint against England, or her lament for her own sorrows or for the loss of her Stuart lover, spoken of sometimes as 'the bricklayer', or 'the merchant's son'.[14]

Ireland, under the conventions of the Aisling form, was also frequently described as the 'droimeann donn dílis' or loyal brown cow, and it is from this eighteenth-century fashion that the personification of the country as Róisín Dubh and as Caitlín Ní Houlihan comes, and from which Joyce draws for his character of the old milk woman in the opening episode of *Ulysses*: 'Silk of the kine and poor old woman, names given her in old times' (*U* 15).[15]

---

12 Lady Augusta Gregory, *Poets and Dreamers: Studies and Translations from the Irish* (Dublin: Hodges, Figgis; London: John Murray, 1903), 68.

13 The best-known example of such engagement from the later twentieth century is Richard Murphy's long poem *The Battle of Aughrim* (London: Faber and Faber, 1968).

14 Lady Gregory, *Poets and Dreamers*, 69.

15 Declan Kiberd, in his study of *Ulysses*, describes this moment as 'a sort of anti-*aisling*'. See Kiberd, *Ulysses and Us: The Art of Everyday Living* (London: Faber and Faber, 2009), 324.

Aisling and 'After the Race'

When starting to write the stories that would become *Dubliners*, the allegory that most interested Joyce and that he chose to put to use himself shortly after reading Lady Gregory's essay on the Aisling in his story 'After the Race' was that of the Stuart pretender as 'the merchant's son' or 'Mac an Ceannuidhe'.[16] Though there is some controversy over the first usage of this term, it seems likely that it has its roots in the sixteenth century with the poet Tadhg Dall Ó Huiginn (1550–91) and his poem 'Do Mhac Í Dhomhuill'. It became popularized by Eoghan Ruadh Ó Súilleabháin in the mid-eighteenth century.[17] The poems take the form of a dream vision in which aid is sought by Ireland from overseas, usually from France or Spain, and the 'merchant's son' is seen as the country's saviour. The merchant's son is usually interpreted to be James III, son of the defeated King James II and father of Bonnie Prince Charlie, though Edward Walsh in his *Reliques of Jacobite Poetry* (1844) reads 'Mac an Cheannuidhe' as 'a poetical allegory for the king of Spain, from whom the Irish expected aid to shake off the Saxon yoke'.[18] More recently Owen Dudley Edwards sees any of Patrick Sarsfield, James Francis Sarsfield or James II's illegitimate son, the Duke of Berwick, as likelier candidates than James III. The identity of the merchant's son is not important for us here – the knowledge that he is Jacobite code for the Pretender is all we need to know, and, most likely, all that Joyce, courtesy of Lady Gregory's *Poets and Dreamers*, knew.

'After the Race', on first reading, is an unremarkable story; were it to be one's only exposure to Joyce, it would make any talk of him as a literary genius seem laughable. It is, perhaps unsurprisingly, the least critically examined of the stories in *Dubliners*. Joyce himself, as Stanislaus tells us, did not like it.[19] Yet he revised it only very slightly between initial publication in the *Irish Homestead* of February 1904 and the publication of *Dubliners* in 1914. Stanislaus is wrong in thinking that this was

16 I am not the first reader to see elements of the Aisling form in *Dubliners* though I am unaware of any such application to 'After the Race'. See Cóilín Owens, '"Clay" (2): The Myth of Irish Sovereignty', *James Joyce Quarterly*, 27.3 (Spring 1990), 603–14.

17 For a learned account of the origins and meaning of the 'merchant's son' allegory, see Owen Dudley Edwards, 'Who was Mac an Cheannuidhe? A Mystery of the Birth of the Aisling', *North Munster Antiquarian Journal*, xxxiii (1991), 55–77.

18 Edward Walsh and John Daly, *Reliques of Irish Jacobite Poetry; with biographical sketches of the authors, interlinear literary translations, and historical illustrative notes* (Dublin: Samuel J. Machen, 1844), 14.

19 See Stanislaus Joyce, *My Brother's Keeper: James Joyce's Early Years*, ed. Richard Ellmann (1958) (Cambridge, MA: Da Capo Press, 2003), 199–200.

because Joyce saw the published word as sacrosanct or lapidary. We know, of course, that he did a great deal of meddling with his first published story, 'The Sisters', in the same period. Peter K. Garrett grouped 'After the Race' as one of what he called *Dubliners*' 'lesser stories', of interest only because it was part of a collection that represented a revolution in artistic technique that left the nineteenth century behind and became a hugely influential part of twentieth-century writing in English. Stories such as 'After the Race' and 'A Mother' only receive critical attention, argues Garrett, because of their place 'in the larger design of *Dubliners* and the fact that their author went on to become the century's greatest writer of fiction in English'.[20] That may be so, though such neglect seems potentially rather a dangerous oversight given what we know about Joyce's perfectionism and minute attention to detail. If 'A Mother' can be read as a reasonably straightforward sneer at modish revivalism, what are we to make of 'After the Race' other than a simple vignette of frustrated youth? Why did Joyce write 'After the Race'? What was he trying to tell us that made it worth fighting for the story's retention in a form very close to its original? The decision not to significantly change this story in the ten years between first and last publication is a puzzling one and makes a reconsideration worthwhile.

'After the Race' sees Joyce tapping into the Aisling tradition to give the story an added historical resonance. I am not the first to suggest a submerged historical layer: Donald Torchiana, in linking the phrase that appears in the first paragraph, 'their friends, the French', with the title of the story, posits a hidden allusion on Joyce's part to the 1798 rebellion in which aid was provided to the United Irish rebels in the form of a small French force of approximately 1,200 men landed at Kilcummin, near Killala, County Mayo, on 23 August 1798 under the command of General Humbert.[21] These troops, joined by a number of Irish rebels, won a victory against a much larger British force at Castlebar on 27 August in a skirmish that became popularly known as 'the Races of Castlebar' as a result of the hurried retreat of the British troops – or when 'they got the bump at Castlebar' (55.32), as the battle is characterized in *Finnegans Wake*. Torchiana links the motor 'race' of Joyce's story in which 'the French were virtual victors' with the 'Races' of Castlebar. Joyce's interest in the failed French mission to County Mayo is further evidenced by his efforts, during

20 Peter K. Garrett, 'Introduction', in Garrett (ed.), *Twentieth-Century Interpretations of 'Dubliners'* (Englewood Cliffs, NJ: Prentice Hall, 1968), 17.

21 See Donald T. Torchiana, *Backgrounds for Joyce's 'Dubliners'* (Boston: Allen and Unwin, 1986), 80–1.

his final visit to Ireland, to source a postcard of Killala for his Triestine student Count Francesco Sordina.[22]

Torchiana's is an intriguing theory and he is right to draw our attention to the phrase 'their friends, the French'. Joyce had first used this phrase in writing the year before he wrote 'After the Race' in a review that appeared in the *Daily Express*. The review, titled 'Today and Tomorrow in Ireland', looked at a book of the same name by the minor revivalist figure Stephen Gwynn. As with most books offered for review to Joyce, he was not impressed and wondered at the author's confused politics. 'It is hard to say', wrote Joyce, 'into what political party Mr Gwynn should go, for he is too consistently Gaelic for the Parliamentarians, and too mild for the true patriots, who are beginning to speak a little vaguely about their friends the French.'[23] What is the Franco-Irish friendship to which Joyce refers? Kevin Barry, in his notes to the review, refers us to *Stephen Hero* where Arthur Griffith, founding father of Sinn Féin and editor of one of Joyce's favourite newspapers, the *United Irishman*, is seen keeping a close watch on Philocelticism in Paris in the hope that rebellion may be fomenting.[24] Barry's is certainly an attractive theory if we look again at *Stephen Hero*, and in particular at the way in which France and Hungary briefly merge, as they do in 'After the Race'. The nationalist circles with which Stephen's friend Madden is intimate are strongly Francophile in their sympathies:

> The orators of this patriotic party were not ashamed to cite the precedents of Switzerland and France. The intelligent centres of the movement were so scantily supplied that the analogies they gave out as exact and potent were really analogies built haphazard upon very inexact knowledge. The cry of a solitary Frenchman (A bas l'Angleterre!) at a Celtic re-union in Paris would be made by these enthusiasts the subject of a leading article in which would be shown the imminence of aid for Ireland from the French Government. A glowing example was to be found for Ireland in the case of Hungary, an example, as these patriots imagined, of a long-suffering minority, entitled by every right of race and justice to a separate freedom, finally emancipating itself. (*SH* 66–7)

Richard Ellmann thinks that the phrase 'their friends, the French' refers to 'Maud Gonne and her faction, who had long been hoping to secure the support of French arms for an Irish revolution'.[25]

---

22 See James Joyce to Stanislaus Joyce (7 August 1912), in Joyce, *Letters*, vol. II, ed. Richard Ellmann (London: Faber and Faber, 1966), 300.
23 James Joyce, 'Today and Tomorrow in Ireland', in Joyce, *Occasional, Critical, and Political Writing*, 65.
24 See Kevin Barry, in Joyce, *Occasional, Critical, and Political Writing*, 303, fn. 1.
25 Richard Ellmann, in Joyce, *Letters*, vol. II, 28, fn. 1.

Certainly, both Griffith and Gonne saw France as a possible source of assistance – ideological and material – for Irish revolution. Both had been deeply involved in the 1898 centenary celebrations of the United Irish rebellion. Their admiration for the United Irishmen is reflected in the title of Griffith's newspaper and in the unveiling of a plaque at Kilcummin pier and a statue in nearby Ballina by Maud Gonne to commemorate the French landing. General Humbert's 1798 proclamation on arrival in Mayo had played on the history of Franco-Irish alliance: 'You know what efforts France has made to assist you. Her affections for you, her desire for avenging your wrongs, and assuring your independence can never be impaired.'[26] One hundred years later Irish hopes of French help were still vibrant. Deirdre Toomey has written of the very real expectations among certain Irish nationalists that France was once again preparing to come to Ireland's assistance, having fallen out with England over the Fashoda incident in far-off North Africa:

> On 29 October the *Irish Weekly Independent* published a front-page cartoon, 'Should Auld Acquaintance be Forgot', which depicts 'Pat' addressing 'Miss La Belle France': 'Sure, Miss, if you have any trouble with yer neighbours you might like to step over here for a time, bring a few traps with you'. The 'traps' at La Belle France's feet contain guns and bayonets. The accompanying editorial assumed an imminent invasion of Britain by France and urged the French to come via Ireland, where they would be sure of a welcome.[27]

When he came to write his *Dramatis Personae*, Yeats recalled the tumult of the closing years of the nineteenth century and the pull of France on the popular imagination:

> A man I met in Sligo dreamed that he was entrenched in a swamp, fighting against invaders. 'What will you do', somebody asked the *Express* Editor, 'if the French land at Killala?' 'I will write the best article of my life', was the answer. 'I will call upon readers to remember their great traditions, to remember their own ancestors, to make up their minds with the utmost resolution, without a moment's hesitation, which side they are going to take.'[28]

26 Quoted in Stephen Dunford, in collaboration with Guy Beiner, *In Humbert's Footsteps: Mayo 1798* (n. pl.: Fadó Books, 2006), 49.

27 Deirdre Toomey, 'Moran's Collar: Yeats and Irish Ireland', *Yeats Annual 12: That Accusing Eye. Yeats and his Irish Readers*, ed. Warwick Gould and Edna Longley (London: Macmillan, 1996), 47.

28 W. B. Yeats, *Autobiographies*, ed. William H. O'Donnell and Douglas N. Archibald (New York: Scribner, 1999), 312–13.

As late as 1914 British army recruitment posters in Mayo appealed to county natives to consider their indebtedness to France and to join the war effort against Germany: 'Remember how the French helped us in Killala Bay in 1798. Remember Castlebar and ask yourselves: shall we desert the French people now?'[29]

In addition to all this 1798 centennial sabre rattling, Joyce, when referring to 'their friends, the French' in 'After the Race', is remembering a long and complex history of alliances between Ireland and France that reverberates through all of his work. The notion of a Franco-Irish alliance appears in *Ulysses* where it is raised for comic purposes in the 'Cyclops' chapter as the drinkers in Barney Kiernan's pub, led by the bombastic nationalist 'Citizen', talk rubbish about Ireland and her history.

> — We are a long time waiting for that day, citizen, says Ned. Since the poor old woman told us that the French were on the sea and landed at Killala.
> — Ay, says John Wyse. We fought for the royal Stuarts that reneged us against the Williamites and they betrayed us. Remember Limerick and the broken treaty-stone. We gave our best blood to France and Spain, the wild geese. Fontenoy, eh? And Sarsfield and O'Donnell, duke of Tetuan in Spain, and Ulysses Browne of Camus that was Fieldmarshal to Maria Teresa. But what did we ever get for it?
> — The French! says the citizen. Set of dancing masters! Do you know what it is? They were never worth a roasted fart to Ireland. Aren't they trying to make an *Entente cordiale* now at Tay Pay's dinnerparty with perfidious Albion? Firebrands of Europe and they always were.
> — *Conspuez les Français*, says Lenehan, nobbling his beer. (*U* 428)

Again, as with Yeats's 'September 1913', we get that conflation of a whole series of disparate historical moments and figures, from Killala to Fontenoy to nineteenth-century Irish noblemen in Spain, into one unitary narrative. But while Yeats is serious, Joyce finds the whole thing preposterous and hilarious.

Joyce, like any Irish schoolboy of the day, would have been familiar with the history of French aid but he also had a more personal knowledge of the alliance through his beloved father, John Joyce. Stanislaus Joyce tells us in *My Brother's Keeper* that his father might never have come to Dublin from his native Cork were it not for his rash desire to take up arms for France, and for a watchful mother determined to see him settle and succeed. 'After an abortive attempt to volunteer with three college friends for the French Army in 1870', writes Stanislaus, 'including a flight to London with his

---

29 Quoted in Guy Beiner, *Remembering the Year of the French: Irish Folk History and Social Memory* (Madison, WI: University of Wisconsin Press, 2007), 11.

mother in stern chase and a crestfallen return, he got mixed up with a Fenian group in rebel Cork, so that his harassed mother decided to leave for Dublin.'[30] John's wish to fight for France took place within the context of the Franco-Prussian war, a conflict that had aroused intense sympathy among Irish Catholics for their old Gallic ally and that saw extensive coverage in Ireland's national and provincial press.[31] In addition to this youthful quest for adventure on John Joyce's part, he was also very friendly with the old Paris-based Fenian Joseph Casey who had been involved in the dynamiting of Clerkenwell jail and who is remembered in *Ulysses* as 'the wild goose, Kevin Egan of Paris' (*U* 51). Thus Paris, long a home for exiled revolutionaries, would have been keenly and affectionately seen as a home for romantic adventurism in the Joyce household.

But, all of this Franco-Irish friendship acknowledged, it is important to be clear-eyed about the tone of that key phrase in 'After the Race'. Here is the relevant passage:

> The cars came scudding in towards Dublin, running evenly like pellets in the groove of the Naas Road. At the crest of the hill at Inchicore sightseers had gathered in clumps to watch the cars careering homeward and through this channel of poverty and inaction the Continent sped its wealth and industry. Now and again the clumps of people raised the cheer of the gratefully oppressed. Their sympathy, however, was for the blue cars – the cars of their friends, the French. (*D* 35)

Irish identification with the French cars is a pathetic kind of love, the unrequited gaze of a loser for a winner. And so the phrase 'their friends, the French' is not a comment on the Gallic victors but is instead a sneer at the 'gratefully oppressed' onlookers. There is more than a suggestion that, were the tables to be turned, French automobile enthusiasts would be slow to return these rather desperate feelings of affection. The tone of the paragraph problematizes any sense of a proud and mutual *entente* between the two countries. Misplaced Irish faith or love for the French is, for Joyce, a fact of Irish history: Humbert came in 1798 too late and with too few troops. But it is not just to the United Irish rebellion that Joyce is alluding but to an earlier French intercession, one recalled by John Wyse Nolan as he sinks his pint in Barney Kiernan's: the period of the Williamite War of 1689–91.

---

30 Stanislaus Joyce, *My Brother's Keeper*, 25.

31 For discussion of Irish interest in the Franco-Prussian war, see Dónal Ó Luanaigh, 'Ireland and the Franco-Prussian War', *Éire-Ireland: A Journal of Irish Studies*, IX.1 (Earrach 1974), 3–13.

Joyce provides us with several clues towards a Jacobite subtext in 'After the Race'. The chief protagonist of the story is James, or Jimmy, Doyle. This choice of name is meant as a prompt towards King James, as it is in another story published in the same year, 'The Sisters', where the paralysed priest is also named James.[32] Jimmy Doyle allies himself with the French, as King James did during the war in Ireland, and gets nothing but empty pockets and a vague sense of being a loser in a game he has not the wit to understand. The big winner in the card game at the end of the story is an Englishman named Routh. Stanislaus tells us that his brother chose this name because it was that of a young English bohemian he had socialized with in Paris during his first sojourn there.[33] Ellmann agrees but says that Eugene Routh was 'of origin unknown'.[34] Whatever Routh's nationality, in 'After the Race' Joyce has him as a victorious Englishman, but I suspect that the name is there to remind us of a historical Frenchman: General St Ruth, commanding officer of the Jacobite army that took the field at Aughrim on 12 July 1691. St Ruth was a French career soldier who had served with distinction in Savoy and had a reputation as an effective persecutor of Hugenots.[35] Historians are in general agreement that he had the upper hand at Aughrim before he was decapitated by a Williamite cannonball. His death led to widespread confusion in the Jacobite ranks and crushing defeat soon followed. The 'Irish historiographical tradition', comments one recent account, 'has considered the decapitation of St Ruth as the effective end of Irish Jacobite militarism'.[36] Popular nationalist myth had it, even into the early twentieth century, that Jacobite defeat could be put down simply to faulty command. Stopford Brooke is unequivocal about this in his introduction to Emily Lawless's 1902 collection *With the Wild Geese*: 'Had Sarsfield commanded and not St Ruth, the French General, it is probable that neither the town [Athlone] nor the battle [Aughrim] would have been lost.'[37]

The fact of Routh's Englishness should not put us off. John V. Kelleher, one of the most astute exegetes of *Dubliners*, has described Joyce's allusive

32 Robert M. Adams argues that the name and the character of Jimmy Doyle are chosen by Joyce as a version of himself. See Adams, *James Joyce: Common Sense and Beyond* (New York: Random House, 1966), 66–7.
33 Stanislaus Joyce, *My Brother's Keeper*, 200.
34 Richard Ellmann, *James Joyce* (Oxford: Oxford University Press, rev. edn, 1982), 123.
35 See J. G. Simms, *Jacobite Ireland, 1685–91* (1969) (Dublin: Four Courts Press, 2000), 196–7.
36 Éamonn Ó Ciardha, *Ireland and the Jacobite Cause, 1685–1766: A Fatal Attachment* (Dublin: Four Courts Press, 2nd edn, 2004), 34.
37 Stopford A. Brooke, 'Preface', in Emily Lawless, *With the Wild Geese* (London: Isbister, 1902), x.

technique as one that is not dependent on exhaustive historical exactitude but rather on a sense of half-heard prompts: 'Everyone of course knows that Joyce was fond of weaving into his work parallels with myth, saga, and epic. It is, however, a mistake to assume, when such a parallel is identified, that it must be complete. [...] Usually Joyce is content with a few salient indications.'[38] Importantly for Joyce's pessimistic view of Irish history, St Ruth's defeat at Aughrim was usually put down to treachery, the guilty party in this case being the cowardly and fickle Jacobite cavalry officer, Henry Luttrell, who withdrew the troopers under his command from the left flank of St Ruth's army at a crucial moment, allowing Williamite troops to pour through the line.[39] The land held by Luttrell has since been known as Luttrell's pass and is remembered by Joyce in *Finnegans Wake*: 'Luttrell sold if Lautrill bought, in the saddle of the Brennan's (now Malpasplace?) pass' (81.14–15).[40] Joyce's hard feelings about defeat at Aughrim run, it is clear, from his earliest to his final published work, as is underlined by the *Wake*'s Thomas Moore-inspired lament: 'Forget not the felled! For the lomondations of Oghrem!' (340.8–9).[41]

Along with the name 'James', the desultory French alliance and the allusion to St Ruth, the other pointer to 'After the Race' as a type of misshapen Aisling is the description of Jimmy Doyle's father: 'His father, who had begun life as an advanced Nationalist, had modified his views early. He had made his money as a butcher in Kingstown and by opening shops in Dublin and in the suburbs he had made his money many times over' (D 36). So, Mr Doyle senior is a turncoat like so many of the canvassers in 'Ivy Day in the Committee Room', the type of character most despised by Joyce, whose hot-headed Parnellism remained his only lifelong political passion. And, of course, it is no accident that we see him associated with the British monarchy in his early success at *Kings*town. But there is worse to come: 'He had also been fortunate enough to secure some of the police

---

38 John V. Kelleher, 'Irish History and Mythology in James Joyce's "The Dead"', in Charles Fanning (ed.), *Selected Writings of John V. Kelleher on Ireland and Irish America* (Carbondale, IL: Southern Illinois University Press, 2002), 46.

39 For an exemplary nineteenth-century interpretation of Luttrell's part in the battle, see Charles ffrench Blake-Forster, *The Irish Chieftains; or, A Struggle for the Crown: with numerous notes and a copious appendix* (Dublin: McGlashan and Gill, 1872), 243–6.

40 James Atherton, while agreeing with the Aughrim allusion, argues that the Luttrell reference may also point to a manuscript – the Luttrill Psalter – held in the British Library and known to Joyce. See Atherton, *The Books at the Wake: A Study of Literary Allusions in James Joyce's 'Finnegans Wake'* (London: Faber and Faber, 1959), 68. On Luttrell's treachery, see Simms, *Jacobite Ireland*, 225.

41 Moore's ballad 'Forget not the Field' is a typical nationalist romantic lament.

contracts and in the end he had become rich enough to be alluded to in the Dublin newspapers as a merchant prince' (*D* 36). Along with being politically fickle, then, Mr Doyle is also a collaborator, like the repulsive and sweaty Corley of 'Two Gallants' who is known to keep company with plainclothes policemen. Finally, Mr Doyle is slavishly anglophile, with Jimmy having been sent to boarding school in England, followed by a period in Trinity College, Dublin, and then a term at Cambridge, 'to see a little life' (*D* 36).

It is clear enough why Joyce provides us with the details on the provenance of Mr Doyle's wealth but it is easy to pass over one important detail: the description of him as a 'merchant prince'. Joyce thought a good deal about using this phrase. In the initial *Irish Homestead* version of the story of 17 December 1904, he chose to highlight the phrase by placing it between inverted commas. He removed these punctuation marks for his abortive attempt to have the story published by Maunsel in 1910–12 and the quotation marks are also absent from the final version of the story as published by Grant Richards in 1914.[42] In drawing attention to the phrase in the initial version he was thinking of Lady Gregory's *Poets and Dreamers*, which he had reviewed the previous year and which provided him with the information that the Stuart pretender, the hero of the Aisling, is often alluded to as 'the merchant's son'. Jimmy Doyle, then, loser at cards, ally of the French, son of the merchant prince, is a coded artistic version of James III, Stuart pretender and son of the last Stuart monarch, King James II, vanquished leader of the Franco-Irish armies at the Boyne and last Catholic king of England.

Poor James: 'The Sisters' and the Stuarts

If 'After the Race' were the only story to exhibit these Jacobite tendencies it would be harder to make the argument stick, but they are present also, and more clearly so, in both 'The Sisters' and 'The Dead'. 'The Sisters' comes from the same period of composition as 'After the Race' and along with 'Eveline' was one of only three stories published in the *Irish Homestead*. Between this first publication and the final version of 1914, 'The Sisters' was revised more often, and more completely, than any other story in *Dubliners*, and it is in these revisions that the Jacobite traces are most clearly visible. As with 'After the Race' we have a character named James as a loser – in this case Father James Flynn who begins the story as a

---

42 See James Joyce, *Dubliners: A Facsimile of Drafts and Manuscripts*, ed. Hans Walter Gabler (New York and London: Garland, 1978), 3c–3d; and James Joyce, *Dubliners: A Facsimile of Proofs for the 1910 Edition*, ed. Michael Groden (New York and London: Garland, 1977), 58.

paralytic and ends it as a corpse. Father Flynn's death in a house on Great Britain Street is an example of Joyce being relatively kind to the reader in terms of leaving clues to easier interpretation of the story. The only other indication of a historical undercurrent in the original version is the repetition – Aisling-like – by the dead priest's sisters at the end of the story of the phrase 'poor James' three times in quick succession. By the time of the final version of the story, Joyce's interest in Jacobitism is clearer and, unusually for him, he actually makes 'The Sisters' easier, rather than more difficult, to interpret as he revises.[43] He does this in three main ways. First, he doubles the frequency of the phrase 'poor James' to a jarring six times, thus underlining the sense of the story as a kind of lament. Secondly, he decides to utilize street names and places even more transparently than in the original by telling us not only of Father Flynn's death on Great Britain Street but also of his birth in Irishtown, thus underlining the damaging historical relationship between Ireland and her conqueror. Thirdly, and most importantly for the Jacobite subtext, Joyce alters the card pinned to the crape bouquet on the dead priest's front door.

The *Irish Homestead* version of 'The Sisters' is evasive about the exact date on which Father Flynn died, with the card reading 'July 2nd, 189- The Rev. James Flynn (formerly of St. Ita's Church), aged 65 years. R.I.P.' In an intermediate version of the story probably written late in 1905, since it incorporates some details – most notably what the dead priest ought to be dressed in – that Joyce asked Stanislaus to verify in October 1905, the card has been revised to read 'July 2nd 1890 The Rev. James Flynn (formerly of S. Catherine's Church, Meath Street) aged sixty-five years. R.I.P.' The final version revises both day and year of death to read July 1st, 1895. Marvin Magalaner, who was the first critic to seriously ponder Joyce's motivations behind the various revisions in *Dubliners*, was stumped by this meddling with Father Flynn's funeral card. 'It is possible', he wrote, 'that there is no logical answer.'[44] Florence L. Walzl unconvincingly argues that Joyce made the changes in order to have the boy of the story become a replica of himself: 'Born in 1882, Joyce would have been thirteen years old in 1895 and he sought an identification with his protagonist.'[45]

43 This way of reading the story pushes against the commonly held critical view of 'The Sisters' that 'The *Homestead* text was simple. [...] By contrast the *Dubliners* version increases uncertainty everywhere.' See L. J. Morrissey, 'Joyce's Revision of "the Sisters": From Epicleti to Modern Fiction', *James Joyce Quarterly*, 24.1 (Fall 1986), 48.

44 Marvin Magalaner, *Time of Apprenticeship: The Fiction of Young James Joyce* (London: Abelard-Schuman, 1959), 85.

45 Florence L. Walzl, 'Joyce's "The Sisters": A Development', *James Joyce Quarterly*, 10.4 (Summer 1973), 404.

William Bysshe Stein was the first to understand the implications of the change of date from 2 to 1 July. The first day of July has a double significance for Joyce and for the story. Given that Father Flynn's breaking of the chalice was the catalyst that led to his paralysis and death, it is significant that 1 July is the Feast of the Most Precious Blood of Our Lord Jesus Christ. We can be certain that Joyce, with his in-depth knowledge of Saints days, was aware of this feast. And 1 July also carries a heavy historic resonance in the Irish context. It is the date on which the armies of King James were defeated by the armies of Prince William of Orange at the Boyne.[46] 'Thus', argues James Fairhall, 'Father Flynn's demise resonates with political as well as spiritual failure, bringing to mind turn-of-the-century Ireland's continuing status as a colony.'[47] Though the Boyne was a much less catastrophic defeat than that at Aughrim the following summer, it has taken on greater symbolic power in Irish history in part because it represented the last stand of King James, who departed the battlefield and the country with unseemly haste. The battle appears repeatedly in *Finnegans Wake* as, variously, 'the prodestung boyne' (126.22), 'Buckily buckily, blodestained boyne!' (341.5–6), and even acts as a kind of before and after historical pivot: 'both before and after the battle of the Boyne it was a habit not to sign letters always' (114.35–115.1).

James's cowardice was long remembered in Ireland where in ballad and song he became known as *Séamas an Chaca*, or James the Shit. The feelings were mutual, with James despising and distrusting his Irish subjects in equal measure:

> His instructions to his son, written in 1692, show a distrust of the Irish that is reminiscent of Henry VIII. The principal garrisons should never be entrusted to Irish governors or Irish troops; the sons of old families should be given an English education so that they should 'be weaned from their natural hatred against the English'; schools should be set up in Ireland to teach English and 'by degrees wear out the Irish language, which would be for the advantage of the body of the inhabitants'; the Os and Macs should be firmly told that estates forfeited by James I and his predecessors could not be restored; no native of Ireland should be lord lieutenant.[48]

46 Today, of course, the Battle of the Boyne is commemorated on 12 July. The change in date is due to the British decision to convert from the Julian to the Gregorian calendar in September 1752, a decision met with some hostility in Jacobite circles. For an interesting account of this, see Robert Poole, '"Give Us Our Eleven Days!": Calendar Reform in Eighteenth-Century England', *Past and Present*, 149 (November 1995), esp. 131–7.

47 James Fairhall, *James Joyce and the Question of History* (Cambridge: Cambridge University Press, 1993), 91.

48 Simms, *Jacobite Ireland*, 153–4.

There is something rather pathetic, then, about the burning desire among many of the Catholic Irish to see another Stuart on the throne. We are reminded of this unrequited and worthless love for the Stuarts in an early scene of *Ulysses* when Stephen enters the bigoted Deasy's office in search of his wages:

> Stale smoky air hung in the study with the smell of drab abraded leather of its chairs. As on the first day he bargained with me here. As it was in the beginning, is now. On the sideboard the tray of Stuart coins, base treasure of a bog: and ever shall be. (*U* 35)

Here Joyce is remembering James Stuart's 1689 debasement of Irish coinage in order to help his war effort, a move derided in the Orange toast to William III, 'who saved us from brass money and wooden shoes', again referred to early in the *Wake* in the phrase 'his quarterbrass woodyshoes' (8.19).

The eponymous sisters of Joyce's opening story are types of the 'gratefully oppressed' of 'After the Race', and their misguided lamentations for 'poor James' will see them remain prostrate. As for Joyce's decision to use the year 1895 on the funeral card, Stein feels that it is chosen to remind the reader of the continuing decline of the Home Rule dream with the success of the unionist Conservative party in the general election of that year.[49] A more likely explanation is that provided by John Kelly: Father Flynn dies aged sixty-five in 1895; that makes his year of birth 1829 or 1830 and thus Joyce is inviting us to associate the priest's life with the winning of Catholic emancipation under the political leadership of Daniel O'Connell, a figure who will make a reappearance at the end of *Dubliners* as Gabriel and Gretta pass his snow-covered statue at the foot of Sackville Street. 'His life', writes Kelly, 'is therefore coterminous with the revived Catholic Church in Ireland, and his paralysis, and the effect it has on others, symbolic of the Church's influence in Ireland.'[50] A further possible reason for the choice of year – linking Joyce with Yeats – will be considered in the next chapter.

Joyce was by no means the only Irish writer thinking about James II's legacy at this time and here we must return again to Lady Gregory. The Gregory and Persse families had been among those to benefit from Jacobite defeat in the 1690s. As part of the eighteenth-century Protestant ascendancy, they saw their estates in County Galway grow and prosper as their Catholic neighbours came under the scrutiny of the Penal laws, which

49 William Bysshe Stein, 'Joyce's "The Sisters"', *The Explicator*, XXI.1 (September 1962), n.p. [3 and 5].
50 John Kelly, 'Introduction', in James Joyce, *Dubliners* (New York: Everyman, 1991), xxx.

restricted their right to practise their religion, to bear arms and to hold property. Lady Gregory, through books such as *Poets and Dreamers* and essays such as 'Jacobite Ballads', wished to distance herself from the worst excesses of her colonial ancestry on both sides of the family tree. Though she had begun her writing career with a stern attack on Home Rule and with supportive biographical pieces on her powerful and much-despised late husband, by the later 1890s she had become more recognizably the Lady Gregory of the Revival who is, for the most part, fondly remembered in Ireland today. While Gregory had revealed her interest in Jacobitism through her essay on the Aisling tradition, she had a more personal interest in the events of the Williamite War as is evident in her naming of her beloved young son Robert's first horse 'Sarsfield' after the popular nationalist hero of the war. Her focus on this period reaches its clearest manifestation with the publication in 1905 of her play *The White Cockade*.

The White Cockade, one of those rather unremarkable but very popular comedies that made up much of the Abbey's early repertoire, was written in three acts and revolves around division within the Kelleher family of Duncannon regarding their wavering loyalty to the cause of King James, the white cockade being a favourite Jacobite emblem. The immediate inspiration for the play came from work that Lady Gregory had carried out the previous year in translating Douglas Hyde's one-act Gaelic play, *Righ Seumas* (*King James*). This short farce follows the comical efforts of an old man and young boy to smuggle King James aboard a French ship. James is concealed in a barrel that becomes coveted by three Jacobite soldiers fleeing from the Boyne. While James hides in the barrel the soldiers vent their fury regarding their cowardly king: 'King James, the ugly cur; he did treachery on us. He ran away with himself out of the battle. He forsook the Gael. The coward; O, if his skull was under my heel now it is well I would pound it under my feet.'[51] Ultimately the boy dupes the soldiers into letting James make his escape.

The White Cockade also deals with the aftermath of the Battle of the Boyne, with King James depicted as a bumbling coward and Patrick Sarsfield as a virtuous hero. And, as in *Righ Seumas*, James seeks refuge in a barrel. A key character of *The White Cockade* is Lady Dereen, a Catholic aristocrat who has lost her land and longs to see restitution under a Stuart king. Lady Dereen is a type of the female speaker of the traditional Aisling, a forlorn representative of a defeated Ireland who looks to the Stuarts for salvation. The Aisling motif is underlined in the play's epigraph, 'I saw a vision

---

51 An Craoibhín Aoibhinn [Douglas Hyde], *Righ Seumas*, trans. Lady Gregory (n.pl. [Dublin]: n.p., n.d. [1904]), 7.

through my sleep last night.'[52] Through the character of Lady Dereen, *The White Cockade* operates as a comic inversion of the much better known Lady Gregory/W. B. Yeats collaboration, *Cathleen Ni Houlihan*. In *Cathleen Ni Houlihan* a crooked old woman arrives at the cottage of the Gillane family at a crucial moment in Irish history, the 1798 landing of the French in Killala. She succeeds in persuading the son of the family, Michael Gillane, to leave his family and his young bride in order to fight for Ireland. The play became an immediate success with nationalist audiences and famously prompted Yeats to ponder many years later whether the play had sent out 'certain men the English shot'[53] – a phrase that is so often quoted now that it has hardened into cliché.

Whether *Cathleen Ni Houlihan* prompted anyone to pick up a rifle must remain a moot point, but we can say for sure that *The White Cockade* had no one reaching for their revolver. Again, an old lady representing nationalist Ireland arrives at a cottage in an Irish port and seeks assistance from the son of the family. But this time the boy in question, Owen Kelleher, stays put, Ireland is betrayed by the fleeing James Stuart, and Lady Dereen is left lamenting another defeat. James, in his desperate bid to quit the country by any means necessary, is a pantomime villain. 'I would prefer to be elsewhere', he declares, and goes on: 'It is all very well for those who have a taste for fighting. I had it once myself – when I was a boy. But it has gone from me now with the taste of unripe apples.' Owen might have been another Michael Gillane were it not for the hard-headed realism of his mother. The start of the play sees him with the typical optimism of youth as he waits for Stuart salvation:

> The cuckoo had no word to say,
> Sharp grief has put us under rent,
> The heavy cloud is on the Gael,
> But comely James will bring consent!

Such faith ought to provide rich pickings for Lady Dereen who wanders the land in search of youths willing to sacrifice themselves for Ireland. 'The young men are leaving the scythes in the meadows', she chants, 'the old men are leaving the stations and the blessed wells. Give me some white thing – some feathers – I have to make cockades for the King's men.' But Mrs Kelleher is not seduced by this vision and the romantic nationalism so prominent in *Cathleen Ni Houlihan* is subverted by chary realism:

---

52 Lady Gregory, *The White Cockade* (Dublin: Maunsel, 1905), n.p. [1].
53 W. B. Yeats, 'Man and the Echo', in Yeats, *Poems*, 392.

LADY: (taking feathers and beginning to fasten them together with shaking hands) James, our own King, will bring prosperity to us all.
MRS KELLEHER: So long as we get it, I wouldn't mind much what King brings it. One penny weighs as good as another, whatever King may have his head on it.[54]

The White Cockade, though published after 'The Sisters' and 'After the Race', and therefore not an influence, does reflect an intense revival of interest in the Jacobite period of Irish history among many of those writers at the centre of the Literary Revival. The published play was one of four Lady Gregory books that Joyce had in his Trieste library and its concerns become in part the concerns of his last and greatest story, 'The Dead'.[55]

Jacobitism and the Literary Revival

The Revival's interest in Jacobitism evident in *The White Cockade*, *Poets and Dreamers*, 'September 1913', George Moore's story 'The Wild Goose', Douglas Hyde's *Songs of Connacht*, Emily Lawless's *With the Wild Geese* and elsewhere goes back to the late 1880s and early 1890s, to the beginnings of the movement and its indebtedness to Young Ireland romanticism, and in particular to the figure of Thomas Davis.[56] In early May 1888 W. B. Yeats wrote to his friend, the poet and novelist Katharine Tynan, about the importance to the writer of having a particular theme of one's own: 'I think you will be right to make your ballad Irish, you will be so much more origonal [sic] – one should have a speciality. You have yours in Ireland and your Religion. I cannot now think of a subject but will be on the look out – perhaps in the Sarsfield age their [sic] was something.'[57] On first reading there is a straightforward generosity of spirit about these remarks; however, by turning his attention to 'the Sarsfield age', that is, the period of the Williamite War of 1689–91 and its aftermath, Yeats is merely picking up on a prompt already dropped by Tynan in her first collection of poetry, *Louise de la Vallière*, published some three years earlier. That book's

54 Lady Gregory, *The White Cockade*, 22–3, 8, 9, 10.
55 The other Lady Gregory titles held by Joyce in Trieste in 1920 were *The Kiltartan Wonder Book* (1910); *Poets and Dreamers* (1903); *Spreading the News, The Rising of the Moon, The Poor House* (1906). See Richard Ellmann, *The Consciousness of Joyce* (London: Faber and Faber, 1977), 110–11.
56 A large number of Jacobite ballads are contained in Douglas Hyde, *Abhráin atá Leagtha ar an Reachtúire. Songs Ascribed to Raftery, being the fifth chapter of 'The Songs of Connacht'* (1903) (Shannon: Irish University Press, 1973).
57 W. B. Yeats to Katharine Tynan (May 1888) in W. B. Yeats, *The Collected Letters, vol. I: 1865–1895*, ed. John Kelly and Eric Domville (Oxford: Oxford University Press, 1986), 66.

preoccupations with Catholic sensibility and pastoral retreat predicted much of what was to flow from Tynan's pen over the following years. At this early stage in her career, however, she occasionally permitted herself a more political note.

The soft nationalism of the early Tynan is evident in *Louise de la Vallière* via a poem titled 'The Flight of the Wild Geese', which carries a footnote: 'The Irish soldiery, who, after the Williamite conquest and the treachery of the broken "Treaty of Limerick", sailed away from Ireland and took service in the armies of France and Austria and Spain, were called "The Wild Geese".'[58] The poem is interesting as perhaps the earliest instance of a Revival focus on the period of Jacobite defeat. As so often in such poems, Patrick Sarsfield is the hero, with the poem concluding thus:

> Ah! Patrick Sarsfield, when you lay,
> With your life-blood following amain,
> You looked at the dark stain on your hand,
> And 'Would it were shed for mine own dear land!'[59]

Thirty years after the composition of this poem Tynan's affection for Sarsfield remained intact, as is evident from her *Book of Irish History*, written for the Educational Company of Ireland:

> Sarsfield went back to the service of the King of France. Two years later he fell on the field of Landen, in the very moment of victory, charging the retreating army of England. As he lay dying, he looked at his life-blood which had stained his hand. 'Would God it were for Ireland!' he said, and passed to take his place for ever in the long gallery of Irish heroes.[60]

And, intriguingly, in her hagiographical biography of Lord Edward Fitzgerald, published in 1916, Tynan attempts to draw a rather spurious lineage from Fitzgerald and his ancestors back to the Stuarts and then forward again to another of her heroes, the former Chief Secretary George Wyndham.[61]

Yet for all Tynan's interest in Fitzgerald, Sarsfield and other romantic Irish heroes, her experimentation with Jacobite-themed poetry did not last very long, and only one of her hundred-plus novels, *For the White Rose*

58 Katharine Tynan, *Louise de la Vallière and other poems* (London: Kegan Paul, Trench, 1885), 21. I am grateful to Kieron Winterson and Whitney Standlee for drawing my attention to Tynan's Jacobite interests.

59 Tynan, *Louise de la Vallière*, 24.

60 Katharine Tynan, *Book of Irish History* (Dublin and Belfast: The Educational Company of Ireland, n.d. [1918?]), 149.

61 See Katharine Tynan, *Lord Edward: A Study in Romance* (London: Smith, Elder, 1916).

(1905), used the Jacobites for background. 'The Wild Geese (A lament for the Irish Jacobites)', included in her *Ballads and Lyrics* of 1891, sums up Tynan's enthusiasm for the subject with typical sentiment:

> O sore in the land of the stranger
> They'll pine for the land far away!
> But Day of Aughrim, my sorrow,
> It was you was the bitter day![62]

The waning of interest may in part be due to difficulties she experienced in having this poem accepted for publication. Before eventually appearing in the Irish-nationalist inclined *Boston Pilot*, it had been rejected by the *Scots Observer*. Yeats, always the pragmatist, points out this miscalculation to Tynan: 'You should not have sent the poem to the Scots Observer it was too political – Irish exiles are out of their range I think.'[63] Edited by W. E. Henley, the *Scots Observer* had a reputation for elitism and was given the name the 'Snobserver' by Arnold Bennett.[64] It was certainly not the kind of periodical to publish anything smacking of Irish nationalism. Yeats, who had a very good sense of who would publish what, knew this very well and was frequently published by Henley, who he cultivated as a friend while living in Bedford Park.[65]

Writing at the same time as Tynan but from the other side of the religious divide, the unionist Emily Lawless, daughter of Lord Cloncurry, also saw in the legacy of the defeated Jacobites a theme worthy of poetic focus. As early as her historical study of 1887, simply titled *Ireland*, Lawless showed an even greater enthusiasm for Patrick Sarsfield than had Tynan. 'Sarsfield', she wrote, 'is the one redeeming figure upon the Jacobite side. His gallant presence sheds a ray of chivalric light upon this otherwise gloomiest and least attractive of campaigns.'[66] *Ireland* is dedicated to 'the Earl of Dufferin, K.P., G.C.B., F.R.S., &c., Viceroy of India'. This gloriously imperial address is, oddly as it might seem, followed by a few words in unorthodox Irish: 'Sgeul na H-Éireann don Éireannach as fiú', which translates as 'The story of Ireland for the best of Irishmen'. So we seem to have a number of mixed messages: a Protestant unionist writing in praise of rebellious seventeenth-century Catholics; an enthusiastic imperialist

---

62 Katharine Tynan, *Ballads and Lyrics* (London: Kegan Paul, Trench, Trübner, 1891), 93.

63 W. B. Yeats to Katharine Tynan [c. 18 May 1890], in Yeats, *Letters*, vol. I, 217.

64 See Yug Mohit Chaudhry, *Yeats, the Irish Literary Revival and the Politics of Print* (Cork: Cork University Press, 2001), 133.

65 For a useful discussion of Yeats's relationship with the *Scots Observer*, see Chaudhry, *Yeats, the Irish Literary Revival and the Politics of Print*, 132–83.

66 Emily Lawless, *Ireland* (London: T. Fisher Unwin, 1887), 289–90.

with an interest in the Irish language. Jacobitism here provides a curious bridging ground between the two main traditions in Ireland.

As a type of authentic royalism, supportive of an aristocratic Ireland, Jacobitism appeals to Lawless and to other Protestant grandees such as Lady Gregory. As a form of Catholic separatist rebelliousness it appeals to writers like Tynan and to the early Sinn Féiner William Rooney who also, though damning King James, praised the Jacobite enterprise in a speech delivered in January 1900 to the Celtic Literary Society in Dublin:

> That such men as Tyrconnell had no other object than the mere resurgence of Catholic rule should in no sense blind us to the fact that all the Gaelic soldiers and chiefs, and the semi-Gaelic like Sarsfield, favoured a more complete independence. Aughrim was fought, not for James' pretensions, but for the preservation of all the characteristics and privileges of the Gael. In the rout there was settled the fate not only of James, but of Irish nationhood for that generation. It is more than doubtful if even the relieving of the siege of Limerick could have preserved the cause. Sarsfield was simply a soldier; he was not even an elementary statesman, and the diplomats scored again. '*Briseadh Eachdhroma*' is even to-day the Gaelic peasants' synonym for disaster.[67]

While there is an immediacy and a stringency about Rooney's wish to remember this period in Irish history – an immediacy shared by Joyce – what is appealing about Jacobitism to both Tynan and Lawless is its remoteness: it allows for a very easy and tepid kind of patriotism, its main events having occurred some two hundred years in the past. Much safer to praise Patrick Sarsfield than, say, their contemporary, Michael Davitt. Sir Walter Scott had enacted a similar aesthetic bowdlerization for Scottish Jacobitism some ninety years earlier in *Waverley* (1814), a novel in which, writes G. J. Watson, Scott 'reduces the convulsion of the '45 to the stasis of art [...] to matter for passive and romantic contemplation'. As with Tynan, Lawless and other Irish revivalists, Jacobitism is, to borrow from Watson, 'all so attractively *distant*'.[68]

While Jacobitism goes out of favour with Tynan by the turn of the century, it is given full voice by Lawless in her 1902 collection *With the Wild Geese*. This collection has a substantial section of poems about the war of 1689–91 and the subsequent actions of the vanquished armies in the pay of the royal courts of France, Austria and Spain. There are two

---

67 William Rooney, *Prose Writings* (Dublin and Waterford: M. H. Gill and Son, n. d. [1902]), 93–4.
68 G. J. Watson, 'Celticism and the Annulment of History', in *Celticism*, ed. Terence Brown (Amsterdam and Atlanta, GA: Rodopi, 1996), 212, 213.

poems, for example, on the Battle of Fontenoy, but the best-known poem of the collection is the frequently anthologized 'After Aughrim', in which the figure of Éire or Ireland laments her treatment of her bravest sons:

> She said, 'They gave me of their best,
> They lived, they gave their lives for me;
> I tossed them to the howling waste,
> And flung them to the foaming sea.'[69]

Not long after the publication of this collection Lawless, tiring of an increasingly nationalist Ireland, became something of a wild goose herself and decamped for self-imposed exile in England, where she died in 1913.

It was in that year that Yeats was putting together the poems that would form *Responsibilities*, published in 1914, a collection that contained the poem 'September 1913'. Opening *Responsibilities* is an untitled italicized poem, which attempts to establish Yeats's pedigree:

> *Pardon, old fathers, if you still remain*
> *Somewhere in ear-shot for the story's end,*
> *Old Dublin merchant 'free of the ten and four'*
> *Or trading out of Galway into Spain;*
> *Old country scholar, Robert Emmet's friend,*
> *A hundred-year-old memory to the poor;*
> *Merchant and scholar who have left me blood*
> *That has not passed through any huckster's loin,*
> *Soldiers that gave, whatever die was cast:*
> *A Butler or an Armstrong that withstood*
> *Beside the brackish waters of the Boyne*
> *James and his Irish when the Dutchman crossed;*[70]

This poem was written in angry response to George Moore's teasing remarks about Yeats's delusions of aristocratic lineage in the *Vale* volume of what would become *Hail and Farewell*, originally printed in the *English Review* of January and February 1914.[71]

Naturally, for Yeats, an important part of establishing a good bloodline was evidence of martial vigour, hence the part played in Williamite victory at the Boyne. Bizarrely, however, Yeats had originally believed, or wished to believe, that his forebears had fought on the losing, Jacobite side, the first version of lines 9–12 reading thus:

---

69 Lawless, *With the Wild Geese*, 13.
70 W. B. Yeats, 'Pardon, old fathers', in Yeats, *Poems*, 148.
71 See A. Norman Jeffares, *A Commentary on the Collected Poems of W. B. Yeats* (London: Macmillan, 1968), 115.

> Pardon, and you that did not weigh the cost,
> Old Butlers when you took to horse and stood
> Beside the brackish waters of the Boyne,
> Till your bad master blenched and was lost.[72]

In later life Yeats recanted any affection he may have had for the particular strain of nationalism associated with the Stuart cause and credited his move away from political extremism to his reading of Balzac 'who saved me from Jacobin and Jacobite'.[73]

The lineage of Yeats's *Responsibilities*, picking up on Tynan's early sympathies and Lawless's loyalties, is just one strand in a complicated web of revivalist Jacobite symbols and allusions. One other key strand in the Jacobite revival is the Charles Gavan Duffy-controlled New Irish Library. This series of cheap books, meant to inspire patriotic fervour and educate the masses on the subject of their country's history and culture, is another signal example of passionate late nineteenth-century interest in the story of Sarsfield, the Wild Geese and the bumbling King James. Gavan Duffy and Yeats, though ostensibly sharing the same ambitions for Ireland's future, soon fell out over control of this scheme. Ultimately it was a case of two clashing egos with Gavan Duffy emerging victorious: the types of book finally issued in the series were not all that different to the titles Yeats originally had in mind, in spite of what the poet may have wished to believe in retrospect.[74]

For our purposes what is important about the New Irish Library is its enthusiasm for the Jacobite cause. Though the series ran to only a dozen titles between launch in 1893 and close in the early years of the new century, two of its publications concentrated on the period of the Williamite War and the presence of the English King James II in Ireland, with a third reprinting an array of Jacobite ballads. Significantly, the opening title of the series was a book by Thomas Davis that had originally appeared as a run of articles in the *Dublin Magazine* of 1843. The book, a shilling paperback published by T. Fisher Unwin and titled *The Patriot Parliament of 1689*, was meant for wide circulation among Irish nationalists.

The Dublin parliament of 1689, which was called by King James on his arrival in Ireland after having fled England upon the invasion of William of Orange, was designed to win favour with James's Irish Catholic subjects

---

72 See Jeffares, *Commentary*, 119.

73 W. B. Yeats, 'Louis Lambert', in Yeats, *Essays and Introductions* (New York: The Macmillan Company, 1961), 447.

74 For a summary of the 'Library of Ireland' controversy, see R. F. Foster, *W. B. Yeats: A Life, I: The Apprentice Mage, 1865–1914* (Oxford: Oxford University Press, 1997), 117–24.

chiefly through the restoration of title and land lost in the previous decades, most particularly as a result of the Cromwellian confiscations. It was seen by some nationalists as a high point in Catholic dignity and power, and certainly Gavan Duffy did not spare the hyperbole in his introduction: 'There is scarcely in human history a more touching or impressive spectacle than the genuine fairness and moderation of this maligned parliament.'[75] And if the Jacobite parliament was a singular example of benign governance, then the Glorious Revolution that had brought William to power – and that Joyce would discuss many years later in his essay on Defoe – was, for Davis, repugnant. 'It seems not excessive to say', he wrote, 'that there never was a revolution in which so much ingratitude, selfishness, and meanness were displayed.' Just as Yeats telescoped Irish history in 'September 1913', so too Davis saw in the 1680s the beginning of a nationalist relay race that concluded a hundred years later. The parliament, wrote Davis, 'boldly announced our national independence, in words which Molyneux shouted on to Swift, and Swift to Lucas, and Lucas to Flood, and Flood and Grattan redoubling the cry, Dungannon church rang, and Ireland was again a nation'.[76] Whatever the accuracy of Davis's account, the book proved a huge success and was the best-selling title of its era.[77]

The second overtly Jacobite title in the New Irish Library series was John Todhunter's biography of Patrick Sarsfield.[78] While James II was remembered in nationalist circles as a coward, Sarsfield was thought of as almost saintly, the military hero who, as legend had it, died fighting for the King of France, wishing with his final words that he had sustained his fatal wounds for Ireland. Sarsfield, wrote J. G. Simms in his classic study of the period, *Jacobite Ireland*, was 'the one Irishman spoken of with respect and admiration in Williamite writings: the Rommel of the Jacobite war'.[79] R. Barry O'Brien, in his preface to Todhunter's book, gives the party line on the greatest of the Wild Geese:

> The name of Sarsfield is not only a household word in every Irish home, but his memory is revered wherever his deeds are known, and patriotism

75 Charles Gavan Duffy, 'Introduction', in Thomas Davis, *The Patriot Parliament of 1689* (London: T. Fisher Unwin, 1893), lxxxviii.
76 Davis, *Patriot Parliament*, 10, 152.
77 See W. B. Yeats, *The Collected Letters, Volume Four 1905–1907*, ed. John Kelly and Ronald Schuchard (Oxford: Oxford University Press, 2005), 941, fn. 1.
78 See John Todhunter, *The Life of Patrick Sarsfield, Earl of Lucan, with a short narrative of the principal events of the Jacobite war in Ireland* (London: T. Fisher Unwin; Dublin: Sealy, Bryars and Walker, 1895).
79 Simms, *Jacobite Ireland*, 159.

and valour are prized. Struggling under immense difficulties, and thwarted at every turn by incompetent superiors, he redeemed the honour of his country, and vindicated the gallantry of his race.[80]

James II, on the other hand, 'inherited the dregs of the Stuart nature, its arrogance, its meanness, its shifty futility'.[81] Joyce, almost inevitably, given the reverence with which Sarsfield was remembered by his contemporaries, finds place for him in *Finnegans Wake*, mainly through repeated references to the Wild Geese but also in the place name Lucan, the neighbouring village to HCE's Chapelizod and, according to Todhunter, Sarsfield's birth-place: 'Before there was a patch at all on Ireland there lived a lord at Lucan' (452.28–9). R. Barry O'Brien, well known to Joyce through his two-volume *Life of Charles Stewart Parnell 1846–1891* (1898), went on, in 1904, to publish *Irish Memories*, a volume of essays on Irish history covering figures such as Shane O'Neill, Brian Boru and Owen O'Neill. To give some further indication of the preoccupation among contemporary popular historians with the era of the Williamite War and its aftermath, three of O'Brien's twelve essays – 'Sarsfield', 'Cremona' and 'Fontenoy' – concern themselves with the period. 'Sarsfield and Limerick', wrote O'Brien, 'are still names to conjure with in Ireland.'[82] James Joyce would prove the ideal conjuror.

In his insistence on remembering the damage done to the Irish psyche by crushing defeat, Joyce differs from the likes of Tynan, Lawless and Yeats. For them, writing about defeated Jacobites is a kind of safety valve that allows harmless hero worship and a rather idle patriotism that offends no one (except maybe the *Scots Observer*). But Joyce is more disgruntled and feels the salt of defeat still, hence his decision to open *Dubliners* with a nod towards the Battle of the Boyne and to close it with thoughts of Aughrim. It is important to acknowledge that this Joycean strain ought not to be seen as an isolated enthusiasm. All around him in varying ways his contemporaries of varying political hue were busy retrieving aspects of the disastrous collapse of Catholic Ireland associated with the Williamite War and putting them to use – sometimes as polemic, more often as dreamy romance – in their writing. The failure to recognize such a consistent strain in Irish writing of the period leads not only to an inaccurate understanding of some important revivalist motivations, but to misinterpretations of Joyce's

---

80 R. Barry O'Brien, 'Prefatory Notes', in Todhunter, *Life of Patrick Sarsfield*, vi.
81 Todhunter, *Life of Patrick Sarsfield*, 9.
82 R. Barry O'Brien, *Irish Memories* (London: T. Fisher Unwin, 1904), 73. O'Brien also published a textbook for schools on the Stuart kingship, *The Educational History of the Stuart Period, English and Irish*, in which the standard tragic interpretation of Sarsfield was to the fore.

attitude to Irish nationalism and of his engagement with Ireland's history. This Joycean sense of historical wrong becomes apparent again in his use of Thomas Davis's famous ballad 'The West's Asleep'.

Thomas Davis and the Mutinous Shannon Waves

The third and final volume of the New Irish Library that revisits the Jacobite cause and, more particularly, Thomas Davis's espousal of that cause was *The New Spirit of the Nation* (1894), edited by Martin MacDermott.[83] The original *Spirit of the Nation* was one of the best-selling and most popular books in nineteenth-century Ireland. First published in 1845 to make the ballads that were being printed in *The Nation* newspaper more widely available, it went into dozens of reprints over the following months and years and was widely read by both Catholic and Protestant nationalists. A young Augusta Persse caused scandal in her Roxborough home by asking for it as a birthday present. Her sister Arabella, unsure what to make of such militancy, inscribed the book, 'Patriotism is the last refuge of a Scoundrel'.[84] Many of the better-known ballads that formed the collection were written by Thomas Davis, the best-known being 'A Nation Once Again' and 'The West's Asleep'. Both these ballads were very commonly sung in Joyce's youth and he was intimately familiar with them; they appear prominently in *Finnegans Wake* as, respectively, 'A nation wants a gaze' (43.21) and 'the waste's a'sleep' (64.1). 'The West's Asleep' is mentioned or quoted at least three more times in the *Wake*, with the phrases 'rouse him out o'slumber deep' (64.12), 'Till Irinwakes from Slumber Deep' (321.17) and the neologism 'westasleep' (449.35).

Repeated use by Joyce of any individual song, book or name in this way ought to alert the reader to a deeper significance than mere authorial whimsy, though James Atherton has argued that 'Joyce's attitude to such songs is doubtful', quoting another section of the *Wake* in support of his position. '[T]he Gillooly chorus, from the Monster Book of Paltry-attic Puetrie' (178.16), writes Atherton, 'is a phrase suggesting strongly that he disliked them'.[85] Atherton's position, however, is unsustainable if we think, for instance, of the centrality of the 1798 ballad 'The Croppy Boy' to the 'Sirens' episode of *Ulysses*, or if we are attentive to a 1935 letter

83 See Martin MacDermott (ed.), *The New Spirit of the Nation; or, ballads and songs by the writers of 'The Nation'. Containing songs and ballads published since 1845* (London: T. Fisher Unwin; Dublin: Sealy, Bryers and Walker; New York: P. J. Kenedy, 1894).

84 Quoted in Judith Hill, *Lady Gregory: An Irish Life* (Stroud: Sutton Publishing, 2005), 12.

85 Atherton, *Books at the Wake*, 105–6.

to his daughter-in-law, Helen Joyce, in which he tells her that 'I have an enormous collection of Irish folk music collected by Petrie and another lot by Joyce (P.W.)'.[86] Whether Joyce liked or disliked the sort of nationalist balladry on show in collections such as *The Spirit of the Nation* and *Moore's Melodies*, he made extensive and repeated use of them.[87] Perhaps Joyce's friend Arthur Power should have the final word on the subject of Joyce's attachment to song as he describes in his remembrances a typical evening spent with the writer in Paris: 'Towards midnight Joyce would go over to the piano and try running his fingers in a ripple over the keys. He would sing in a light and pleasant tenor voice many Irish ballads in which romance and lament and satire were combined, and which were the secret source of his inspiration.'[88]

Of course, in trying to extract meaning from the *Wake*, several frequently opposing interpretations are possible, even inevitable. But in the case of 'The West's Asleep', Joyce's affection for, and interest in, the ballad goes back in his published work to the closing paragraph of 'The Dead'. In order to make this point it will be necessary to quote at length from this still much-loved song.[89] The first of the four verses pictures Ireland's western province of Connacht in a state of lethargy, unready for war:

> When all beside a vigil keep,
> The West's asleep, the West's asleep –
> Alas! and well may Erin weep,
> When Connaught lies in slumber deep.
> There lake and plain smile fair and free,
> 'Mid rocks – their guardian chivalry –
> Sing oh! Let man learn liberty
> From crashing wind and lashing sea.

Designed both to recall past historic events and to rouse present and future generations to service of Ireland, the ballad goes on in verse three to give a potted history of the west, before concluding in verse four with the province's awakening, leading to a common misconception by many

---

86 Letter to Helen Joyce (18 January 1935), in Joyce, *Letters*, vol. III.
87 For discussion of Joyce's use of song in his work, see Zack Bowen, *Musical Allusions in the Works of James Joyce: Early Poetry Through Ulysses* (Albany, NY: State University of New York Press, 1974), and Ruth Bauerle (ed.), *Picking Up Airs: Hearing the Music in Joyce's Text* (Urbana, IL: University of Illinois Press, 1993).
88 Arthur Power, *Conversations with James Joyce* (1974) (Dublin: Lilliput Press, 1999), 50.
89 The enormous popularity and intense historical resonance of 'The West's Asleep' for natives of Connacht was memorably demonstrated after Galway won the 1980 All-Ireland hurling final and Joe McDonagh, player and future GAA President, sang the song to rousing acclaim.

that the song's title is 'The West's Awake'.[90] Those last two verses run as
follows:

> For often in O'Connor's van,
> To triumph dashed each Connaught clan –
> And fleet as deer the Normans ran
> Through Corlieu's Pass and Ardrahan.
> And later times saw deeds as brave;
> And glory guards Clanricarde's grave –
> Sing oh! they died their land to save,
> At Aughrim's slopes and Shannon's wave.
>
> And if, when all a vigil keep,
> The West's asleep, the West's asleep –
> Alas! and well may Erin weep,
> That Connaught lies in slumber deep.
> But, hark! Some voice like thunder spake:
> 'The West's awake! the West's awake!' –
> 'Sing oh! hurra! let England quake,
> We'll watch till death for Erin's sake!'[91]

We cannot know for certain from which of the many collections of nationalist ballads Joyce was familiar with the song. It was first anthologized in
The Spirit of the Nation but was reprinted in many subsequent books, the
best-known and most widely available being a collection made up entirely
of Davis's songs and some of his essays titled *National and Historical Ballads,
Songs, and Poems.*

   This collection, edited by the anonymous T. W. (presumably T. W.
Rolleston, the revivalist and later assistant editor on the New Irish
Library scheme), brought together most of the poetry of Thomas Davis,
a writer described memorably by Seamus Deane as 'probably among the
most important and worst of Irish poets'.[92] That he was a bad poet is clear
enough from a quick perusal of his oeuvre; that he was important for later
generations of Irish writers becomes evident chiefly through his influence
on Yeats. His impact on Joyce was of a much smaller order but is nonetheless worth noting. The posthumously published *National and Historical*

---

90 See, for instance, Keith Duggan, 'Burning Passion Hard to Quench', *Irish Times Sports
   Supplement*, 6 May 2006, 8.
91 Thomas Davis, *National and Historical Ballads, Songs, and Poems* (1846) (Dublin: James
   Duffy and Sons, new rev. edn, n.d. [1870]), 38–9.
92 Seamus Deane, 'Poetry and Song 1800–1890', in *The Field Day Anthology of Irish Writing*,
   vol. II, gen. ed. Seamus Deane, assoc. eds Andrew Carpenter and Jonathan Williams
   (Derry: Field Day Publications, 1991), I.

Ballads was divided into sections reflecting Davis's varying interests. The longest of these sections was devoted to Jacobite songs of the Irish Brigade, or Wild Geese. Some of the songs included in this section are 'A Ballad for Ireland, May, 1689', 'The Battle of Limerick, August 27, 1690', 'The Death of Sarsfield: A Chant of the Brigade', 'The Surprise of Cremona, 1702', 'The Battle Eve of the Brigade' and 'Fontenoy, 1745', to name but a few. And to further underline this emphasis on Jacobitism, Appendix XIII of the collection, titled 'A Rally for Ireland', regrets that 'There is no period in Irish, or in English History, which has been so much misrepresented, or of which so utterly discordant opinions are still entertained, as the Revolution of 1688–91.'[93] An 1890 collection of Davis's prose writings, edited by T. W. Rolleston, also noticed Davis's affinity with the Wild Geese.[94]

Joyce, coming to manhood in an Ireland acutely aware of Davis, Sarsfield, St Ruth, Ginkel, the Wild Geese and all the rest of the cast and characters of the Williamite War, nods in 'The Dead' towards Davis's lines: 'Sing oh! they died their land to save, / At Aughrim's slopes and Shannon's wave'. Aughrim's presence is clear enough through Bartell D'Arcy's singing of 'The Lass of Aughrim', to which I shall return at length in a moment. As for the Shannon waves, they make their appearance in the famous sentence describing the falling snow: 'It was falling on every part of the dark central plain, on the treeless hills, falling softly upon the Bog of Allen and, farther westward, softly falling into the dark mutinous Shannon waves' (*D* 225). Perhaps not surprisingly, those waves have created considerable confusion among the critics who, in search of a choppy river surface, have Gabriel's putative crossing all the way down in County Limerick at the estuary of the Shannon. This literalness is particularly marked in what has become the accepted copy text of *Dubliners*, the 1969 Scholes and Litz edition, where the note for 'Shannon waves' reads 'The estuary of the river Shannon, on the south-west coast of Ireland.'[95] The misreading has been followed by subsequent readers to the extent that it has become a critical commonplace.[96]

---

93 No author [T. W.], 'A Rally for Ireland', in Davis, *National and Historical Ballads*, 236.

94 See Thomas Davis, *Prose Writings*, ed. T. W. Rolleston (London: Walter Scott, n.d. [1890]), 104–7.

95 James Joyce, *Dubliners: Text, Criticism and Notes*, ed. Robert Scholes and A. Walton Litz (1969) (Harmondsworth: Penguin Books, 1976), 492.

96 See, for instance, Terence Brown, 'Notes', in Joyce, *Dubliners* (Harmondsworth: Penguin Books, 1992), 317; Jeri Johnson, 'Explanatory Notes', in Joyce, *Dubliners* (Oxford: Oxford University Press, 2000), 279; and Daniel R. Schwarz (ed.), *James Joyce, The Dead: Complete, Authoritative Text with Biographical and Historical Contexts, Critical History, and Essays from Five Contemporary Critical Perspectives* (New York and Boston: Bedford Books, 1994), 59.

A more satisfactory explanation for Joyce's waves is provided by John Wyse Jackson and Bernard McGinley, who find the source in Thomas Moore's 'Oh, Ye Dead', a ballad that both Stanislaus Joyce and Richard Ellmann have argued provides both title and theme to 'The Dead'. Though Wyse Jackson and McGinley also feel that '"Waves" implies the Shannon estuary', they point to these lines from Moore's ballad:

> Oh, ye Dead! oh, ye Dead! whom we know by
> the light you give
> From your cold gleaming eyes, though you move
> like men who live –
> Why leave you thus your graves,
> In far-off fields and waves,
> Where the worm and the sea-bird only know your bed[97]

Kevin Whelan has linked 'Oh, Ye Dead' to the exiled eighteenth-century Irish Jacobite soldiery. 'Moore's lyric', argues Whelan, 'concerns the Irish folk belief that the shades of men who have died on foreign soil (notably The Wild Geese) return to haunt their familiar and beloved places of origin.'[98] Whelan, though more interested in the shadow of 1798 as it falls upon 'The Dead', has some interesting things to say about a possible earlier historical layer present in the story – an aspect of Joyce's writing to which I shall shortly return.

A further suggestion for the provenance of these puzzling river waves is provided by Richard Ellmann who sees in them a possible reference to the twelfth book of Homer's *Iliad* as translated by Thoreau:

> The snowflakes fall thick and fast on a winter's day. The winds are lulled, and the snow falls incessant, covering the tops of the mountains, and the hills, and the plains where the lotus-tree grows, and the cultivated fields, and they are falling by the inlets and shores of the foaming sea, but are silently dissolved by the waves.[99]

'Where Homer speaks of the waves silently dissolving the snow', writes Ellmann, 'Joyce adds the final detail of "the mutinous Shannon waves" which suggests the "Furey" quality of the west.'[100] While the strictly literal search for waves in the Shannon estuary is unsatisfactory (Gabriel's journey is, after all, westward, not south-westward), it is more than possible that

---

97 Quoted in John Wyse Jackson and Bernard McGinley, *James Joyce's 'Dubliners': An Annotated Edition* (London: Sinclair-Stevenson, 1993), 198.
98 Kevin Whelan, 'The Memories of "The Dead"', *The Yale Journal of Criticism*, 15.1 (Spring 2002), 70.
99 Quoted in Ellmann, *James Joyce*, 251.
100 Ellmann, *James Joyce*, 251.

both the Wyse Jackson–McGinley and Ellmann interpretations are correct. But we need also to see 'The West's Asleep' as a source text for a number of reasons beyond the coincidence of an unsettled Shannon.

Aughrim of the Slaughter

Returning to the lines from Davis's ballad, 'Sing oh! they died their land to save, / At Aughrim's slopes and Shannon's wave', we are forced to look a little further back into 'The Dead' and towards the significance of the singing of 'The Lass of Aughrim'. Stanislaus, in an effort to reinforce his argument that Moore's 'Oh, Ye Dead' is the key shadow text for his brother's greatest story, unconvincingly argues that by the time James came to write 'The Dead' he had replaced Moore with a substitute. Stanislaus misnames the Moore song 'The Dead', describing it as a ballad in which 'It sounded as if the dead were whimpering and jealous of the happiness of the living.' He goes on to write that

> My brother liked the idea and asked me to send him the song. I did so, but when he wrote the story some six or seven years later – so long did it take to mature! – he preferred to use a west of Ireland ballad for the song which is the turning point of the story.[101]

The title of the song is not the only matter on which Stanislaus is wrong. The letter in which he told James of hearing 'Oh, Ye Dead' was written in 1905, just two years before the composition of 'The Dead', and it is fanciful to think that 'The Lass of Aughrim' is just some sort of convenient west of Ireland replacement for the Moore song as clearly so much hinges on it.

In fact James Joyce, whatever his feelings for Moore's ghostly offering, chose to use 'The Lass of Aughrim' as the catalyst for Gretta's heartbreak and Gabriel's subsequent epiphany for three clear reasons. The first and most obvious is that he liked the song very much himself and associated it with Nora Barnacle and with Galway. The second is that he wished to bring to the surface of his story memories of a defeated Catholic Ireland. The third is that he wished to continue the mischievous assault on Lady Gregory and her caste outlined in the previous chapter. Taking his personal liking for the song first, Joyce's sisters recall him knowing a sad ballad called 'The Lass of Aughrim', which he was 'perpetually singing at home' and of which he claimed to know thirty-five verses.[102] Whether he knew thirty-five verses

---

101 Quoted in Torchiana, *Backgrounds for Joyce's 'Dubliners'*, 223–4.
102 On Joyce's ability to sing thirty-five verses, see C. P. Curran, *James Joyce Remembered* (New York and London: Oxford University Press, 1968), 41–2.

or not we cannot know, but the original Scottish song of which 'The Lass of Aughrim' is a version did indeed have thirty-five verses.[103]

It must have been one of those almost sacred coincidences of which Joyce was so fond when he began, in June 1904, to court a girl who also knew the song. Gretta Conroy, the 'country cute' Galway girl so disliked by Gabriel's upwardly mobile mother, is, of course, a version of Nora Barnacle, the baker's daughter from Bowling Green with whom Joyce eloped in 1904. When Joyce eventually got some time alone with Nora's mother in Galway he was keen for her to sing 'The Lass of Aughrim', as he wrote to Nora in a letter of August 1909:

> My dear little runaway Nora, I am writing this to you sitting at the kitchen table in your mother's house!! I have been here all day talking with her and I see that she is my darling's mother and I like her very much. She sang for me 'The Lass of Aughrim' but she does not like to sing me the last verses in which the lovers exchange their tokens. I shall stay in Galway overnight.[104]

And again, five days later, back in his father's house on Dublin's Fontenoy Street, the song still reverberated in his head: 'I was singing an hour ago your song "The Lass of Aughrim". The tears come into my eyes and my voice trembles with emotion when I sing that lovely air. It was worth coming to Ireland to have got it from your poor kind mother.'[105]

The second level at which 'The Lass of Aughrim' works within 'The Dead' is as a trapdoor into Jacobite Ireland. The previous chapter stressed the importance of accuracy in precisely locating Nuns' Island geographically, historically and etymologically. It is equally important, for a fuller understanding of Joyce's motivations in writing *Dubliners*, to dwell upon the geography of another Galway place name that occurs shortly before the mention of Nuns' Island – that place is Aughrim. As briefly discussed earlier, Aughrim became a sort of worry stone for Irish writing, from the composers of the Aisling to the revivalists and right through to the present. Aughrim is a common Irish place name, occurring at least twenty times across the island. P. W. Joyce, a writer familiar to James Joyce, lists Aughrim in his *Irish Names of Places* as 'Each-dhruim', translating it as 'horse-hill'.[106] Much the most storied of the Aughrims, and the one mentioned by P. W.

---

103 On the history of 'The Lass of Aughrim' and its variants, see George L. Geckle, 'The Dead Lass of Aughrim', *Éire-Ireland*, IX.3 (Fomhar 1974), 86–96.

104 James Joyce to Nora Barnacle Joyce (26 August 1909), in Joyce, *Letters*, vol. II, 240.

105 James Joyce to Nora Barnacle Joyce (31 August 1909), in Joyce, *Letters*, vol. II, 242.

106 P. W. Joyce, *The Origin and History of Irish Names of Places*, first series (Dublin: McGlashan and Gill; London: Simpkin, Marshall; Edinburgh: John Menzies, 1875), 524.

Joyce to illustrate his explanation of the name, is a small village in east Galway, three miles west of Ballinasloe and thirty-five miles east of Galway City. It is an anonymous little place, easily missed on the drive from Dublin to Galway, as captured by Richard Murphy in his long poem of 1968, which uses the battle as a lens through which to examine Ireland as it rests on the cusp of a new wave of sectarian unrest:

> A Celtic cross by the road commemorates no battle
> But someone killed in a car, Minister of Agriculture.
> Dairy lorries on the fast trunk-route rattle:
> A girl cycles along the lane to meet her lover.[107]

Yet despite its anonymity, Aughrim is remembered as a place of disaster for the Irish Catholic cause and of great triumph and rejoicing by Irish Protestant loyalists who march in its memory every summer.

Don Gifford, in his notes for *Dubliners* and *A Portrait of the Artist as a Young Man*, rightly asserts that a general knowledge of Irish history is 'indispensable to an informed reading of Joyce's works', and to facilitate the reader in achieving an understanding of this history he provides a time line of significant dates.[108] Surprisingly, under the heading '1688–1714', while briefly discussing the Battle of the Boyne and the Treaty of Limerick that concluded the Williamite War, he makes no mention of the Battle of Aughrim. This battle, more so than the Boyne, proved the decisive turning point in the Williamite campaign to suppress Jacobite support in Ireland. The greatest pitched battle in Irish history, involving perhaps as many as 40,000 soldiers, it accounted for the lives of some 7,000 men and smashed Catholic power in Ireland for another two hundred and thirty years. 'Aughrim of the slaughter' is how it was remembered by one contemporary poet:

> In Aughrim of the slaughter they rest;
> Their skeletons lying there, uncoffined,
> Have caused the women of Ireland to beat their hands,
> The children to be neglected, and the fugitives to wail.[109]

'"It isn't the loss of Aughrim" became a proverb', writes J. G. Simms 'for bearable misfortunes.'[110] Whether Joyce was familiar with this saying we

---

107 Murphy, *The Battle of Aughrim*, 11. Since 2009 the village of Aughrim has been bypassed by the M6 running from Galway to Dublin.

108 Don Gifford, *Joyce Annotated: Notes for 'Dubliners' and 'A Portrait of the Artist as a Young Man'* (Berkeley, CA: University of California Press, 2nd edn, 1982), 18.

109 Séamas Dall MacCuarta, 'Elegy for Sorley MacDonnell', quoted in Simms, *Jacobite Ireland*, 229.

110 Simms, *Jacobite Ireland*, 229.

cannot say, but the near homonyms of 'lass' and 'loss' make the idea very appealing.

Gifford, in his note on 'The Lass of Aughrim', says merely of Aughrim that it is 'a small village in the west of Ireland, about thirty miles east of Galway'.[111] Not to mention the battle that took place there is a surprising oversight on his part, especially given Gabriel's description of his grand-father's old horse, Johnny, circling the statue of King Billy, which comes shortly before the singing of 'The Lass of Aughrim'. This linkage of Williamite superiority with a doleful folk song is as close as Joyce is willing to go in helping the reader sense a Jacobite shadow, though in addition to this clear historical pointer Joyce saturates 'The Dead' in language of a martial and militaristic nature even in the most seemingly innocent moments, such as in the following description of the dinner table:

> In the centre of the table there stood, as sentries to a fruit-stand which upheld a pyramid of oranges and American apples, two squat old-fashioned decanters of cut glass, one containing port and the other dark sherry. On the closed square piano a pudding in the huge yellow dish lay in waiting and behind it were three squads of bottles of stout and ale and minerals, drawn up according to the colours of their uniforms, the first two black, with brown and red labels, the third and smallest squad white, with trans-verse green sashes. (D 197)

These images of soldiery on parade are all very deliberate and designed to prompt the alert reader to thoughts of battle.[112] Joyce, of course, would never be so blunt as to tell us which battle but I think he makes this clear without actually spelling it out.

Gifford is not the only exegete to miss Joyce's Jacobite signals. Robert Scholes and Walt Litz, while giving considerable space to a discussion of 'The Lass of Aughrim', have not commented at all on the place name in their otherwise often useful notes.[113] Warren Beck, in a failed effort to trump Richard Ellmann, moves the battle site across to the east coast:

> Aughrim, says Ellmann, is 'a little village in the west not far from Galway,' and this corresponds with Nora's girlhood knowledge of the song, and

111   Gifford, *Joyce Annotated*, 123.

112   For an examination of military imagery and its significance in 'The Dead', see Rod Mengham, 'Military Occupation in "The Dead"', in John Brannigan et al. (eds), *Re: Joyce: Text, Culture, Politics* (Basingstoke: Macmillan, 1998), 77–86; and Greg C. Winston, 'Militarism and "The Dead"', in Oona Frawley (ed.), *A New and Complex Sensation: Essays on Joyce's 'Dubliners'* (Dublin: Lilliput Press, 2004), 122–32.

113   See Robert Scholes and A. Walton Litz, 'Notes to the Stories', in Joyce, *Dubliners*, ed. Scholes and Litz, 490–2.

Gretta's too, since her people are from Connacht and in her girlhood she like Nora had lived in Galway with her grandmother. Another and more notable Aughrim may come to mind, the one south of Dublin, in County Wicklow, where in 1691 the Irish and their French allies suffered a final defeat that consolidated England's previous victories. Though certainly Joyce is using the ballad with its private matters, an historical association may deepen the melancholy.[114]

While there is no doubting the veracity of that last sentence, the only skirmish that I know of to have taken place in Aughrim, County Wicklow, involved a Gaelic football referee being locked in the boot of his car after a particularly fractious club match in the late 1980s. Other critics have been more attentive. Terence Brown recognizes the significance of the 1691 engagement, locating it correctly in County Galway. 'The title of this song adds therefore', he writes, 'a note of national significance.'[115] Joyce, more than anyone, was awake to this historical resonance.

The third reason, after personal preference and historical significance, why Joyce decided to make use of 'The Lass of Aughrim' in 'The Dead' was as a means to attack Lady Gregory. The previous chapter has already suggested that the swirl of whiskey in *Dubliners* ought to be read as a clever assault on the Persses, the Gregorys and their ascendancy class; 'The Lass of Aughrim' is another, yet clearer, barb. Though several critics have skated around the issue of the Gregorys and their presence in the song, few have pointed sufficiently clearly to the very obvious malicious intent on Joyce's part to fire a winning shot across his one-time patroness's bows. In order to demonstrate this malice, we will have to look closely at the lyrics. All that Joyce permits the reader to see of the song are an abbreviated three lines, interrupted by Mary Jane:

> *O, the rain falls on my heavy locks*
> *And the dew wets my skin,*
> *My babe lies cold...* (D 211)

The same device of hidden song lyrics is used by Joyce at the close of 'Clay' where Maria's misremembrance of Michael William Balfe's much-loved song, 'I Dreamt that I Dwelt', causes her brother Joe to cry. Joyce even goes to the trouble of telling us that Maria has made a mistake by repeating the first verse rather than moving on to the second. Thus he expects the attentive reader to find out what it is that the ageing spinster has forgotten to sing:

---

114 Warren Beck, *Joyce's 'Dubliners': Substance, Vision, and Art* (Durham, NC: Duke University Press, 1969), 348.

115 Terence Brown, 'Notes', in Joyce, *Dubliners*, ed. Brown, 315.

> I dreamt that suitors sought my hand,
> That knights on bended knee,
> And with vows no maiden heart could withstand,
> They pledged their faith to me.[116]

Joe finds Maria's unwillingness or inability to sing these words almost unbearable and the story seems to end in characteristic Joycean inconclusiveness: 'and his eyes filled up so much with tears that he could not find what he was looking for and in the end he had to ask his wife to tell him where the corkscrew was' (D 102). I say that the story 'seems' to end inconclusively because without knowledge of that which is not written down, that is, those lines quoted above, Joe's tears make little sense. But armed with the image of suitors coming to seek the maiden's hand, the reader realizes the implication of Maria's error.

Paul Muldoon has been particularly alert to a similar Joycean evasiveness in the case of 'The Lass of Aughrim' and posits a convincing explanation for the paucity of lyrics. 'This is as far as Bartell goes, as much as Joyce quotes', writes Muldoon. 'He resists continuing with the lines "My babe lies cold in my arms: Lord Gregory let me in" because he resists a direct reference not so much to Lord as *Lady* Gregory.'[117] While Muldoon is the first critic to realize the force of the missing lines as they relate to Lady Gregory, he does not go far enough in tracing the significance of the Gregory name in 'The Dead'. While it will not be necessary to rehearse the thirty-five verses of 'The Lass of Aughrim' reputedly known by Joyce, it will prove helpful to expand a little if we are to get to the point of the song.

Without some knowledge beyond that which Joyce provides on the page, the significance of the song lies beyond the understanding of the reader. In this case it is sufficient for us to know just a few more lines:

> The rain beats at my yellow locks and the dew wets me still,
> Oh, the rain rains on my yellow locks and the dew drops on my chin,
> Let the rain beat my yellow locks, Let the dew beat my skin
> The babe is cold in my arms, Lord Gregory, let me in.
> My baby is cold in my arms, Lord Gregory, let me in.
> Let the bonny lass of Aughrim and her baby come in.[118]

---

116 Quoted in Gifford, *Joyce Annotated*, 80.
117 Paul Muldoon, *To Ireland, I* (Oxford: Oxford University Press, 2000), 57. Muldoon also argues that Gregory's *Gods and Fighting Men* is a presence in 'The Dead'.
118 Quoted in Hugh Shields, 'The History of *The Lass of Aughrim*', in Gerard Gillen and Harry White (eds), *Irish Musical Studies 1: Musicology in Ireland* (Dublin: Irish Academic Press, 1990), 64.

The song is about a young, abandoned mother who has been Lord Gregory's lover, returns to seek his help on a stormy night, is turned away from the house by Gregory's mother – necessarily 'Lady' Gregory – and is left to die with her child in the freezing night. The musicologist Hugh Shields, when researching the history of the song, found that it had become known by the name of its villain rather than by that of its victim. 'Popular tradition still knows it a little', writes Shields, 'though disobligingly it drops the older, more poetic title and labels the song "Lord Gregory", after its relatively inactive hero. It thus discards an evocative Irish toponym in favour of an unfamiliar personal name: a change which Joyce would surely have found unwelcome.' Shields is right in his surmise about Joyce's preferences both because losing 'Aughrim' would have taken away the Jacobite subtext from the song and because getting Bartell D'Arcy to sing a song titled 'Lord Gregory' would, as Paul Muldoon has pointed out, have been giving the game away – not something Joyce was prone to do.

In his essay on the song, Shields stresses that it is Lord Gregory's mother who is the guilty party in the death of the lass of Aughrim:

> Despite obscurity – or circumstantial complexity – in this and other versions, the ballad has a simple dramatic action in the hero's or more usually his mother's rejection of a girl who has borne him a child. 'Annie' knocks for admittance to Lord Gregory's castle and is refused. His mother, speaking as if with his voice, requests tokens of her identity which she, deceived, provides by allusion to their former intimacies. She is still refused and goes away. Lord Gregory wakes from some kind of sleep in which he dreamt with foreboding about Annie. His mother tells him of her visit and receives his curse for not waking him. He goes in search of Annie and finds her and her child dead, usually drowned. [119]

Most critics of 'The Dead' have failed to examine 'The Lass of Aughrim' in the sort of detail necessary to understand the many ways in which it gives meaning to the story. Some readers, such as Richard Ellmann and C. P. Curran, have noticed the name Gregory but have made little of it other than to remark on the coincidence between this and the name of the Revival's leading female figure, and, as George Geckle points out, they both fail to notice that it is Lady rather than Lord Gregory who is primarily at fault for the death of the lass and her child. 'The point of the ballad in fact', writes Geckle, 'is that it is Lord Gregory's *mother* who asks the questions and who deceives the lass while Lord Gregory sleeps, thereby causing tragedy.' [120]

119 Shields, 'History of *The Lass of Aughrim*', 59.
120 Geckle, 'Dead Lass of Aughrim', 89.

'The Lass of Aughrim', for Joyce, as well as being a convenient way to heap yet more scorn on Lady Gregory, is a perfect allegory of the unhappy relationship between Ireland and England, between Catholic and Protestant, colonized and colonizer. A female Ireland is seduced and abandoned by a male England, the peasantry are left to beg and die in the rain while the landlords turn in their beds. In recent years, several Joyceans have attempted to read 'The Dead' as a response in certain ways to memories of the potato famine of the 1840s.[121] The year 1852, which many historians give as the final year of famine, was the year in which Lady Gregory was born. Coming to womanhood on a vast Galway demesne, she was part of one of the few west of Ireland families left relatively unscathed by the Great Hunger. Augusta Persse grew up, wrote one recent set of biographers, 'in a prosperous household, but one shadowed by a catastrophe that eroded the political and social order supporting a small colonial class against the disenfranchised majority'.[122] Joyce was born just thirty years after the end of that catastrophe so he would have grown up around people for whom it was a vivid memory. While I am not convinced by the more determined of such theses, I believe that by indexing Lord Gregory Joyce means us to remember Lady Gregory's reviled husband, author of the notorious 'Gregory Clause' of 1847, which stated that no person in possession of more than a quarter-acre of land qualified for famine relief and which, as suggested in the previous chapter, may also have been referenced in *Finnegans Wake*. This piece of legislation had the effect of making many desperate and starving people unwilling to seek the help that would have meant them having to divest themselves of their smallholdings, thus leading to even greater death and desolation, as was acknowledged in the *First Report of the Irish Poor Law Commissions* (1847):

> The class of poor and destitute occupiers, who are debarred by law unless they give up their land, struggle, notwithstanding their great privations, to retain it, and endeavour by every effort to pass through the season of difficulty, by which they see the prospect of their former mode of subsistence returning, provided they continue in the possession of their land. The use for a long time of inferior food has in such cases sometimes induced disease fatal to the occupier himself or one or more members of his family.[123]

121   See, for instance, Bonnie Roos, 'James Joyce's "The Dead" and Bret Harte's *Gabriel Conroy*: The Nature of the Feast', *The Yale Journal of Criticism*, 15.1 (Spring 2002), 99–126; and Whelan, 'Memories of "The Dead"', 59–97.

122   Lucy McDiarmid and Maureen Waters, 'Introduction', in Lady Gregory, *Selected Writings*, ed. McDiarmid and Waters (London: Penguin Books, 1995), xiii.

123   Quoted in John E. Pomfret, *The Struggle for Land in Ireland 1800–1923* (Princeton, NJ: Princeton University Press, 1930), 38.

John E. Pomfret, in his history of the land question in nineteenth-century Ireland, describes the clause as 'the cheapest and most efficient of the eject-ment acts', and points to the massive increase in evictions between the period 1847–49 (25,700 families) and 1849–52 (58,423 families).[124]

At the time of the enactment of the Gregory Clause, William (later Sir William) Gregory was Conservative MP for Dublin City and had just succeeded to the Coole estate. Though the clause eventually passed through parliament with some ease, there were those who recognized its potential for promoting disaster. George Poulett Scrope, MP for Stroud, was especially clear-eyed:

> Its consequence would be a complete clearance of the small farmers in Ireland – a change which would amount to a perfect social revolution in the state of things in that country. Such a change might be desirable if effected by degrees; but to introduce it at once would have the effect of turning great masses of pauperism adrift on the community – a catastrophe which would undoubtedly not be without its effects in this country.[125]

Gregory was dismissive of this position, declaring that if indeed the clause led to the destruction of small farmers in this way that he did not see of what use such farmers could possibly be. 'Throughout the rest of the famine years', writes James S. Donnelly, 'the Gregory clause, or "Grego-ryism", became a byword for the worst miseries of the disaster – eviction, exile, disease, and death.'[126] John O'Rourke, author of the standard history of the famine available to Joyce and his contemporaries, insisted that 'Mr Gregory's words – the words of [...] a pretended friend of the people – and Mr Gregory's clause are things that should be forever remembered by the descendants of the slaughtered and expatriated small farmers of Ireland.'[127]

In Galway, naturally enough, opposition from the people to Gregory and his hated clause was especially vocal, with the ballad 'Gregory's Quarter Acre' appearing in the *Galway Mercury* in the winter of 1849:

> When ruthless tyrants work so sure,
> To swamp with famine breaker,
> The death surge tumbles o'er the poor,
> In Gregory's Quarter Acre.

124 See Pomfret, *Struggle for Land*, 38.
125 Quoted in James S. Donnelly, Jr, *The Great Irish Potato Famine* (Stroud: Sutton Publishing, 2001), 258, fn. 5.
126 Donnelly, *Great Irish Potato Famine*, 102.
127 John O'Rourke, *The history of the great famine of 1847, with notices of earlier Irish famines* (Dublin: McGlashan and Gill; London: James Duffy, 1875), 332–3. A third edition of this book was issued in Dublin in 1902.

> Bees are done up with smoke and fire,
> The lot of famine's bleaker,
> For famine feeds the funeral pyre,
> In Gregory's Quarter Acre.[128]

When, in 1848, another local newspaper, the *Galway Vindicator*, published an article taking a more favourable view of Gregory, it met with stern opposition – the *Limerick Chronicle* pointing to the 'exterminations' attendant on prosecuting the Gregory Clause – and was forced to make a retraction.[129]

While it is clear enough, then, why a young man like Joyce, from an Irish Catholic family on the slide, could bear a grudge against a powerful imperial figure such as Sir William Gregory, it is hard to understand just why he kicked so hard against the late Governor of Ceylon's widow. Joyce first had contact with Lady Gregory via AE and W. B. Yeats who had begun, both through published pieces such as 'The Day of the Rabblement' and through the Dublin literary rumour mill, to understand that they had a new young genius on their hands. Willing to overlook 'his bad manners', writes Ellmann, Lady Gregory 'invited him, with Yeats and Yeats's father, to dine with her at the Nassau Hotel on November 4 [1902]'.[130] Joyce's first written contact with Lady Gregory of which we have a record was a forlorn letter written shortly before he left for Paris in 1902, seeking her assistance:

> I am going alone and friendless – I know of a man who used to live somewhere near Montmartre but I have never met him – into another country, and I am writing to you to know can you help me in any way. I do not know what will happen to me in Paris but my case can hardly be worse than it is here.[131]

And, as we have already seen, Lady Gregory was kind enough to put in a good word for Joyce with E. V. Longworth, editor of the *Daily Express*. This resulted in a regular though short-lived reviewing slot with the paper. But Joyce very quickly bit the hand that fed him with his pungent review of *Poets and Dreamers*, and his attitude to this early patron seems to have remained at best dismissive and at worst hostile for the rest of his life.

When leaving Ireland for permanent self-imposed exile on the Continent in 1904 Joyce penned a short broadside aimed at literary Dublin

---

128 'Gregory's Quarter Acre', *Galway Mercury*, 27 January 1849.
129 See William Henry, *Famine: Galway's Darkest Years* (Cork: Mercier Press, 2011), 76.
130 Ellmann, *James Joyce*, 104.
131 James Joyce to Lady Augusta Gregory (n.d. [November 1902]), in James Joyce, *Letters*, ed. Stuart Gilbert (London: Faber and Faber, 1957), 53.

titled 'The Holy Office'. In a section that parodies Yeats's 'To Ireland in the Coming Times' and that is meant primarily as an attack on the Revival's most important poet, Lady Gregory is reduced to the status of a 'giddy dame' – and this despite the fact that she had forwarded him five pounds with her best wishes for his coming Continental adventure:

> But I must not accounted be
> One of that mumming company –
> With him who hies him to appease
> His giddy dames' frivolities
> While they console him when he whinges
> With gold-embroidered Celtic Fringes[132]

Again in 1912, after the last of his unsuccessful returns to Dublin, Joyce, ventriloquizing the voice of the Maunsel company's printer, turns his sights on Coole's celebrated hostess in 'Gas from a Burner':

> I printed the table-book of Cousins
> Though (asking your pardon) as for the verse
> 'Twould give you a heartburn on your arse:
> I printed folklore from North and South
> By Gregory of the Golden Mouth[133]

But the best-known and funniest of Joyce's public pronouncements on Lady Gregory comes in the 'Scylla and Charybdis' episode of *Ulysses* when, this time, he has Buck Mulligan do his dirty work as he chastises Stephen Dedalus in the National Library for giving *Poets and Dreamers* a bad review. 'Longworth is awfully sick, he said, after what you wrote about that old hake Gregory. O you inquisitional drunken jew jesuit! She gets you a job on the paper and then you go and slate her drivel to Jaysus. Couldn't you do the Yeats touch?' (*U* 277–8). Passages such as this tell us as much about Joyce's attitude towards revivalism as they do about his feelings for his great *bête noir*, Oliver St John Gogarty; my next chapter will have a good deal more to say about Joyce and his feelings towards the Revival. While the scorn heaped on the unfortunate Lady Gregory feels like overkill, she got off lightly in comparison with Gogarty, Joyce's one-time cohabitant in the Martello tower.

Naturally enough, it was not just in his published work that Joyce was critical of Lady Gregory, as a quick examination of his collected letters reveals. In April 1905, as he stews in Trieste, we find him aggrieved that Nora

---

132 James Joyce, 'The Holy Office', in Joyce, *Critical Writings*, 150.
133 James Joyce, 'Gas from a Burner', in Joyce, *Critical Writings*, 244

has chosen Gregory's *Kincora*, a play about Brian Boru, as light reading. 'O blast Kincora!', he writes to Stanislaus, 'Nora is reading the slip by fits and starts to a tune of "Old Tom Gregory, Has a big menagerie", which seems to me what old Thornton would have called a *double entente*.'[134] By early 1907, with the first imaginative stirrings of 'The Dead' at work in his mind, we see Joyce anxious for news of home in the wake of the so-called 'Playboy riots'. Again writing to his faithful correspondent Stanislaus, he is delighted to hear of the Abbey's discomfiture:

> I knew, before now, that there was a schism in the theatre: as all of Columb's plays have been given by the 'Irish Theatre' and the reviews of Yeats and Lady Gregory and Miss HORNYMAN's productions which have appeared lately in Sinn Féin have been hostile. Yeats says the Irish obeyed great leaders in the past but now they obey ignorant committees. I believe Columb and the Irish Theatre will beat Y and L.G. and Miss H: which will please me greatly, as Yeats cannot well hawk his theatre over to London.[135]

A week later we see Joyce even surer that the Abbey is in decline. 'As I told you before', he wrote to Stanislaus, 'I think the Abbey Theatre is ruined. It is supported by the stalls, that is to say, Stephen Gwynn, Lord X, Lady Gregory etc who are dying to relieve the monotony of Dublin life.' But for all of his delight at the demise of Yeats and Gregory's beloved theatre, his letter is also mixed with a distinct sense of exasperation at being out of the literary loop:

> This whole affair has upset me. I feel like a man in a house who hears a row in the street and voices he knows shouting but can't get out to see what the hell is going on. It has put me off the story I was 'going to write' – to wit, 'The Dead'.[136]

Crucially, in addition to being preoccupied with contemporary events at home, 1907 also saw Joyce pondering the difficulties of an earlier Ireland. In a lecture delivered at the Università Popolare on 27 April Joyce was again thinking about the Stuarts and their unfortunate followers. Writing about the April 1900 visit of Queen Victoria, Joyce recalls with some glee the attitude of the waiting crowds on her only previous trip to Dublin in 1849:

> Then the Irish, who had not entirely forgotten their loyalty to the unlucky Stuart family nor to the name of Mary Stuart, the Scottish queen, and the legendary fugitive Bonnie Prince Charlie, had the nasty idea of mocking the queen's consort: poking fun at him for being an uprooted German princeling,

134 James Joyce to Stanislaus Joyce (4 April 1905), in Joyce, *Letters*, vol. II, 88.
135 James Joyce to Stanislaus Joyce ([1?] February, 1907), in Joyce, *Letters*, vol. II, 208.
136 James Joyce to Stanislaus Joyce (11 February, 1907), in Joyce, *Letters*, vol. II, 211–12, 212.

imitating the way he stammered his English as well as cheerfully greeting him the very moment he set foot on Irish soil with a head of cabbage.

Just because, argued Joyce, the Irish had not, like the Americans, risen up against British rule did not mean that they would not at some future point. Indeed the wandering Irish had already played their part in freeing America:

> From the time of the Treaty of Limerick, or rather, from the time it was broken by the Punic faith of the English, millions of Irish have left their homeland for other shores. These fugitives who, centuries ago, were called the Wild Geese, enlisted in all the foreign garrisons of European Powers, mainly France, Holland and Spain, and won many a victor's laurel on the battlefields for their adoptive masters. In America they found another homeland. The ancient Irish tongue could be heard in the ranks of the American rebels, and Lord Mountjoy himself said in 1784: 'We lost America because of the Irish emigrants.'[137]

Within six months of delivering this lecture Joyce would be writing 'The Dead', turning the base metal of history into the gold of fiction, using his story to avenge the defeated and downhearted.

Yet why should that vengeance be so pronounced and so focused in the case of Lady Gregory? Given her kindnesses to him, it is hard to put Joyce's dislike for Gregory down to purely private or personal spleen. Joyce, the down-at-heel Catholic, feels himself, like the lass of Aughrim, an abandoned waif outside the walls of the Big House, 'outcast from life's feast' (*D* 113), as he says of James Duffy in 'A Painful Case'. In literary Dublin he saw an ascendancy-backed Revival winning garlands with landlords such as Edward Martyn, George Moore and Lady Gregory at its helm. No amount of assistance from them could make him feel less aggrieved; indeed help from those quarters would amount to charity, the worst possible benevolence to bestow on the proud son of a once-wealthy Catholic man of property. 'The members of the Irish literary movement were doing their best for Joyce', as Richard Ellmann memorably puts it, 'but all were to discover that he was not a man to be helped with impunity.'[138]

In recent years scholars such as Len Platt, Willard Potts and Colm Tóibín have emphasized to varying degrees a certain sectarian elitism about Lady Gregory's personality; this is an aspect of her character that would have proved especially repugnant to Joyce. Tóibín takes the title

---

137 James Joyce, 'Ireland: Island of Saints and Sages', in Joyce, *Occasional, Critical, and Political Writing*, 117, 123–4.

138 Ellmann, *James Joyce*, 104.

of his compelling short study, *Lady Gregory's Toothbrush* (2002), from his subject's division of the world into those – like herself and Yeats – who used toothbrushes and those who did not. Joyce, a man, coincidentally, who suffered much with his teeth, would have fallen into the latter category. While Tóibín and others see this proclivity on Gregory's part as relatively harmless given all that she achieved, Willard Potts is more inclined to judge Gregory's snobbery and sectarianism a serious flaw:

> In spite of what appear to be strong feelings of identification with Catholics, Lady Gregory also shared the Protestant sense of their inferiority. When asked by an American if she were Catholic, she quickly replied, 'All who do anything are Protestants.' Another version of her belief that Catholics couldn't do anything turns up in a letter to Yeats, where she accuses her friend Edward Martyn of that failing. Speaking of Martyn's reluctance to support the Abbey directors in a quarrel with the actors, she told Yeats, 'These RC's haven't the courage of a mouse, and then wonder how it is we go ahead.'[139]

Lady Gregory's friend and sometime lover, Wilfred Scawen Blunt, was similarly harsh in his judgement of her after a visit of June 1886 to Coole. 'It is curious', he writes, 'that she, who could see so clearly in Egypt when it was a case between the Circassian Pashas and the Arab fellahin, should be blind now that the case is between the English landlords and Irish tenants in Galway.' It is to class and sectarianism that Blunt looks for an explanation of the cooling in the friendship:

> But property blinds all eyes, and it is easier for a camel to pass through the eye of a needle, than for an Irish landlord to enter into the kingdom of Home Rule. She comes of a family, too, who are 'bitter Protestants', and has surrounded herself with people of her class from Ireland, so that there is no longer room for me in her house.[140]

At this point in her life Lady Gregory was still decidedly unionist in outlook, a position that would change much over the following decades.

Of Lady Gregory's contemporaries, George Moore, himself an apostate – or, as he is described in 'The Oxen of the Sun' episode of *Ulysses*, a 'papish' who is now 'a good Williamite' (*U* 519) – was the only figure to make seriously damaging public accusations about her religious practice when, in early drafts of *Hail and Farewell*, he remembered her as an over-zealous

---

139 Willard Potts, *Joyce and the Two Irelands* (Austin, TX: University of Texas Press, 2000), 22–3.

140 Diary entry (10 June 1886), in Wilfred Scawen Blunt, *The Land War in Ireland* (London: Swift, 1912), 146. I am grateful to Anna Pilz for drawing my attention to this book.

proselytizer in her Roxborough youth. She was, wrote Moore, 'an ardent soul gatherer in the days gone by but abandoned missionary work when she married'.[141] Acutely sensitive to such accusations because of her unhappy childhood memories of a devout evangelical mother, the statement caused enormous offence to Gregory, legal action was threatened, and the remark was softened in the final version of the book; W. B. Yeats would wait more than twenty years to avenge his dear friend when he filleted Moore as a man and as a writer in his delightfully cruel *Dramatis Personae*. On New Year's Day 1912 the writer and fellow member of the Protestant landed elite, Violet Martin, wrote in sympathy to Gregory:

> I have been affronted by what he says of you [...] It is a pity that such a gift as his should be set in an earthen vessel – at its best it is very hard to beat – & then comes a feeling as of tasting suddenly a lump of garlic – Paris, on top of R.C. Mayo ancestry can produce these things – but this is for your private ear. The second rate R.C. with the French admixture is a blend peculiar to itself & betrays itself sooner or later.[142]

The landlord's disdain and distrust for both Roman Catholics and the French could not be made any clearer. While nationalists such as Maud Gonne, Arthur Griffith and the 'gratefully oppressed' of Joyce's 'After the Race' may have looked to Paris for salvation, the embattled Irish ascendancy viewed the French with suspicion.

Wild Geese and Orangemen

These contrasting attitudes to France bring us back to the widespread revival of Jacobite tropes in Irish literature and historiography in the period of Joyce's composition of *Dubliners*. If 'The Lass of Aughrim' is the most reverberative tremor of late seventeenth-century Irish history contained within 'The Dead', it is not the most clear-cut, and there are two other instances of Jacobite resonance that we need to examine before moving on. The first of these – a reference to the Wild Geese – is fleeting and need not delay us long. Kevin Whelan has commented on it in a perceptive essay on Irish history and 'The Dead'. As well as seeing a nod to Sarsfield's exiled troops in the place name Aughrim, he also finds the Wild Geese encoded in Nora Barnacle's surname and in the goose that forms the main part of the

---

141 Quoted in Colm Tóibín, *Lady Gregory's Toothbrush* (London: Picador, 2003), 13.

142 Quoted in Adrian Frazier, *George Moore, 1852–1933* (New Haven, CT: Yale University Press, 2000), 370. For an account of Moore's attack on Lady Gregory, see Frazier, *George Moore*, 369–70 and 390–1.

meal on Usher's Island.[143] Barnacle geese were at one time commonly eaten by Irish Catholics on Friday as they were taken to be fish rather than fowl – a rather fanciful notion for those tired of a diet of dried herring. Gabriel Conroy's odd declaration to his aunts that he is 'ready to carve a flock of geese, if necessary' (*D* 197) has in the past been taken by John V. Kelleher as a pointer to an underlying current in 'The Dead' of the Irish saga *Togail Bruidne Da Derga*, or 'The Destruction of Da Derga's Hostel', in which King Conaire is forbidden to hunt birds. Gabriel Conroy, as Joyce's version of Conaire, breaks this taboo by carving the goose and thus brings ruin on himself.[144] While Kelleher's thesis is both elegant and persuasive, I agree with Whelan that there is a further undercurrent that links Gabriel's 'flock of geese' to the Wild Geese who stocked the armies of Catholic Europe in the years after defeat at Aughrim.

One final way in which I would like to tentatively suggest the presence of these exiled Jacobites in 'The Dead' is in the place name Nuns' Island, which was discussed at length in the previous chapter. Though called Nuns' Island after becoming home to the Poor Clare order in Galway, the original Gaelic name for this strip of land surrounded by Corrib waters was Oileán Altanach, as is indicated in Hardiman's history of Galway and in today's bilingual street signs. Oileán Altanach in translation has nothing to do with convent life but rather means 'the island of flocking birds'.[145] Whether Joyce knew this or not one cannot say, but given his Jacobite hints seeded throughout *Dubliners*, it is a tempting connection to make. Galway – and the Poor Clare settlement on Nuns' Island – suffered greatly as a result of James's defeat; its status as the last Irish city in which Catholics held the reins of power quickly changed after 1691, a point of which Hardiman is conscious in the dedication to his *History*:

> James Daly, esq. of Dunsandle, one of the representatives in parliament for the county of Galway [...] Whose venerable forefather, Denis Daly, Esq. (the counsellor and steadfast friend of the ill-fated James II) suggested those measures which would have led to the general pacification of this part of the kingdom, and, perhaps, have prevented the sanguinary battle of Aughrim, unless frustrated by the prevalence of that party which led Ireland into danger, and then abandoned her to her fate.[146]

143   See Whelan, 'Memories of "The Dead"', 71.
144   See Kelleher, 'Irish History and Mythology', 47.
145   See Peadar O'Dowd, *Old and New Galway* (Galway: Connacht Tribune and the Archaeological, Historical & Folklore Society, Regional Technical College, Galway, 1985), 71.
146   James Hardiman, *The History of the Town and County of the Town of Galway, from the earliest period to the present time, Embellished with several Engravings. To which is added, a*

These Jacobite memories found in Galway's history may feed in some small way into Joyce's all-absorbing imagination. They would be unworthy of consideration were it not for the already examined significance of Galway as a place of loss and sadness, of Michael Furey's singing of 'The Lass of Aughrim' on Nuns' Island, and of the final and strongest reminder of Jacobite ruin contained within 'The Dead', Gabriel's humorous story about his grandfather's uncooperative horse, Johnny.

The tale of Johnny comes at the end of the party as Freddy Malins is outside on the street in search of cabs, prompting Aunts Kate and Julia to remember an old horse that was owned by the Morkan family in their youth. Present as Gabriel recounts the strange tale of the horse and its master, his grandfather Patrick Morkan, are the three hostesses, Mrs Malins, his wife Gretta and Mr Browne. The story shows Gabriel in high good humour now that his duties as after-dinner speaker are over:

— Why, what was wonderful about Johnny? asked Mr Browne.
— The late lamented Patrick Morkan, our grandfather, that is, explained Gabriel, commonly known in his later years as the old gentleman, was a glue-boiler.
— O, now, Gabriel, said Aunt Kate, laughing, he had a starch mill.
— Well, glue or starch, said Gabriel, the old gentleman had a horse by the name of Johnny. And Johnny used to work in the old gentleman's mill, walking round and round in order to drive the mill. That was all very well; but now comes the tragic part about Johnny. One fine day the old gentleman thought he'd like to drive out with the quality to a military review in the park.
— The Lord have mercy on his soul, said Aunt Kate compassionately.
— Amen, said Gabriel. So the old gentleman, as I said, harnessed Johnny and put on his very best tall hat and his very best stock collar and drove out in grand style from his ancestral mansion somewhere near Back Lane, I think.
Everyone laughed, even Mrs. Malins, at Gabriel's manner and Aunt Kate said:
— O now, Gabriel, he didn't live in Back Lane, really. Only the mill was there.
— Out from the mansion of his forefathers, continued Gabriel, he drove with Johnny. And everything went on beautifully until Johnny came in sight of King Billy's statue: and whether he fell in love with the horse King Billy sits on or whether he thought he was back again in the mill, anyhow

copious appendix, containing the principal charters and other original documents (Dublin: W. Folds and Sons, 1820), iii. On Galway's post-Aughrim decline, see Simms, *Jacobite Ireland*, 13–14.

he began to walk round the statue.

   Gabriel paced in a circle round the hall in his galoshes amid the laughter
of the others.

— Round and round he went, said Gabriel, and the old gentleman, who was
a very pompous old gentleman, was highly indignant. *Go on, sir! What do
you mean, sir? Johnny! Johnny! Most extraordinary conduct! Can't understand
the horse!* (*D* 208–9)

Joyce makes this entire passage work hard for its keep and it has attracted
considerable critical attention over the years, attention that requires
further comment.

   The first reader to understand fully the historical significance of Gabriel's story was John V. Kelleher, who interpreted his narrative and behaviour
as a blundering betrayal of nationalist Ireland. Pointing out that Gabriel,
in his earlier unhappy encounter with the Gaelic revivalist, Miss Ivors, had
been forced to admit that 'I'm sick of my own country, sick of it!' (*D* 190),
Kelleher then turns to the story of Johnny to demonstrate further Gabriel's
insensitivity and crassness. Much of Kelleher's critique revolves, as so often
in the study of Joyce, around place names – in this case Usher's Island and
Back Lane. Again, Aughrim rears its head, when Kelleher points out that
while Gabriel is in Usher's Island, 'he is now in that part of the city where
Catholics, his own ancestors among them, emerging from the century of
defeat and helotry in which they were sunk after Limerick and Aughrim,
stood up, straightened their backs, and moved into the modern world'. It
is, therefore, unfair of the comfortably bourgeois Gabriel to poke fun at his
Catholic grandfather's attempts to climb a social ladder in a Protestant-
dominated city in times much more difficult than his own. Aunt Kate, in
her gentle and unheeded efforts to correct Gabriel, first regarding Patrick
Morkan's profession and, secondly, over the accuracy of the starch mill's
location, shows a certain pride in her father's achievements – a pride absent
from that of the 'West Briton' Gabriel. Kelleher is especially well attuned
to the historical significance of Joyce's choice of Back Lane as the location
of the mill:

   There, from 1628 to 1630, the Jesuits maintained the only Catholic college in
   Ireland previous to the one in which Gabriel now teaches. In the eighteenth
   century the site was occupied by Tailors Hall, where, in 1792, the Catholic
   Association convened what their enemies contemptuously called 'the Back
   Lane Parliament' and demanded and got the Relief Act, passed in 1793, by
   which all the remaining punitive clauses of the Penal Code were abolished
   and Catholics were admitted to the franchise and university degrees.

'Clearly', concludes Kelleher, 'Back Lane is not to be treated lightly.'[147] To underline the street's educational significance Joyce again mentions it many years later, this time as 'Backlane Univarsity' (287.30), in *Finnegans Wake*.

Of Joyce's choice of Usher's Island, Kelleher tells us that the 'quay itself was a fashionable quarter to the very end of the eighteenth century, chiefly occupied by Moira House, the most splendid residence in the city'. In addition to this it is adjacent to the Guinness brewery, which lies on an old roadway called Lord Galway's Walk. 'Considering all the emphasis in the story about going west, going to Galway', writes Kelleher, 'it would be odd if this bit of lore were absent from Joyce's mind.'[148] Kevin Whelan is similarly interested in this path and finds in it another Jacobite trace, pointing out that the first Lord Galway had been Henri Massue, second Marquis de Ruvigny, who was installed as Viscount Galway in 1693 and elevated to Earl of Galway in 1697 by William of Orange. 'The Huguenot Lord Galway', writes Whelan, 'had been the victor at the Battle of Aughrim and the principal instigator of the Penal Laws, seen in Catholic narrative as a betrayal of the Articles of Limerick.'[149] The Articles of Limerick, better remembered as the Treaty of Limerick from which that city takes its sobriquet, 'the Treaty City', was the final peace of the Williamite War and became a notorious emblem of English treachery among nationalists in the centuries that followed. Joyce, as much as anyone, was aware of the treaty's symbolic importance and I will shortly conclude this chapter with some comments on a possible link between Jacobitism and whiskey via the broken treaty of 1691. Before doing that, though, a few more words on Whelan's intriguing interpretation of 'The Dead'.

While Kelleher, Donald Torchiana and Whelan consider that Joyce's choice of Usher's Island for the location of the Christmas party that concludes *Dubliners* has something to do with the location there of Moira House, others, less convincingly, sense that its 'island' location is what is significant.[150] Whelan feels that Joyce is triggering memories of the United Irish rebellion of 1798, a revolt that plays heavily on the mind of anglophilic Tom Kernan in the 'Wandering Rocks' chapter of *Ulysses*:

147 Kelleher, 'Irish History and Mythology', 49.
148 Kelleher, 'Irish History and Mythology', 53.
149 Whelan, 'Memories of "The Dead"', 80.
150 One critic argues that Joyce's use of Usher's Island suggests the Morkan sisters' 'ironic entrapment in Dublin'. See Martha Fodaski Black, 'Joyce on Location: Place Names in Joyce's Fiction', in Michael Begnal (ed.), *Joyce and the City: The Significance of Place* (Syracuse, NY: Syracuse University Press, 2002), 23.

> Somewhere here Lord Edward Fitzgerald escaped from major Sirr. Stables
> behind Moira House. Damn good gin that was. Fine dashing young
> nobleman. Good stock, of course. That ruffian the sham squire, with his
> violet gloves, gave him away. Course they were on the wrong side. They
> rose in dark and evil days. (*U* 309)

Whelan points to a book published in 1892 that had caused a stir by
unmasking Lord Edward Fitzgerald's betrayer, which again strengthens the
argument that Joyce had history on his mind when choosing the location
of the Morkans' party:

> A great sensation was accordingly created by the publication in 1892 by
> W. J. Fitzpatrick of *Secret Service Under Pitt* which 'outed' Francis Magan
> as the Catholic informer who had betrayed the Protestant Lord Edward
> Fitzgerald for blood money. Magan had been recruited by the 'Sham Squire'
> Francis Higgins. Magan, the secretive betrayer, was a respectable Catholic
> barrister who lived at 20 Usher's Island. [151]

Whelan goes on to make a range of other fascinating connections between
'The Dead' and Irish history, particularly the period of the United Irish
unrest. Kevin Barry, too, is forceful on this point as he sees in the story 'a
web of allusions to Irish political history: the victory of William of Orange
at the Battle of Aughrim; the Back Lane Parliament, called in 1792 in answer
to the revolution in France'; he makes an intriguing connection between
Gabriel's chief tormentor, Miss Ivors, and 'the United Irishmen's password
"Is Ivers of Carlow come?"'[152]

   While Joyce almost certainly knew of *Secret Service under Pitt*, the book
from which he is most likely to have taken his knowledge of Lord Moira's
house is John T. Gilbert's *History of the City of Dublin* (1854–9), a three-
volume exploration of the city that remained a firm favourite of Joyce's
throughout his writing life.[153] Gilbert goes to considerable lengths in the
first volume of his *History* to describe Moira House, home of the Rawdon
family who had been favourites of the Stuart king Charles I and 'whose

---

151 Whelan, 'Memories of "The Dead"', 81.
152 Kevin Barry, *The Dead* (Cork: Cork University Press, 2001), 24. Joyce could have known
     about the 'Ivers' password from a reading of P. O'Kelly, *General History of the Rebellion of
     1798 with many interesting occurrences of the two preceding years. Also a brief account of the
     insurrection in 1803* (Dublin: J. Downes, 1842), 29–30.
153 Joyce used Gilbert in writing both *Ulysses* and *Finnegans Wake*. Interestingly, Gilbert
     also edited a contemporary Jacobite account of the Williamite War, usually known as 'A
     Light to the Blind', which is likely to have been known to Joyce. See John T. Gilbert (ed.),
     A Jacobite Narrative of the War in Ireland, 1688–1691 (1892) (Shannon: Irish University
     Press, 1971).

services in the royal cause were recompensed in 1665 by the baronetcy of Moira'. Gilbert, in quoting Hardy's *Life of Charlemont*, provides a portrait of Moira House as a place of remarkable charm: 'it was for many years the seat of refined hospitality, of good nature, and good conversation'. This is a description of which Joyce may have been conscious when describing the Morkan sisters' home and in composing Gabriel Conroy's speech: 'I feel more strongly with every recurring year that our country has no tradition which does it so much honour and which it should guard so jealously as that of its hospitality' (*D* 203). If Gabriel dishonours his grandfather's memory with the story of Johnny and the Back Lane mill, as Kelleher argues, then he gives further affront to his country by telling such tales at a site associated by Gilbert with acts of great patriotism undertaken by the second Earl of Moira in the late eighteenth century:

> Lord Moira was a strenuous advocate of Parliamentary Reform and Roman Catholic Emancipation, and at his mother's mansion on Ussher's Island he frequently entertained Wolfe Tone, William Todd Jones, William Sampson, Thomas Russell and others of their party who laboured to advance those objects. [...] In November, 1797, Lord Moira in the English Parliament denounced the system of torture and coercion practised by the Ministers in Ireland; and in February, 1798, in the Irish House of Peers, with great eloquence and humanity, he again endeavoured to arrest the cruelties by which the insurrection of the populace was precipitated.

Gilbert goes on at length to tell of Lord and Lady Moira's attempts to help the rebel leader Lord Edward Fitzgerald in 1798, of Lord Moira's opposition to the Act of Union, and of the subsequent fall of the family and their magnificent house into rack and ruin:

> 'Moira House,' which was maintained as a family mansion for some years subsequent to the death of the Countess in 1808, was let in 1826 to the Governors of the Institution for the suppression of Mendicancy in Dublin. Under the superintendence of this body, the upper story of the edifice was taken off, the magnificent internal decorations removed, the handsome gardens covered with offices; and every measure adopted to render it a fitting receptacle for the most wretched paupers.[154]

It is descriptions such as this – perhaps this very account – that led Joyce to despair of his once-proud hometown, which now merely 'wore the mask of a capital' (*D* 39), and whose decline is most memorably captured

---

154 John T. Gilbert, *A History of the City of Dublin*, 3 vols (1854–59) (Dublin: Gill and Macmillan, 1978), I, 392, 395, 396, 400.

as Little Chandler leaves work in 'A Little Cloud': 'He emerged from under the feudal arch of the King's Inns, a neat modest figure, and walked swiftly down Henrietta Street. [...] He picked his way deftly through all that minute vermin-like life and under the shadow of the gaunt spectral mansions in which the old nobility of Dublin had roistered' (*D* 66).

While Joyce draws on Gilbert's description of Lord Moira's house on Usher's Island in order to lend sharper historical resonance to 'The Dead', he makes even greater use of Gilbert's comments on King William III's statue for Gabriel's story about his grandfather's circling horse. The equestrian statue of William of Orange that stood for over two centuries in College Green, and that was the most important symbol of Protestant domination in Dublin right up to Joyce's time, is given inordinate attention by Gilbert over sixteen pages of his third volume. He begins by describing the inaugu-ration of the statue on 1 July 1701, eleven years to the day after William's victory at the Boyne. The date – which is also, remember, the date on which Father James Flynn of 'The Sisters' dies – was a public holiday of great festivity among Dublin's loyalists. On that first day of William's unveiling the custom began of circling the statue in homage to the Orange Prince:

> The Lord Mayor, aldermen, sheriffs, masters, wardens, and common councilmen of the city, having assembled at the Tholsel at 4 p.m., walked thence in formal procession to College-green, preceded by the city musicians, and by the grenadier companies of the Dublin Militia. Some time after the city officials had reached College-green, the Lords Justices arrived, and were conducted through a line, formed by the grenadiers, to the statue, round which the entire assembly, uncovered, marched three times; the kettle-drums, trumpets, and other music playing on a stage erected near the front of the monument. After the second circuit, the Recorder deliv-ered an eulogy on King William, expressing the attachment of the people of Dublin to his person and government, and at the conclusion of this oration a volley was fired by the grenadiers, succeeded by a discharge of ordnance. At the termination of the third circuit round the statue, the Lords Justice, the Provost and Fellows of the University, with numbers of the Williamite noblemen and gentry, were conducted by the Lord Mayor, through a file of soldiers, to a large new house on College-green prepared for the reception, where they were entertained, the ordnance again discharging twice while they drank the King's health and prosperity to Dublin; the surrounding crowd being regaled with cakes thrown amongst them, and several hogsheads of claret were placed on stilts and set running.

This custom continued for most of the eighteenth century but, Gilbert tells us, was discontinued by the republican-minded Volunteers in the early 1790s. 'Desirous of no longer outraging the feelings of their Catholic countrymen', Gilbert writes, 'the Volunteers discontinued their annual procession round the statue on the 4ᵗʰ of November, 1792, on which day some of them appeared on parade with green cockades, instead of the orange ribbons which they had previously worn.' This change in habit on the Volunteers' part led to fears that the statue would become a focus for rebellion: 'During the panic of the Government in 1793, it was rumoured that the signal for the rising of the people was to be the pulling down of the statue with ropes.'

The statue 'regained its original notoriety when religious and political rancour was revived after the formation of the Orange Association in 1795, on whose medals and certificates representations of this monument were engraved'. And so, far from being a subject of mirth as it is for the clumsy Gabriel, the circling of King William's statue became the *ne plus ultra* of Orange pomp and posturing in nineteenth-century Dublin. On 12 July, the anniversary of the Battle of Aughrim, and on 4 November, the birthday of King William, the statue was 'annually coloured white, decorated with orange lilies, and with a flaming cloak and sash [...] and every person who passed through College-green on these occasions was obliged to take off his hat to the statue'.[155] Days such as this, on which Protestant power was restated and reinforced in a city that was still predominantly Catholic, naturally led to trouble, and defacement of the statue became a common goal both among disgruntled nationalists and, for a period in the eighteenth century, among a Protestant Jacobite rump in Trinity College. There was a dangerous affray in 1822 on the anniversary of Aughrim and three attempts were made in 1836 to blow up the statue, the third such effort on 7 April proving successful. The king and his horse were fully restored and strengthened in 1855 but were finally, and inevitably, removed in 1928, seven years after the foundation of the Irish Free State, after having been irreparably damaged in a Remembrance Day explosion. The site of the statue was subsequently used for the raising of a memorial to the nationalist icon Thomas Davis in 1966.[156]

While King William was removed from public view in Dublin, he remains a real presence in Belfast and among the Orangemen of Ulster and beyond. His victories are passionately remembered and celebrated

---

155 Gilbert, *History of the City of Dublin*, III, 40–1, 51, 51, 51.
156 See Yvonne Whelan, 'Written in Space and Stone: Aspects of the Iconography of Dublin after Independence', in Howard B. Clarke, Jacinta Prunty and Mark Hennessy (eds), *Surveying Ireland's Past: Multidisciplinary Essays in Honour of Anngret Simms* (Dublin: Geography Publications, 2004), 597–9.

each July as those still loyal to the crown recall the events of 1690–91, from the Boyne to Aughrim to final victory at Limerick. Alfred Barnard, whose *Whisky Distilleries of the United Kingdom* was discussed at length in the preceding chapter, and whom I suspect Joyce read, travels, after his visit to Nuns' Island, to a distillery in Limerick. Struck at first by the barrenness and poverty of the land, he is relieved on seeing the majesty of the Shannon, but this buoyancy is pricked on entering Limerick as he writes about the city's sad history of treachery and defeat:

> The history of the Old City of Limerick, for many centuries, is full of romance and tragical events; it is the only city that has never been taken by the English. It is called the 'City of the Violated Treaty,' from the following event: General Ginckle invested it in the year 1691, and after six weeks, failing of success, negotiations for a treaty were set on foot, amicable intercourse was established, and articles of capitulation signed, the garrisons were to march out with the honours of war, the Roman Catholics of the kingdom were to enjoy every privilege of King Charles the Second's time, and a parliament was to be summoned in Ireland. Alas, these stipulations were not fulfilled, and King William's successor enacted far more oppressive laws.

The breaking of the Treaty, for Barnard, acts like a curse against his native land and prompts him to wonder how it might all have been different had it been honoured. 'What miseries, rebellions, cruelties, and midnight murders', writes Barnard, 'might have been prevented by these concessions of civil and religious rights; and Ireland to-day would have been a loyal and happy country.'[157] The surrender of Limerick was in part brought about by the failure of French aid to arrive at the besieged city. 'It is evident', argues J. G. Simms, 'that there was no love lost between the allies, and that the idea of prolonging resistance into the winter simply to suit French long-term strategy had little appeal for the Irish.'[158] Joyce's ironic phrase from 'After the Race', 'their friends, the French', once more comes to mind.

In a description of the Irish peasant mentality, Joyce was vividly conscious of the Limerick betrayal and all it entailed. The peasant, he wrote, 'does not forget [...] the false oath that the English made on the broken rock of Limerick. How could he forget? Does the slave's back forget the rod?'[159] For an Anglo-Irish boy like the young W. B. Yeats, Limerick was not something he could forget, for it was not a name that meant anything

---

157 Alfred Barnard, *The Whisky Distilleries of the United Kingdom* (1887) (Edinburgh: Birlinn, 2003), 399, 401.
158 Simms, *Jacobite Ireland*, 255.
159 Joyce, 'Ireland: Island of Saints and Sages', in Joyce, *Occasional, Critical, and Political Writing*, 121.

to him in the first place, thus causing him to be distanced from the Catholic boys of Sligo as much as he was from English boys:

> I was divided from all those boys, not merely by the anecdotes that are everywhere perhaps a chief expression of the distrust of races, but because our mental images were different. I read their boys' books and they excited me, but if I read of some English victory, I did not believe that I read of my own people. They thought of Cressy and Agincourt and the Union Jack and were all very patriotic, and I, without those memories of Limerick and the Yellow Ford that would have strengthened an Irish Catholic, thought of mountain and lake, of my grandfather and of ships.[160]

But for Joyce, as for the Irish peasant, the events of the Williamite War were not to be forgotten, and the 'mutinous Shannon waves' of 'The Dead' are rebelling against Williamite conquest as that great river guards Ireland's last bastion of Catholic power.

As Gretta is sneered at for being 'from Connacht', so too the ghosts of a vanished Ireland are betrayed by Gabriel and his upwardly mobile, university-educated, West British friends. Joyce – always the realist – knows that there is no Pretender, no Stuart to free the island from English Protestant domination, no French army in waiting, and 'The Dead' works as an elegy, not just for the dead love between Gabriel and Gretta, nor for the consumptive Michael Furey, but for the fallen of Aughrim and the last of Gaelic Ireland. As Sarsfield and his Wild Geese saw no option but to board the French ships on the banks of the Shannon and serve Ireland and her 'friends' on the Continent, so Joyce saw his country as a dead, defeated, paralysed place, and he too would become a wild goose and decamp for the adventures and opportunities of Europe. As he opened that little package from Mrs Gorman on an autumn day in 1930 in his Parisian quarters and admired his new tie's Stuart tartan, Joyce had Aughrim on his mind. Paradoxically, while Sarsfield and Joyce set out on their journey eastward, Gabriel Conroy would realize that it was time to go west, to cross the Shannon and to feel the Galway wind on his face.

160 Yeats, *Autobiographies*, 61.

3

'He would put in allusions':
The Uses and Abuses of Revivalism

It is often annoying the way people will blunder on what you have elaborately planned for.

— James Joyce, 'The Sisters'

I am quite content to go down to posterity as a scissors and paste man.

— James Joyce

Perhaps the most striking and, in a sense, disappointing thing about James
Joyce's Trieste library as it is held today by the Harry Ransom Center
in Austin, Texas, is its pristine condition.[1] While the bibliophile might
enjoy the almost unmarked and near-perfect condition of the collection,
the Joycean scholar longs for something messier: scribbles in the margins,
turned-down pages, broken spines. But there is almost nothing there for
the forensic detective to ponder. Other than the haunting and exciting
experience of reading the books that Joyce read, and imagining him lifting
those very same volumes down from their shelves over a century ago, there
is not a great deal to be had in the way of a eureka moment. An exception
to this general pattern is a well-thumbed, loose-leafed, card-covered copy
of Douglas Hyde's *Love Songs of Connacht* published in 1905.[2] Cóilín Owens
argued with his usual flair some twenty years ago for seeing the first song
in this collection, 'If I Were to Go West', as a hidden and oblique ghost
text behind 'The Dead', informing, in particular, Gabriel's epiphany and
realization that the time has come to journey westward.[3] Owens' argument

---

1　On this collection, see Michael Patrick Gillespie and Erik Bradford Stocker, *James Joyce's
Trieste Library: A Catalogue of Materials at the Harry Ransom Humanities Research Center,
The University of Texas at Austin* (University of Texas at Austin: Harry Ransom Humani-
ties Research Center, 1986).

2　The full bibliographical details of this volume are as follows: Douglas Hyde, *Abhráin
Grádh Chúige Connacht or Love Songs of Connacht (Being the Fourth Chapter of the 'Songs
of Connacht'), now for the first time Collected, Edited, and Translated*, fourth edition (Baile
Átha Cliath: Clóbhuailte le Gill & a Mhac; London: T. Fisher Unwin, 1905).

3　See Cóilín Owens, 'The Mystique of the West in Joyce's "The Dead"', *Irish University
Review*, 22.1 (Spring–Summer 1992), 80–91.

is convincing, all the more so if one considers not just the song (which is narrated by a western girl wishing to leave the city where she gave her love to a man who never understood it) but Hyde's introductory remarks on the nature of the Irish spirit:

> Not careless and light-hearted alone is the Gaelic nature, there is also beneath the loudest mirth a melancholy spirit [...] The same man who will to-day be dancing, sporting, drinking and shouting, will be soliloquising by himself to-morrow, heavy and sick and sad in his poor lonely little hut, making a croon over departed hopes, lost life, the vanity of this world, and the coming of death.[4]

Could there be a neater description of Gabriel Conroy's change in mood over the course of 'The Dead'? This possible use of Hyde by Joyce is just one in a very complex pattern of nods and winks at revivalism throughout *Dubliners* and his wider oeuvre.

We know that Joyce, while on the one hand rejecting some of the central tenets of the Revival in essays such as 'The Day of the Rabblement' and 'Ireland, Island of Saints and Sages', was nevertheless intrigued by it as a cultural movement. In the spring of 1907 Joyce was invited by his friend and student Attilio Tamaro to deliver three lectures at the Università Popolare in Trieste. The first of these lectures, the above-mentioned 'Ireland, Island of Saints and Sages', was given on 27 April. The other two lectures remained, because of financial constraints at the university, undelivered. The putative second lecture, 'James Clarence Mangan', survives in incomplete manuscript form, though it still provides the scholar with much to mull over. The final lecture, 'The Irish Literary Renaissance', survives only as a few incomplete sentences in the Slocum Collection at Yale University. That we have come so tantalizingly close to possessing Joyce's considered opinion on the Revival stands as a singular pity but also as a marvellous joke against the critics, and sets us on an even more difficult hunt than usual to uncover Joyce's feelings about his Irish artistic contemporaries.

At least as far back as 1948 scholars were bringing to attention the fact that Joyce encoded within his work a mischievous series of allusions and references to revivalist works beyond the straightforward engagement with figures such as George Russell, Lady Gregory and George Moore evident in *Ulysses*. In that year Marion Witt pointed out the jocose reference to W. B. Yeats, his sisters and their printing operations contained within the opening 'Telemachus' episode of the novel, when Buck Mulligan, talking high nonsense over breakfast, suggests an approach for

4 Hyde, 'Fourth Chapter: Love Songs', in *Abhráin Grádh Chúige Connacht*, 3.

Haines to take with his hibernophilic studies: 'That's folk, he said very earnestly, for your book, Haines. Five lines of text and ten pages of notes about the folk and the fishgods of Dundrum. Printed by the weird sisters in the year of the big wind' (*U* 14).[5] The allusion is, as Witt pointed out, to the colophon to the Dun Emer edition of W. B. Yeats's *In the Seven Woods* (1903). Yeats had, by that early stage in the novel, already been quoted directly as Stephen, prompted by Buck Mulligan's recital of 'Who Goes With Fergus', recalled his singing of it through the open door of his dying mother's bedroom.

For many, the allusiveness of Joyce's work is its chief intrigue and charm. Commenting on Stanislaus Joyce's now well-rehearsed claim that 'Grace' derives its structure from Dante's *Divine Comedy*, Frank O'Connor, though not always as convinced of Joyce's greatness as some other of his compatriots, reflected on the continuing fascination of the Joycean oeuvre. 'Joyce was an intensely literary man', wrote O'Connor, 'and – in his later work at least – loved to play the well-known literary game of basing his books on underlying myths and theories so that half the reader's fun comes of spotting the allusions.'[6] Scholars such as Don Gifford, Roland McHugh and Adaline Glasheen, to name but a small few, devoted much of their professional lives to tracking down and illuminating Joyce's myriad codes, unacknowledged sources and allusive trapdoors. And, as O'Connor points out, it is on Joyce's later novels that most of this work has been concentrated. I would like to suggest in this chapter that O'Connor's quali-fication about the more allusive nature of the later work is overstated – as one recent critic has put it of the Joyce who wrote *Dubliners*, 'his ability to amalgamate a multiplicity of different texts to his apparently simple narrative is dizzying'.[7] *Dubliners*, despite welcome and pioneering work by critics such as Gifford, Torchiana and Muldoon, still has a host of allusions yet to be uncovered – allusions that, once unpicked, will reveal a number of new emphases on the part of the book's author, and help us to arrive at some clearer idea of how Joyce felt about his writing contemporaries in Ireland and their project of pursuing a cultural revival.

---

5 See Marion Witt, 'A Note on Joyce and Yeats', *Modern Language Notes*, 63 (November 1948), 552–3.

6 Frank O'Connor, 'Work in Progress', in Robert Scholes and A. Walton Litz (eds), *Dubliners: Text, Criticism and Notes* (Harmondsworth: Penguin Books, 1996), 299.

7 Cóilín Owens, *James Joyce's Painful Case* (Gainesville, FL: University Press of Florida, 2008), 9.

Yeats and Joyce

Witt's observations, as discussed above, on the presence of Yeats in *Ulysses* are irrefutable and quickly became critical orthodoxy. Joyce's friend and fellow Dubliner, C. P. Curran, in his memoir of the great writer, comments on this aspect of the man and his work:

> He was diligent in following up clues and the modish allusions to more esoteric writers in Yeats and the French Symbolists. His extraordinary memory and natural acuteness did the rest in the way of preserving for use immediately, or after a great space of years, what came his way.[8]

A Portrait of the Artist as a Young Man is a case in point and is open in its use of Yeats, with one of Stephen's last diary entries making reference to the poet's mystic creation Michael Robartes. And Joyce's interest in Yeats becomes even clearer from an examination of drafts for *A Portrait*, subsequently published posthumously as *Stephen Hero*, where Yeats's mystical, *fin-de-siècle* stories, 'The Tables of the Law' and 'The Adoration of the Magi', are referenced. These stories are among a small part of Yeats's published output that actually formed part of Joyce's library. When, in the mid-1970s, Richard Ellmann performed the valuable task of cataloguing the Trieste library as it stood in 1920 he discovered that, among the very many books present, just six were by Yeats. Those six were a 1912 edition of *The Countess Cathleen*; *The Hour-Glass* (1907); *John Sherman and Dhoya* (1891); *The Land of Heart's Desire* (1912); 'The Tables of the Law' and 'The Adoration of the Magi' published together in one 1904 volume; and *Ideas of Good and Evil*, of which Joyce owned not the original 1903 volume but the edition published by Maunsel in 1905.[9] This seems an odd collection – particularly so in its lack of poetry – but if considered carefully reveals some interesting aspects of the nature of influence between the older and the younger writer.

As in *A Portrait* and *Ulysses*, the lead character of *Stephen Hero* is young Stephen Daedalus (Joyce still preferred this spelling of the name at this early stage in his career), and here we meet him strolling through Dublin's streets:

> During his wanderings Stephen came on an old library in the midst of those sluttish streets which are called old Dublin. The library had been founded by Archbishop Marsh and though it was open to the public few people seemed aware of its existence. [...] He had found on one of the

---

8 C. P. Curran, *James Joyce Remembered* (New York and London: Oxford University Press, 1968), 35–6.
9 See Richard Ellmann, *The Consciousness of Joyce* (London: Faber and Faber, 1977), 134.

carts of books near the river an unpublished book containing two stories by W. B. Yeats. One of these stories was called *The Tables of the Law* and in it was mentioned the fabulous preface which Joachim, abbot of Flora, is said to have prefixed to his Eternal Gospel. This discovery, coming so aptly upon his own researches, induced him to follow his Franciscan studies with vigour. [...] one evening while talking with a Capuchin, he had over and over to restrain an impulse which urged him to take the priest by the arm, lead him up and down the chapel-yard and deliver himself boldly of the whole story of the *Tables of the Law*, every word of which he remembered. (*SH* 181–2)

It would seem that Joyce, like Stephen, could indeed recite the entirety of 'The Tables of the Law' – an almost unbelievable feat of memory from any ordinary mortal. In his own radical artistic innovations, Joyce saw himself as isolated from the throng – like Joachim or another of his favourite heretics, Giordano Bruno. Yeats wrote in 'The Tables of the Law' that Joachim's *Eternal Gospel* had been found and was in the possession of one of his fictional creations, the mystic Owen Aherne. 'When he and I had been students in Paris', writes the narrator of the story, 'we had belonged to a little group which devoted itself to speculation about alchemy and mysticism. More orthodox in most of his beliefs than Michael Robartes, he had surpassed himself in a fanciful hatred of all life.' For Aherne, 'the beautiful arts were sent into the world to overthrow nations, and finally life herself, by sowing everywhere unlimited desires, like torches thrown into a burning city'.[10] Like Aherne, Joyce's alter ego Stephen Daedalus sees in art a transcendent and all-powerful medium through which to view the world. Besides the idea of Paris as a seedbed for aesthetic excellence – a notion that recurs in 'The Adoration of the Magi' – Joyce would also have been attracted to the elitist isolation of this seeker of truth. For Joyce, as for Yeats, this searcher in the modern world is the artist.

Stephen's – and Joyce's – fascination with these mystical Yeatsian tales is reinforced a little later in *Stephen Hero*:

Stephen was still a lover of the deformations wrought by dusk. Late autumn and winter in Dublin are always seasons of damp gloomy weather. He went through the streets at night intoning phrases to himself. He repeated often the story of *The Tables of the Law* and the story of the *Adoration of the Magi*. The atmosphere of these stories was heavy with incense and omens and the figures of the monk-errants, Ahern and Michael Robartes strode through it with great strides. (*SH* 183)

10 W. B. Yeats, 'The Tables of the Law', in *Mythologies* (New York: The Macmillan Company, 1959), 294.

For Joyce, the arch-realist and admirer of Daniel Defoe, devotion to the metaphysical and spiritual world so beloved of Yeats and so luxuriously painted in these two stories seems oddly out of character, but there can be little doubt of Joyce's enthusiasm for aspects of Yeats's work at this point in his life.

Joyce's marked interest in Yeats as exhibited in *Stephen Hero* makes it surprising that, until relatively recently, scholars have been unlikely to see Yeats or other revivalist texts shadowing the pages of *Dubliners*. That trend has begun to change now with the emergence of a new wave of Joyceans, such as Paul Muldoon and Kevin Whelan, eager to demonstrate that *Dubliners*, and in particular 'The Dead', carries a marked pattern of allusions and references to the work of Yeats and to other contemporary revivalists.[11] It has been suggested throughout this book that the delay on scholarship's part to look for literary allusions in *Dubliners* is largely down to the book's apparently realist surface. On the question of the book's allusive texture, one is reminded of a prompt provided by Joyce in 'A Little Cloud'. Along with 'A Mother', 'A Little Cloud' is the story that most directly lampoons revivalism, with its central character, Little Chandler, a would-be poet of 'the Celtic school', fantasizing about the positive reviews to come: '*Mr Chandler has the gift of easy and graceful verse... A wistful sadness pervades these poems... The Celtic note*' (D 69). Little Chandler knows his market and realizes that his verse will need two key characteristics to merit critical consideration: 'The English critics, perhaps, would recognise him as one of the Celtic school by reason of the melancholy tone of his poems; besides that, he would put in allusions' (D 68–9). The talentless clerk will have to rely on modish sentimentalism and on the trickery of allusiveness to establish himself as a writer. Joyce's unmerciful scalpel here exposes his creation as a pathetic, delusional mediocrity while also suggesting that the tepid romanticism beloved of revivalism is worthless. Yet while he has Chandler vaguely think that the use of allusions will render him somehow a more serious poet, Joyce himself was acutely allusive in his style throughout his writing career. The difference between Joyce and Chandler (had the unfortunate clerk got around to fulfilling his literary ambitions) would be one of degree. While, one suspects, the use of other writers' work by a man such as Chandler would have been quite clearly open and traceable, for Joyce there is a delight in obscurity, in hidden meaning and in gnomic subterfuge. T. S. Eliot's dictum on allusion is particularly informative here: 'One of the surest of tests is the way in which a poet borrows. Immature

---

11 See Paul Muldoon, *To Ireland, I* (Oxford: Oxford University Press, 2000), 50–66, and Kevin Whelan, 'The Memories of "The Dead"', *Yale Journal of Criticism*, 15.1 (2002), 59–97.

poets imitate; mature poets steal; bad poets deface what they take, and good poets make it into something better, or at least something different.'[12] Nowhere is Joyce's deft thievery better illustrated than in his use of Yeats in the opening story of *Dubliners*, as we shall see shortly.

Popular myth had it for many years that Joyce was no admirer of Yeats, the younger writer telling the older at an early meeting that he was too old to be helped. Joyce at the time was twenty years of age. Joyce's hastily penned broadside of 1904, 'The Holy Office', seems to confirm a lack of respect on his part for Yeats, as is evident in his comic corruption of 'To Ireland in the Coming Times' to undermine the great poet. Djuna Barnes, a fellow resident of 1920s and '30s Paris, recalls Joyce on the subject of Yeats: 'A good boy and a fine poet, but too proud in his clothes, and too fond of the aesthetic.'[13] Certainly, at this point in his life, Joyce's youthful enthusiasm for certain aspects of Yeatsian revivalism had waned, as is evident throughout *Ulysses*. In the 'Oxen of the Sun' chapter, for example, Joyce laughs again at the Yeats sisters and their Dundrum-based Dun Emer, later Cuala, printing press, which stressed the importance of the book itself as artifice: 'To be printed and bound at the Druiddrum press by two designing females. Calf covers of pissedon green. Last word in art shades. Most beautiful book come out of Ireland in my time' (*U* 556). That last phrase is, of course, a direct attack on Yeats's over-enthusiastic praise for Lady Gregory.

But for all of that mockery, it would be a mistake to take Djuna Barnes as the last word on the subject. Stanislaus Joyce tells us a rather different story about his brother, who 'considered that he was more gifted than his coevals, but he recognized that Yeats had more poetical talent, and to me he said so repeatedly'.[14] When, in the spring of 1903, Joyce returned from Paris to be with his dying mother he met with Yeats and confessed his great admiration for 'The Tables of the Law' and 'The Adoration of the Magi'. These two stories had had a chequered publishing history, as Yeats explained in a 1925 note when trying to draw together an anthology of his tales:

> 'The Tables of the Law' and 'The Adoration of the Magi' were intended to be part of *The Secret Rose*, but the publisher, A. H. Bullen, took a distaste to them and asked me to leave them out, and then after the book was published liked them and put them into a little volume by themselves.[15]

12 T. S. Eliot, *The Sacred Wood: Essays on Poetry and Criticism* (1920) (London: Methuen, 1960), 125.

13 Djuna Barnes, *Vagaries Malicieux: Two Stories* (New York: Frank Hallman, 1974), 12.

14 Stanislaus Joyce, *My Brother's Keeper: James Joyce's Early Years*, ed. Richard Ellmann (1958) (Cambridge, MA: Da Capo Press, 2003), 109.

15 Yeats, *Mythologies*, 1.

When the two stories were republished in 1904 Yeats referred to Joyce, though not by name, in a prefatory note: 'I do not think I should have reprinted them had I not met a young man in Ireland the other day, who liked them very much and nothing else that I have written.'[16] It was this edition that formed part of Joyce's library.

'The Tables of the Law' and 'The Adoration of the Magi' come from that period of the closing decade of the nineteenth century that saw Yeats's most energetic and prolific efforts at storytelling, the best-known products of the time being his folk-inspired tales of Red Hanrahan. One of these tales, 'The Twisting of the Rope', was adapted by Douglas Hyde as *Casadh an tSúgáin*, the Literary Theatre's first Irish-language play and target of Joyce's ire in the 1901 broadside 'The Day of the Rabblement'. John Paul Riquelme has argued that the Red Hanrahan stories ought to be read as a source text for *Dubliners* and in particular for 'The Dead'. 'As Joyce brings his own volume of Irish tales to closure', writes Riquelme, 'even though they are not drawn overtly from the folk tradition, Joyce takes that tradition and Yeats's stories as his own implied heritage, as part of the origin of his own voice.' Joyce does this, argues Riquelme, by basing many of the concluding details of 'The Dead' on stories such as 'Red Hanrahan', 'The Twisting of the Rope', 'Hanrahan's Vision' and 'The Death of Hanrahan'.

Riquelme writes that the 'grey mist' that the poet encounters in 'Hanrahan's Vision' is what Joyce in 'The Dead' calls 'that region where dwell the vast hosts of the dead' (*D* 224). And, as with Gretta's remembered love raising the ghost of Michael Furey, Yeats's Hanrahan thinks of lovers 'that were awakened from the sleep of the grave itself by the strength of one another's love', and has a vision in the grey wavelike mist. This vision includes a procession of the dead. Near the end of 'The Death of Hanrahan' the poet has a vision in which he sees old women holding four symbols: cauldron, stone, spear and sword. 'At least two of the four symbols, stone and spear', notes Riquelme, 'are mentioned in the final paragraphs of "The Dead".'[17] In addition to this allusion, Riquelme sees Yeats's old women in 'The Death of Hanrahan' as paralleling the elderly Morkan sisters of 'The Dead'.

While not entirely convinced by Riquelme's theory, I do think that his instincts are right in pursuing Yeatsian allusions in *Dubliners*, and in this regard another of Yeats's mystical stories, 'Rosa Alchemica', is worth

---

16 W. B. Yeats, *The Tables of the Law and The Adoration of the Magi* (London: Elkin Mathews, Vigo Street, 1904), n. p. [4].

17 John Paul Riquelme, *Teller and Tale in Joyce's Fiction: Oscillating Perspectives* (Baltimore, MD: Johns Hopkins University Press, 1983), 128–9.

considering.[18] Those symbolical spears of 'The Death of Hanrahan' that Riquelme sees present in 'The Dead' are here again as decorations on an ornate book given to the narrator as he awaits initiation into a mystical order of alchemists: 'In the box was a book bound in vellum, and having upon the vellum and in very delicate colours, and in gold, the Alchemical Rose with many spears thrusting against it, but in vain, as was shown by the shattered points of those nearest to the petals.' More interesting from the point of view of unlocking the coded last paragraph of 'The Dead' is the location of the narrator at this point: the Temple of the Alchemical Rose. He has been transported there by Michael Robartes as he describes in the following passage:

> I fell at last into a feverish sleep, waking up from time to time when we rushed past some little town, its slated roofs shining with wet, or still lake gleaming in the cold morning light. I had been too preoccupied to ask where we were going, or to notice what tickets Michael Robartes had taken, but I knew now from the direction of the sun that we were going westward; and presently I knew also, by the way in which the trees had grown into the semblance of tattered beggars flying with bent heads towards the east, that we were approaching the western coast.[19]

This description is another possible forerunner of Gabriel Conroy's ambiguous journey westward, which he realizes it is time to take at the conclusion of 'The Dead'. Earlier in that story Gabriel had been dismissive of an invitation to travel west to the Aran Islands with Miss Ivors and her Gaelic revivalist friends, thus alienating both her and his Galway-born wife Gretta.

Several critics have read Gabriel's imagined journey westward as a softening of attitude on Joyce's part towards his native country generally and towards revivalism specifically. Certainly, Joyce's great enthusiasm for 'The Adoration of the Magi' does not suggest someone who is antipathetic to the Revival's mythologizing of the west. The Magi of that story are described as 'three old men [who] were three brothers, who had lived in one of the western islands from their early manhood, and had cared all their lives for nothing except for those classical writers and old Gaelic writers who expounded an heroic and simple life'.[20] It is as clear-cut a

18 'Rosa Alchemica' ought to be considered part of a triumvirate with 'The Tables of the Law' and 'The Adoration of the Magi' and was packaged as such in the original 1897 volume, only to be stripped away in 1904 and then reinstated in the posthumously published anthology of Yeats's shorter prose pieces, *Mythologies*.
19 W. B. Yeats, 'Rosa Alchemica', in Yeats, *Mythologies*, 283, 279.
20 W. B. Yeats, 'The Adoration of the Magi', in Yeats, *Mythologies*, 309.

picture of Yeats's ideal Irishman as one could get, and very different indeed
to the frightening old western man visited by Mulrennan towards the end
of *A Portrait of the Artist as a Young Man*:

> John Alphonsus Mulrennan has just returned from the west of Ireland.
> European and Asiatic papers please copy. He told us he met an old man
> there in a mountain cabin. Old man had red eyes and short pipe. Old man
> spoke Irish. Mulrennan spoke Irish. Then old man and Mulrennan spoke
> English. Mulrennan spoke to him about universe and stars. Old man sat,
> listened, smoked, spat. Then said:
> — Ah, there must be terrible queer creatures at the latter end of the world.
> I fear him. I fear his red-rimmed horny eyes. It is with him I must struggle
> all through this night till day come, till he or I lie dead. (*P* 251–2)

In this instance the old man represents the idealized and constricting Irish
Ireland from which Stephen Dedalus is so desperate to escape. But Stephen
Dedalus is not quite James Joyce, and Joyce's attitude towards the west is,
as this study has repeatedly suggested, considerably more ambiguous than
many critics have allowed. We would do well to note how Stephen closes
his diary entry on Mulrennan's ancient westerner: 'I mean him no harm'
(*P* 252).

Rather than fighting with the old man of the west, Richard Ellmann
suggests that the young Joyce had a somewhat different adversary. 'Even in
adolescence', argues Ellmann, 'Joyce recognized that Yeats was the writer
with whom he must finally compete.'[21] That first meeting between the two
men during which Joyce reputedly told Yeats that his age put him beyond
help made a considerable impact on Yeats's mind, so much so in fact that he
considered reproducing an account of it for his new book of essays, named
in homage to William Blake, *Ideas of Good and Evil.*[22] Though he eventually
rejected this idea for a more orthodox introduction, he continued to follow
closely Joyce's career and became a firm admirer of his work both in his
early poetry, published as *Chamber Music* in 1907, and beyond.

Ellmann has argued that *Ideas of Good and Evil* is on Joyce's mind when
coming to consider the composition of *Ulysses*. In particular he points to
'The Autumn of the Body', in which Yeats disagreed with Mallarmé that
their artistic age should make its one medium the lyric and argued instead
for a new *Odyssey*:

> I think that we will learn again how to describe at great length an old man
> wandering among enchanted islands, his return home at last, his slowly

---

21 Richard Ellmann, *Yeats and Joyce* (Dublin: Dolmen, 1967), 447.
22 See W. B. Yeats, 'William Blake and the Imagination', in Yeats, *Essays and Introductions*
   (New York: The Macmillan Company, 1961), 113.

gathering vengeance, a flitting shape of a goddess, and a flight of arrows, and yet to make all these so different thing [...] become [...] the signature or symbol of a mood of the divine imagination.[23]

That Joyce achieves such an effect with his Bloom of *Ulysses* is clear: his joking in 'Scylla and Charybdis' about the need for an Irish national epic may be a nod, in part, towards Yeats's essay. And if Ellmann is correct about the influence, then it is as well to consider another of the essays in *Ideas of Good and Evil*, 'The Return of Ulysses', a review of a Robert Bridges play that points perhaps to Joyce's Homer-inspired masterpiece: 'those closing books of the *Odyssey* which are perhaps the most perfect poetry of the world, and compels that great tide of song to flow through delicate dramatic verse, with little abatement of its own leaping and clamorous speed'.[24] Though Joyce never acknowledged any Yeatsian influences beyond Stephen Dedalus's enthusiasms, I believe that there are strong reasons to agree with Ellmann in seeing *Ideas of Good and Evil* as an influence not just on *Ulysses* but, as the previous chapter began to consider, on *Dubliners* too.

Four Fathers: Priests in *Dubliners*

The influences of *Ideas of Good and Evil* emerge in the opening story of *Dubliners*, 'The Sisters', where the short Yeats essay from 1895, 'The Body of the Father Christian Rosencrux' (first issued in book format in *Ideas of Good and Evil*), makes a glancing appearance. In this essay Yeats compares the fabled fifteenth-century mystic Father Rosencrux, or Rosenkreutz – inspiration for the order of Rosicrucianism, whose symbols of the rose and cross remained so attractive to Yeats through the 1890s – to the imagination that has been buried in modern times by criticism:

> The followers of the Father Christian Rosencrux, says the old tradition, wrapped his imperishable body in noble raiment and laid it under the house of their Order, in a tomb containing the symbols of all things in heaven and earth [...] It seems to me that the imagination has had no very different history during the last two hundred years, but has been laid in a great tomb of criticism, and had set over it inextinguishable magical lamps of wisdom and romance, and has been altogether so nobly housed and apparelled that we have forgotten that its wizard lips are closed, or but opened for the complaining of some melancholy and ghostly voice. [...] I cannot get it out of my mind that this age of criticism is about to pass, and

23 W. B. Yeats, 'The Autumn of the Body', in Yeats, *Essays and Introductions*, 194. Ellmann makes his argument in *The Consciousness of Joyce*, 10–11
24 W. B. Yeats, 'The Return of Ulysses', in Yeats, *Essays and Introductions*, 199.

an age of imagination, of emotion, of moods, of revelation, about to come in its place; for certainly belief in a supersensual world is at hand again.[25]

Joyce's 'The Sisters' also features a dead priest, in this case Father James Flynn. Before death he has suffered from paralysis, a word that fascinates the nameless boy narrator. In private correspondence with his publisher, Joyce was clear about the significance of the word, famously calling Dublin 'the centre of paralysis' and claiming that by writing the book he was recording 'a chapter of the moral history' of Ireland.[26] Joyce – usually reluctant to provide the baffled reader with any help towards unlocking his dense array of symbol and allusion – gives us in 'The Sisters' two direct signposts back towards 'The Body of the Father Christian Rosencrux'. The first of these comes in the following passage of conversation between the boy's uncle, aunt and a visitor to their house, Old Cotter, who has come to break the news of Father Flynn's death:

> — I wouldn't like children of mine, he said, to have too much to say to a man like that.
> — How do you mean, Mr Cotter? asked my aunt.
> — What I mean is, said Old Cotter, it's bad for children. My idea is: let a young lad run about and play with young lads of his own age and not be... Am I right, Jack?
> — That's my principle, too, said my uncle. Let him learn to box his corner. That's what I'm always saying to that Rosicrucian there: take exercise. (D 2)

By any measure, it is a very odd way for the slow-witted Uncle Jack to refer to the youngster, and Joyce, we can be certain, did not just pull it out of the air, meaning it, rather, as a prompt towards Yeats.

The other signal left by Joyce is the date of Father Flynn's death, a date that, as shown in the previous chapter, Joyce repeatedly revised. One reason for his final choice of 1895 is in order to align it with the year of publication of Yeats's essay on the death of Father Rosencrux. This theory is favoured by Donald Torchiana, who argues that Father Flynn 'serves as an ironic parallel' to Yeats's mystical priest. Yeats's 'age of imagination', thinks Torchiana, is being mocked by the young Dubliner: 'I hold Joyce's first story to be a strong demurrer against such a possibility in the Dublin of 1895 and after. Part of Joyce's method would then seem to be his setting

25 W. B. Yeats, 'The Body of the Father Christian Rosencrux', in Yeats, *Essays and Introductions*, 196–7.
26 James Joyce to Grant Richards (5 May 1906), in Joyce, *Letters*, vol. II, ed. Richard Ellmann (London: Faber and Faber, 1966), 134.

his face against such extravagant hopes.'[27] While Yeats's essay seems the most likely reason for Joyce's final and very deliberate choice of 1895, it is unclear how ironic he intends the allusion to be. Just as Yeats in his essay bemoans the burial of the imagination and awaits keenly its resurrection at the close of the nineteenth century, so too Joyce wishes to bring about spiritual and artistic regeneration in Ireland, albeit via a radically different artistic route. For Yeats the new Ireland might be invigorated by exposure to the fountainhead of myth and magic, while for Joyce what the Irish people need, famously, is to turn to the mirror of realism for 'one good look at themselves'.

If the nod to Father Rosencrux is meant to be taken at least partly seriously, another priest beloved of the Revival is dropped into the story for more playful reasons. Chapter Two argued that Joyce names his paralysed priest James in order to summon up remembrance of the Catholic King James II, but what about the fallen clergyman's surname of 'Flynn'? There were Flynns on Joyce's mother's side of the family; indeed, one critic has argued that it was from these relations that, 'Joyce was to derive most of the details for his long story "The Dead", in which he describes these ancestral Dubliners of his under the name of Morkan'.[28] But there is a more obvious source for the name in a popular poem and song of the time, Alfred Perceval Graves's 'Father O'Flynn'. A line from the poem is summoned up in Bloom's head as he wanders Dublin in the 'Lestrygonians' episode of *Ulysses*: 'Rub off the microbes with your handkerchief. Next chap rubs on a new batch with his. Father O'Flynn would make hares of them all' (*U* 217). 'Father O'Flynn' is a lighthearted and frivolous piece and was very popular in its day, prompting Yeats to include it in his canon-forming revivalist anthology, *A Book of Irish Verse*, published, like 'The Body of the Father Christian Rosencrux', in 1895.

Father O'Flynn, in the eponymous poem, is famous for his erudition, his merriment and his social skills. Like Father James Flynn of 'The Sisters' he is expert in interpreting the more arcane mysteries of the church:

> Talk of your Provost and Fellows of Trinity,
> Far renowned for Greek and Latinity,
> Gad! and the divils and all at Divinity,
> Father O'Flynn would make hares of them all.
> Come, I venture to give you my word,
> Never the likes of his logic was heard

---

27 Donald T. Torchiana, *Backgrounds to Joyce's 'Dubliners'* (Boston: Allen and Unwin, 1986), 2, 3.

28 Peter Costello, *James Joyce: The Years of Growth 1882–1915* (London: Kyle Cathie, 1992), 23.

Similarly, Father Flynn, remembers the unnamed boy narrator of 'The Sisters', 'had studied in the Irish college in Rome and he had taught me to pronounce Latin properly. [...] His questions showed me how complex and mysterious were certain institutions of the Church which I had always regarded as the simplest acts' (*D* 5). The other strong similarity between Fathers Flynn and O'Flynn is their ability to get along with youngsters. Old Cotter of 'The Sisters' considers this aspect of Father Flynn's character to be vaguely scandalous, and impropriety in his friendship with the boy narrator is hinted at but never openly stated. Graves's poem carries no such sinister note, but an examination of it acts to further strengthen the allusion:

> Father O'Flynn, you've the wonderful way with you,
> All the old sinners are wishful to pray with you,
> All the young children are wild for to play with you,
> You've such a way with you, Father *avick*![29]

In our twenty-first-century days of priest-focused paranoia these lines might just cause some unease; in late nineteenth-century Ireland not even Old Cotter could object. But as with all Joycean allusions, perfect symmetry is unnecessary. As to Joyce's motivation in alluding to the poem, I shall speculate on this later in the chapter after having considered a number of other similar moments in *Dubliners*.

If, at the beginning of *Dubliners*, 'The Sisters' alludes to one now largely forgotten poem of the Revival period, then the book also closes with another such poem and another hidden clergyman, Father Andrew Conroy of Lahardane. Father Conroy was an important leader of the 1798 uprising against British rule in County Mayo. A plaque on Daly's Hotel in the county town of Castlebar commemorates the fact that the rebel priest was hanged from a tree on the Mall opposite for his part in the rising. Thus, while Father Conroy's deeds have long been forgotten through most of Ireland and beyond, there are still those in Mayo who hold his name sacred. For James Joyce, a precocious schoolboy at the time of the fervent centenary celebrations of the rising, Conroy would have been a notable, patriotic name and Joyce borrows it for the family name at the heart of 'The Dead', both for Gabriel and Gretta, but also for Gabriel's priestly brother Constantine.

Though he plays a slightly more prominent part in *Ulysses* than in *Dubliners*, the first time we come across Father Conroy in Joyce is in the early pages of 'The Dead' where, as Gabriel's brother, he is referred to in

---

29 Alfred Perceval Graves, 'Father O'Flynn', in W. B. Yeats (ed.), *A Book of Irish Verse* (1895) (London: Routledge, 2002), 123–4, 124.

order to illustrate the upwardly mobile and snobbish nature of his mother. The paragraph in question begins with a description of the anglophilic pictures – one a scene from *Romeo and Juliet*, the other of the Princes in the Tower – that hang on the wall above the piano in the Morkans' home on Usher's Island, and then moves to the photograph of the late Ellen Conroy, the 'proud and matronly' (*D* 186) sister of Kate and Julia Morkan, that stands before the pierglass. In the photograph we are told that 'She held an open book on her knees and was pointing out something to Constantine who, dressed in a man-o'-war suit, lay at her feet' (*D* 186). This smartly dressed child is the boy who will become Father Conroy, who owes his grandiose name and his position as senior curate in Balbriggan to his mother's ambition, and whose brother Gabriel is the central character of the story.

If Bloom is right, then Gabriel's clergyman brother did not remain long in Balbriggan but was moved within six months to the church of Mary, Star of the Sea in Sandymount.[30] Lingering on Sandymount strand in the wake of his Gerty MacDowell-prompted masturbatory fantasies, Leopold remembers an error in property valuations made while he worked at Thom's: 'Yes, there's the light in the priest's house. Their frugal meal. Remember about the mistake in the valuation when I was in Thom's. Twentyeight it is. Two houses they have. Gabriel Conroy's brother is curate' (*U* 492). And again, at the chapter's close, we have another mention of this priest as the cuckoo clock in the parochial house mocks Leopold's cuckolding while the priests tuck into an anything but frugal meal: 'The clock on the mantelpiece in the priest's house cooed where Canon O'Hanlon and Father Conroy and the reverend John Hughes S.J. were taking tea and sodabread and butter and fried mutton chops with catsup' (*U* 499). If Leopold is wrong in assuming meagre rations for the priesthood he may also be wrong in assuming that the Father Conroy of Star of the Sea is the same Father Conroy who was or is senior curate in Balbriggan – Leopold is, after all, as often wrong as he is right throughout *Ulysses*. A Reverend Bernard Conroy was one of two curates attached to Sandymount in June 1904 and Joyce may have used this knowledge to introduce one more inaccuracy into Bloom's confused memory.[31] Whether it is Constantine or Bernard who is enjoying the chops

30 The action of *Ulysses* takes place in June 1904 while the Christmas party of 'The Dead' occurs five months earlier in January 1904. For a convincing dating of the party, see Don Gifford, *Joyce Annotated: Notes for 'Dubliners' and 'A Portrait of the Artist as a Young Man'* (Berkeley, CA: University of California Press, 2nd edn, 1982), 119.

31 See Don Gifford with Robert J. Seidman, *'Ulysses' Annotated: Notes for James Joyce's Ulysses* (Berkeley, CA: University of California Press, 2nd edn, revised and enlarged, 1989), 401.

matters little for the purposes of illustrating this allusion – it is their surname and vocation that attracts my interest.

It has long – and reasonably – been argued that Joyce's source for the name of the central character in 'The Dead' is *Gabriel Conroy*, an 1876 novel of the American West by Bret Harte. The novel opens with a description of snow falling silently, reminiscent of the famous last paragraph of Joyce's story, thus lending more weight to the suggested connection. A second theory for Joyce's use of the name Conroy that I mentioned in my introduction was provided by John V. Kelleher when he argued that the name is meant to prompt the alert reader to thoughts of an ancient Irish chieftain, King Conaire, and the part he plays in the story 'The Destruction of Da Derga's Hostel'. Kelleher's complex and brilliant theory provides, among other things, an explanation for Lily, the caretaker's daughter, using three syllables to pronounce Gabriel's two-syllable surname at the start of the story.[32] Chapter One has already considered some of Kelleher's other findings in relation to the role of Mr Browne in the story. Along with King Conaire and Harte, there is a third source for the name Conroy – a source drawn from a book with which we know Joyce was intimately familiar as a result of reviewing it for the *Daily Express*. The book, by William Rooney, was titled *Poems and Ballads* and was published posthumously in 1902, with Joyce's review of it appearing in the *Express* on 11 December of that year.

In 'The Dead' Joyce chooses to make Gabriel a version of himself in a number of important ways, the clearest being via their mutual involvement as reviewers for the *Daily Express*. Gabriel is unhelpfully revealed to Molly Ivors as a reviewer with the paper as a result of the printing of his initials at the end of a review of Browning, and so too, as we have seen in the previous chapter, Joyce was exposed by the paper's editor, E. V. Longworth, as the reviewer of Lady Gregory's *Poets and Dreamers* when his unfavourable review of it appeared in the paper on 26 March 1903. Joyce's nod towards that controversy within 'The Dead' has long been critically acknowledged while the connection to the Rooney review of three months earlier has so far remained elusive to readers of the story.

The Rooney review, titled simply 'An Irish Poet', is, like the Gregory review, also largely negative about its subject. Joyce argues that Rooney's desire to write patriotic poetry has been at the price of suppression of the individual spirit and imagination. 'He has no care then', writes Joyce, 'to create anything according to the art of literature.' 'Patriotism' is alluded

---

32 For Kelleher's full thesis, see John V. Kelleher, 'Irish History and Mythology in James Joyce's "The Dead"', in Charles Fanning (ed.), *Selected Writings of John V. Kelleher on Ireland and Irish America* (Carbondale, IL: Southern Illinois University Press, 2002), 40–56.

to by Joyce in the review as one of 'those big words which make us so unhappy'.[33] This description irritated Rooney's friend and editor Arthur Griffith so much 'that he used it derisively to advertise the book' in the *United Irishman* of 20 December.[34] Such hostility from Griffith is hardly surprising – he had, after all, in his preface to *Poems and Ballads*, described Rooney as 'the greatest Irishman whom I have known or whom I can ever expect to know'.[35]

William Rooney had, along with Griffith, been the prime mover in the nationalist, protectionist ideologies that blended to form the Sinn Féin party, and died prematurely in 1901 at the age of twenty-eight. What role he might have played in the new Ireland must remain moot, but it is likely that he would have become a prime mover on the road to independence: his best friend Griffith, after all, became the Free State's first leader in 1922. Rooney had been a key figure in the effort to provide a fitting memorial for the centenary of the 1798 rebellion. The single most important event in these centenary celebrations also turned out to be the most pitiful: the laying of a foundation stone for a planned statue of 1798's romantic leader Wolfe Tone at St Stephen's Green. Of the £14,000 the statue was projected to cost, only £561 had been raised and it would take another almost seven decades before the memorial would finally be completed.[36] Stephen Dedalus, wandering and late for a lecture, remembers this singular failure on the part of Irish nationalists to honour the dead hero in *A Portrait*:

> In the roadway at the head of the street a slab was set to the memory of Wolfe Tone and he remembered having been present with his father at its laying. He remembered with bitterness that scene of tawdry tribute. There were four French delegates in a brake and one, a plump smiling young man, held, wedged on a stick, a card on which were printed the words: *Vive l'Irlande!* (P 183–4)

While there is no doubt that such a description is an exaggeration on Stephen's part, the failure to quickly and efficiently raise a memorial was a cause of great embarrassment. But a crowd of several thousand did turn out to see the laying of the foundation stone on 15 August 1898, presided over by the grand old man of Irish separatist nationalism, John O'Leary

---

33 James Joyce, 'An Irish Poet', in Joyce, *Occasional, Critical, and Political Writing*, ed. Kevin Barry (Oxford: Oxford University Press, 2000), 62.

34 See Richard Ellmann, *James Joyce* (Oxford: Oxford University Press, rev. edn, 1982), 112.

35 Arthur Griffith, 'To the Reader', in William Rooney, *Poems and Ballads*, ed. Arthur Griffith (Dublin: The United Irishman, M. H. Gill and Son, O'Donoghue, n.d. [1902]), x.

36 On this subject, see Senia Paseta, '1798 in 1898: The Politics of Commemoration', *Irish Review*, 22 (Summer 1998), 50.

– revered by Yeats in 'September 1913' and described by Joyce as 'the last Fenian' in an admiring 1907 newspaper article.[37] At the event Rooney made a powerful speech in his beloved Irish and the whole spectacle moved W. B. Yeats greatly:

> This immense demonstration is being held at a momentous time in Irish history. England has persuaded herself that Ireland, discredited by dissension, was about to submit. England had persuaded herself that she could settle the Irish question by a handful of arms. We have answered England by this great demonstration. She is no longer deceived. She now knows that Ireland cherishes the same spirit still.[38]

Yeats, like everyone else, was deeply shocked when Rooney died in May 1901. Writing to Lady Gregory about a scheme for a Gaelic-language theatre group originally mooted by Rooney, he wrote warmly of the young nationalist, 'whose death has plunged everybody into gloom. Griffith has had to go to hospital for a week so much did it effect him.'[39] When Griffith composed himself sufficiently to write an obituary he painted a picture of Rooney as the great Irishman of his generation: 'The Davis of the National revival is dead – dead in the spring of his life – a martyr to his passionate love of our unhappy country. Ireland has lost the son she could least have spared, and we have lost our leader, our comrade, and our life-long friend.'[40]

For Joyce to disparage Rooney's writing in his review the year after the young hero's death was a brave and perhaps foolhardy venture, though given the political sympathies of the *Express* – a paper Yeats described as 'the most uncompromising of the Dublin Unionist newspapers' – he knew he was on reasonably safe ground with his editor at least.[41] Rooney's passionate nationalism is writ large through his poetry. But rather than literature, what Rooney presents the reader with, writes Joyce, is 'a weary succession of verses, "prize" poems – the worst of all'.[42] And yet for all Joyce's anger at writing of this sort, it is to one of these very 'prize' poems that we must turn to look for the origins of the Father Conroy of 'The Dead' and of *Ulysses*. The poem in question is titled 'The Priest of Adergool:

37 See James Joyce, 'Fenianism: The Last Fenian', in Joyce, *Occasional, Critical, and Political Writing*, 138–41.

38 Quoted in Paseta, '1798 in 1898', 50.

39 W. B. Yeats to Lady Gregory (21 May 1901), in W. B. Yeats, *The Collected Letters, Volume Three 1901–1904*, ed. John Kelly and Ronald Schuchard (Oxford: Clarendon Press, 1994), 72.

40 Quoted in Yeats, *Collected Letters, III*, 72, fn. 9.

41 W. B. Yeats, *Autobiographies*, ed. William H. O'Donnell and Douglas N. Archibald (New York: Scribner, 1999), 311.

42 Joyce, 'An Irish Poet', 62.

An Incident of the Connacht Rising'; it won a prize offered in 1898 by the *Weekly Freeman* for the best poem written on some incident of the 1798 rebellion.[43] A prefatory note to 'The Priest of Adergool' explains the provenance of the poem and how its hero fits into the story of 1798:

> The arrival of the French in Killala was the occasion of many an act of devotion to Ireland. One of the most notable was that of Father Conroy, P. P. of Adergool, who having intercepted a messenger bearing the tidings of the landing of the French, to Castlebar, wakened his entire district, made a series of maps to guide the French, and headed his parishioners to their support. His name and story are still well-known around the firesides of Mayo. The ballad faithfully follows the history of his act and the sacrifice it occasioned.[44]

John Wyse Jackson and Bernard McGinley, in a note on Constantine Conroy in their 1993 edition of *Dubliners*, point to this same Father Conroy, telling the reader that it was this priest who baptized Archbishop John MacHale of Tuam in 1791 and who went on to be hanged for his support of the rebels during the 1798 rebellion in County Mayo.[45] This is the same John MacHale who is used for comic purposes in 'Grace' when he is recalled by Mr Cunningham holding out against the doctrine of Papal Infallibility until 'at last the Pope himself stood up and declared infallibility a dogma of the Church *ex cathedra*'. At that point 'John MacHale, who had been arguing and arguing against it, stood up and shouted with the voice of a lion: *Credo!*' (D 169)

It is plain to see why 'The Priest of Adergool' might have so irked the increasingly anti-clerical and anti-romantic nationalist Joyce of 1902. In its sincere but clunky doggerel it is typical of its genre – the sentimental nationalist ballad that had reached its apogee under Thomas Davis and his *Nation* newspaper in the 1840s. Joyce shows himself conscious of this lineage in the opening sentence of his review when he writes that 'These are the verses of a writer lately dead, whom many consider the Davis of the latest national movement.'[46] It is likely that Joyce was taking his lead here from Griffith, both from his obituary of Rooney and from his declaration in the preface to Rooney's *Poems and Ballads* regarding 'the greatness and the work of this man, to whom more than to any other, since Thomas Davis,

43 See Patrick Bradley, 'William Rooney – A Sketch of his Career', in Rooney, *Poems and Ballads*, xxiv.

44 Rooney, *Poems and Ballads*, 142.

45 See John Wyse Jackson and Bernard McGinley, *James Joyce's 'Dubliners': An Annotated Edition* (London: Sinclair-Stevenson, 1993), 167.

46 Joyce, 'An Irish Poet', 61.

Ireland owes the saving of her soul'.[47] It will not be necessary to quote the poem in full as the following extract will be sufficient to illustrate the nature of Joyce's allusions to it:

> There's someone at the window. Tap! Tap!
>   tap, anew;
> Sharp thro' the silent midnight it speeds the
>   cottage through;
> 'Some poor soul speeding onward, some sudden
>   call to go
> Unshriven on the pathway we all of us must
>   know.'
> Thus muses he, that sagart, as from his
>   couch he flies
> And opens full the window where wonder-
>   widened eyes
> Look into his, and accents with haste all
>   husky spake –
> 'The French are in Killala – and all the land's awake![48]

Rooney's fascination with the French landing at Killala in August 1798 is, of course, not the only, nor the best-known, of Irish literature's engagements with this final invasion of Ireland. That honour lies with *Cathleen Ni Houlihan*, the nationalist play that Yeats chose to dedicate to the memory of William Rooney.

It has long been argued by critics wishing to read 'The Dead' as partly informed by a series of allusions to previous texts that Joyce is referencing *Cathleen Ni Houlihan* when he has Gretta Conroy say of Michael Furey's death: 'I think he died for me' (*D* 220).[49] This statement of Gretta's chimes with a moment in the Yeats/Lady Gregory play when the title character, the old woman who embodies Ireland, is singing about 'yellow-haired Donough' who was hanged in Galway gaol. When asked by young Michael Gillane, the boy who she is trying to prize from his family in order to assist the French at Killala, what it was that led to Donough's death, the old woman replies, 'He died for love of me: many a man has died for love of

---

47 Griffith, 'To the Reader', xi.

48 William Rooney, 'The Priest of Adergool: An Incident of the Connacht Rising', in Rooney, *Poems and Ballads*, 141–2.

49 The first to make this connection was Adaline Glasheen. It was subsequently taken up by Richard Ellmann in his biography of Joyce, and more recently the case for an allusion to *Cathleen Ni Houlihan* within 'The Dead' has been convincingly restated by Kevin Barry, who sees in the story 'a forceful rewriting of Yeats and Gregory by Joyce'. See Kevin Barry, *The Dead* (Cork: Cork University Press, 2001), 99.

me.'⁵⁰ And that, as discussed in the previous chapter, is by no means Joyce's only nod to the events of August 1798 in County Mayo.

Read through the lens of 'The Priest of Adergool', the famous first sentence of the final paragraph of 'The Dead' is another oblique reference to 1798: 'A few light taps upon the pane made him turn to the window' (*D* 223). These are the same taps heard by Father Conroy in Rooney's poem. For Gabriel Conroy it is the snow that makes the noise on the windowpane while for his priestly namesake it is the stones of rebels rousing him to action. But the effect on both men is similar. The taps are a signal that the west is awake. As Father Conroy, the Mayo priest, is being signalled to arise from his slumber to take up arms on behalf of his country so too Gabriel is being called westward, called to some kind of authentic action to replace the bourgeois trance that his marriage and his life have become.

Again and again in *Poems and Ballads* the Dubliner Rooney looks to the west for salvation. Almost every Irish writer of note was, of course, looking in the same direction at the turn of the nineteenth century but while the standard revivalist sentiment for Connacht was romantic and mystical, Rooney's is martial, as we see in a poem such as 'The Men of the West', another ballad of 1798, and one referenced by Joyce in the 'Sirens' episode of *Ulysses*:

> Though all the bright dreamings we cherished
>   Went down in disaster and woe,
> The spirit of old still is with us
>   That never would bend to the foe;
> And Connacht is ready whenever
>   The loud rolling tuck of the drum
> Rings out to awaken the echoes
>   And tell us – the morning has come.
> So here's to the gallant old West, boys,
> Which rallied her bravest and best,
> When Ireland was broken and bleeding,
> Hurrah, boys! Hurrah for the West.⁵¹

And in the opening stanza of 'Connacht' one is tempted to find a precursor of the dead Michael Furey and his haunting impact on Gabriel's soul:

> Dear land of brake and purple hill
> Broad lake and murmuring river;

---

50 W. B. Yeats and Lady Gregory, *Cathleen Ni Hoolihan* (Dublin: A. H. Bullen, 1902), 19.

51 William Rooney, 'The Men of the West', in Rooney, *Poems and Ballads*, 148. On Joyce's use of this ballad in *Ulysses*, see Zack Bowen, *Musical Allusions in the Works of James Joyce: Early Poetry Through Ulysses* (Albany, NY: State University of New York Press, 1974), 164.

> Dark eyes and vengeance darker still
> Strong hope that flickers never,
> I greet thee, fallen though thy state
> And numbed thine ancient vigour
> Still through thy glens, of good and great
> Stalks many a ghostly figure.[52]

One is reminded of Gabriel's unwillingness to acknowledge Gretta's origins in the face of Miss Ivors' efforts to persuade him to join her and her nationalist friends on a trip to Aran: 'She's from Connacht, isn't she? – Her people are, said Gabriel shortly' (*D* 189). Gabriel will soon regret the disavowal.

It was not in poetry alone that Rooney looked westward for inspiration. In a lecture delivered by him to the Celtic Literary Society in Dublin on 20 January 1899 he spoke in the most exalted terms of the west's purity, its perfect Irishness. Unlike other Irish Irelanders – such as Molly Ivors perhaps – Rooney was quite willing to accept that such a thing as Irish literature written in English was a possibility, so long as it be 'simple and direct'. 'No mystification, no introspective or metaphysical ramblings, can', continued Rooney, 'pass current for Celtic style or spirit'. Rooney's 'Celtic note', then, is very different from Little Chandler's dreamy aesthetics, which Joyce mocks in 'A Little Cloud'; the direct style Rooney demands is closer to Joyce than to Yeats. Rooney then goes on to describe what he calls 'the Celt of to-day' and gives the Irish of the west his greatest regard:

> He, no doubt, has lost much of the simplicity, most of the superstition, and, in great measure, of the optimism of old times, but, in the main, he is the same individual who has been contesting the supremacy of this island for centuries. This is true of the Irishman who has come within the influence of English ideas; it is a million times truer of the men beyond the Shannon and the Galtees, the clansmen of Erris and Inishowen. For them, looking westward over the tumbling waves of the Atlantic, Hy Brasil still comes up on the sunset, for them still the raths and duns are music-full [...] Amongst these people, and in their thoughts, is the real heart of Ireland, the Ireland untouched by time, still fresh and verdant.[53]

This vision of the utopian west is the one so beloved of many revivalists but it is also the west of rebellion, still carrying the torch of republicanism a century after the French landing.

If Joyce is sensitive to the allure of the 1798 rebellion and its evocative power in *Dubliners*, then by the time of composing *Ulysses* the Rising's

52 William Rooney, 'Connacht', in Rooney, *Poems and Ballads*, 149.
53 William Rooney, *Prose Writings* (Dublin and Waterford: M. H. Gill and Son, n. d. [1902]), 68–70.

impact can be seen to have come to a settled maturity in his imagination. Kevin Whelan has done more than any critic of recent years to demonstrate this particular Joycean interest, seeing 1798 at a hidden, reverberative level in 'The Dead' and openly on display in *Ulysses*, coming to a head in the 'Wandering Rocks' episode through the musings of Tom Kernan.[54] Kernan, loyal to the British administration, thinks about the men of '98 and of their successor, Robert Emmet, as he walks around Dublin's south inner city. Though disagreeing with the republican objectives of these rebels, he likes to think of them as gentlemen and is particularly fond of one of their leaders, Lord Edward Fitzgerald: 'Fine dashing young nobleman. Good stock, of course' (*U* 309). He then thinks of one of the best-known political ballads of '98, 'The Memory of the Dead' by John Kells Ingram, a song of which his friend Ben Dollard is known to give a masterly rendition – or so Kernan mistakenly thinks.[55] This memory is followed by what we must assume is a quote from the song: '*At the siege of Ross did my father fall*' (*U* 310). This, in fact, is an error on Kernan's part as the quotation is from another well-known ballad of '98, 'The Croppy Boy' – the song that will form the musical centrepiece of the next chapter, 'Sirens'. Ingram's 'The Memory of the Dead' is also alluded to during Gabriel's after-dinner speech in 'The Dead': 'let us hope, at least, that in gatherings such as this we shall still speak of them with pride and affection, still cherish in our hearts the memory of those dead' (*D* 204). It is likely, given Dollard's singing of 'The Croppy Boy' in 'Sirens', that Kernan does not misremember the line but rather the title of the song.

Before moving on to 'Sirens' another episode from 'Wandering Rocks' ought to be briefly considered if we are to come to some greater clarity about the identity of Father Conroy. Along with Tom Kernan and several others, one of the figures to be seen walking through Dublin in this chapter is Master Patrick Aloysius Dignam, son of Paddy Dignam, buried that morning in Glasnevin cemetery. Young Patrick tries desperately to get his head around the significance of what has happened to him and to his family:

> My father is dead. He told me to be a good son to ma. I couldn't hear the other things he said but I saw his tongue and his teeth trying to say it better. Poor pa. That was Mr Dignam, my father. I hope he's in purgatory now because he went to confession to father Conroy on Saturday night. (*U* 324)

54 See Whelan, 'Memories of "The Dead"', 59–97.
55 Ingram's 'The Memory of the Dead' is, like A. P. Graves's 'Father O'Flynn', included in Yeats's *A Book of Irish Verse* (1895).

This is the first reference to Father Conroy to be found in *Ulysses*. This must be the same Father Conroy later to be seen eating chops in Sandymount, Paddy Dignam's home parish. Whether or not he is – as Leopold believes him to be – Constantine Conroy does not affect what Joyce is trying to achieve here, that is, a delicate allusive connection based on the memories and songs of 1798 between 'The Priest of Adergool' and 'The Croppy Boy', between 'The Dead' and *Ulysses*, between 1798 and 1904.

Both 'The Priest of Adergool' and 'The Croppy Boy' commemorate moments in the 1798 rebellion, one in County Mayo, the other in County Wexford. Both ballads have priests at their centre, albeit a false one in 'The Croppy Boy'. When young Patrick Dignam thinks of his late father, 'I hope he is in purgatory now because he went to confession to father Conroy on Saturday night', he is being used by Joyce as a link between the two ballads. At the centre of 'The Croppy Boy' lies a scene of treachery in which the eponymous young rebel of the ballad attends confession in part to rid himself of guilty memories:

> The youth has knelt to tell his sins:
> '*Nomine Dei*,' the youth begins!
> At '*mea culpa*' he beats his breast,
> And in broken murmers he speaks the rest.
> 'At the siege of Ross did my father fall,
> And at Gorey my loving brothers all.
> I alone am left of my name and race;
> I will go to Wexford and take their place.
> I cursed three times since last Easter day;
> At mass time once I went to play;
> I passed the churchyard one day in haste,
> And forgot to pray for my mother's rest.[56]

The boy having confessed, his confessor promptly reveals himself to be a redcoat yeoman and the boy's tragic fate is sealed. The song contains within it prompts to two major threads that run through *Ulysses*: the guilt carried by Stephen Dedalus who refused to pray at his dying mother's bedside, and Leopold Bloom's memories and regrets over his dead son Rudy:

> All gone. All fallen. At the siege of Ross his father, at Gorey all his brothers fell. To Wexford, we are the boys of Wexford, he would. Last of his name and race.

---

56 'Carroll Malone' (W. B. McBurney) wrote the original song, 'The Croppy Boy', first published in *The Nation* (January 1845). See also http://www.james-joyce-music.com/song16_lyrics.html (accessed 19 November 2011).

I too. Last my race. Milly young student. Well, my fault perhaps. No son.
Rudy. Too late now. (*U* 367)

But the song, in its storyline of croppies, rebellion and the figure of a priest,
is also a subtle reminder of, and return to, William Rooney's Father Conroy.

There is one other way in which the ghost of Father Conroy is present
in 'Sirens', and that is via the 'tap, tap, tap' of 'The Priest of Adergool' that
I have already suggested is present in the final paragraph of 'The Dead'.
For Father Conroy the tapping was of stones at his window, for Gabriel
Conroy the sound was made by snowflakes, also at his window; in *Ulysses*
the sound is made by the cane of a blind stripling piano tuner as he returns
to the music room of the Ormond Hotel to retrieve his tuning fork. This
is revealed to us, if not as repeated noise *on* a window, then *by* a window:
'Tap. Tap. A stripling, blind, with a tapping cane came taptaptapping by
Daly's window where a mermaid hair all streaming (but he couldn't see)
blew whiffs of a mermaid (blind couldn't), mermaid, coolest whiff of all' (*U*
374). Over the last quarter of 'Sirens' the text is frequently disrupted by the
word 'Tap'. At first it is just the solitary word but it is soon repeated and,
as the chapter draws to a close, becomes more and more insistent, inter-
twining itself with Ben Dollard's singing of 'The Croppy Boy':

> Tap. Tap. Tap.
> Pray for him, prayed the bass of Dollard. You who hear in peace. Breathe a
> prayer, drop a tear, good men, good people. He was the croppy boy. (*U* 370)

Three pages later Joyce gives us a little nod to the literary source of the
tapping:

> Tap. Tap. Tap. Tap. Tap. Tap. Tap. Tap.
> Bloom went by Barry's. Wish I could. Wait. That wonderworker if I had. [...]
> But for example the chap that wallops the big drum. His vocation: Mickey
> Rooney's band. (*U* 373)

Here the name Rooney is briefly brought out into the open and then,
finally, as the chapter draws to a close and the last 'tap' is sounded, we are
linked back into thoughts of 1798 and the United Irishmen:

> Tap. A youth entered a lonely Ormond hall.
> Bloom viewed a gallant pictured hero in Lionel Marks's window. Robert
> Emmet's last words. (*U* 375)

And thus, yet again, Joyce has put the rather unpromising material of
Rooney's poetry to good use in his own writing in order to deepen its
allusive texture, thus providing it with greater musical resonance.

Before moving on to a more general review of varying critical approaches to Joyce's richly allusive style let us consider one more poem of which I believe Joyce is conscious that marries both the taps on the windowpane and the journey westward. The poem, 'The Brown Wind of Connaught' (again, brown equals death), is, perhaps not coincidentally, by another revivalist who died tragically young, Ethna Carbery. Another of Carbery's revivalist poems, 'Shiela Ni Gara', is referenced in *Ulysses*.[57] She, like Rooney, is now also largely forgotten. 'The Brown Wind of Connaught' was published under her married name of Anna MacManus in a posthumous collection titled *The Four Winds of Eirinn* (1902). The last three stanzas are particularly germane:

> The brown wind of Connaught,
> When Dermot came to woo,
> (*The brown wind of Connaught*),
> It heard his whispers too;
> And while my wheel goes whirring,
> It taps on my window-pane,
> Till I open wide to the Dead outside,
> And the sea-salt misty rain.
>
> The Brown wind of Connaught
> With women wailed one day
> (*The brown wind of Connaught*)
> For a wreck in Galway Bay;
> And many the dark-faced fishers
> That gathered their nets in fear,
> But one sank straight to the Ghostly Gate –
> And he was my Dermot Dear.
>
> The brown wind of Connaught
> Still keening in the dawn,
> (*The brown wind of Connaught*),
> For my true love long gone.
> Oh, cold green wave of danger,
> Drift him a restful sleep
> O'er his young black head on its lowly bed,
> While his weary wake I keep.[58]

---

57 See Gifford and Seidman, *'Ulysses' Annotated*, 336. Shiela Ni Gara is, like Cathleen Ni Houlihan, a personification of Ireland.

58 Anna MacManus [Ethna Carbery], *The Four Winds of Eirinn*, ed. Seumas MacManus (Dublin: M. H. Gill and Son, 1902), 35–6.

Though this poem has none of the strident patriotism of Rooney's work, it is once again, as in 'The Dead', marked by communication between the living and the dead. We have Galway as the locus for that death and loss, and we have, again, the taps on the windowpane. 'The Brown Wind of Connaught', like 'The Priest of Adergool', is not a great poem, but something about it appealed to Joyce. Why, then, does Joyce so consistently return to the words of others to create his great masterpieces?

Réamh Scéal, Reservoir and Reverberation: The Making of 'The Dead'

If Yeats, Graves, Rooney and Carbery are phantom presences in *Dubliners*, who else might be there? The answer to that question depends on who you ask. Paul Muldoon, for instance, has written that 'One could be forgiven for thinking that all of Irish, and indeed, almost all of world literature had been produced merely as a *reamh sceal*, a prelude or preliminary piece, to the work of the greatest of all Irish writers, James Joyce.' In the specific instance of 'The Dead', he argues strongly for the presence of Samuel Ferguson's *Congal* as well as pointing to what he calls numerous other 'significant feeder-springs into the great reservoir of Joyce's short story'.[59] On the other hand, a critic such as T. H. Gibbons is much queasier about pulling *Dubliners* apart in an effort to find patterns, symbols and allusions beneath the surface. Those who would read it in such a way, he argues, are guilty of 'employing a vocabulary sufficiently "general" or "ambivalent" to give the appearance of equating specific details', and thus, 'allow us to construct apparent analogies between any two events, real or fictional'.[60] Similarly, Samuel Beckett, when thinking about how one might go about a reading of *Finnegans Wake*, warned against seeing overly easy parallels. 'The danger', he wrote, 'is in the neatness of identifications.'[61] While Beckett's words must inform any reading of Joyce's complex texts, this study is drawn towards Muldoon's position. 'It is always unwise', noted James Atherton, one of Joyce's most astute critics, 'to say that Joyce only means one thing.'[62] There is no doubt that Joyce offers unusually tempting

---

59 Muldoon, *To Ireland, I*, 50.

60 T. H. Gibbons, '*Dubliners* and the Critics', *Critical Quarterly*, 9.2 (Summer 1967), 183.

61 Samuel Beckett, 'Dante... Bruno. Vico... Joyce', in Beckett et al., *Our Exagmination round his Factification for Incamination of Work in Progress* (1929) (London: Faber and Faber, 1972), 3.

62 James Atherton, *The Books at the Wake: A Study of Literary Allusions in James Joyce's 'Finnegans Wake'* (London: Faber and Faber, 1959), 32.

ground for critics in search of allusions, and progress must be made with caution. One example of differing critical interpretations from 'The Dead' will serve to demonstrate just how fraught the search can be.

Here Gabriel and Gretta have retired to their hotel room in the Gresham where Gretta has tearfully recounted the story of Michael Furey, his singing of 'The Lass of Aughrim' and his subsequent untimely death. Now she is asleep, her clothes are scattered and Gabriel's disillusion has set in: 'A petticoat string dangled to the floor. One boot stood upright, its limp upper fallen down: the fellow of it lay upon its side. He wondered at his riot of emotions an hour before' (*D* 223–4). Muldoon sees this moment as a nod to perhaps the most celebrated controversy of the Revival and one that captured Joyce's attention in Trieste, the so-called '*Playboy* riots' stemming from the original staging of J. M. Synge's *The Playboy of the Western World* in 1907. 'This seems to me', writes Muldoon, 'to be an extraordinarily effective fusion of the public and the private, the "Playboy" *riot* and the "*riot* of emotions".'[63] Tom Paulin, on the other hand, sees this moment as a homage to *Robinson Crusoe*, a novel that Joyce thought of as the English *Ulysses*. Thinking specifically of the image of Gretta's two boots, Paulin writes: 'This picks up one of the seminal moments in the history of Western realism, when Crusoe, newly landed on the island, laments his drowned comrades [...] and says "I never saw them afterwards, or any sign of them, except three of their hats, one cap, and two shoes that were not fellows."'[64]

Both interpretations may be right: 'riot' is a very deliberately utilized and emotive word, and the fact that Joyce chooses it in the same year as the *Playboy* riots makes Muldoon's argument persuasive. As for Paulin, we know that Defoe was one of Joyce's favourite writers and *Robinson Crusoe* one of his favourite books, as is evidenced by his 1912 lecture on Defoe delivered in Trieste. Paulin provides a nice description of his critical methodology in finding allusions such as this. 'It's less an obscure piece of knowledge', he writes, 'than finding something hidden in the daylight, but that process is picky, at times obsessive, a matter of trusting hunches and intuitions, and weighing particular words that for reasons that aren't immediately apparent seem to stick.'[65] That such differing interpretations of one tiny moment as those provided by these two Irish poets are possible stands testament to Joyce's breadth and complexity.

As briefly mentioned in my introduction, the first critics to attempt a serious non-naturalistic, exegetical reading of *Dubliners* were Richard Levin

---

63 Muldoon, *To Ireland, I*, 58.
64 Tom Paulin, *Crusoe's Secret: The Aesthetics of Dissent* (London: Faber and Faber, 2005), 297.
65 Paulin, *Crusoe's Secret*, xii.

and Charles Shattuck in a 1944 article titled 'First Flight to Ithaca'. They argued that *Dubliners*, like *Ulysses*, ought to be read using the scaffolding of Homer's *Odyssey*. Using this method they equated each of the fifteen stories to an episode in Homer; so, for example, 'The Sisters' is read as a version of Telemachus in Ithaca, and 'The Dead' is Odysseus' destruction of the wooers and reunion with Penelope. While attracting little support and a good deal of hostility, the theory did work as a kind of launching pad for a new generation of Joyceans, as Peter K. Garratt argues in 1968:

> Although few students have fully accepted this thesis, it has served as a stimulus or point of departure for several studies which have also attempted to interpret *Dubliners* in terms of some 'secret technique' or hidden symbolism. [...] There is as yet no critical agreement on how to read *Dubliners*.[66]

That last statement still holds true today despite the grip of realism. An issue for readers of *Dubliners* is that Joyce left no skeleton key for access to the book as he did for his later novels, with studies such as Stuart Gilbert's *James Joyce's 'Ulysses'* (1931) and the multi-authored *Our Exagmination round his Factification for Incamination of Work in Progress* (1929). Donald Torchiana has pondered Joyce's reasons for this decision: 'I suspect, however, that something like the unrelenting artistic independence of his youth kept Joyce from making such like admissions about *Dubliners*, although *Ulysses* does clear up much in that book.'[67] This lack of any key to the stories has, inevitably, led to a multiplicity of interpretations.

The greatest of all Joyceans, Richard Ellmann, in his biography of the writer, pointed to the presence of three hidden texts in the fabric of 'The Dead'. The first of these, Thomas Moore's ballad 'Oh, Ye Dead', in which the living and the dead communicate, was originally suggested by Stanislaus as an influence. The second returns to classical Greece and sees the twelfth book of the *Iliad* as being behind aspects of the story's final paragraph. The third text is a novel, *Vain Fortune*, by Joyce's contemporary, George Moore, a book that, like 'The Dead', features a married couple at an emotional crossroads. Joyce's methodology was, writes Ellmann, 'very like T. S. Eliot's, the imaginative absorption of stray material'.[68] Joyce had, notes Ellmann, overpraised *Vain Fortune* in his 1901 pamphlet 'The Day of the Rabblement'. He had also alluded to another book of Moore's, *Parnell and his Island*, as discussed in my opening chapter. In fact of all writers from the period of

66 Peter K. Garrett, 'Introduction', in Garrett (ed.), *Twentieth-Century Interpretations of 'Dubliners'* (Englewood Cliffs, NJ: Prentice Hall, 1968), 6–7.
67 Torchiana, *Backgrounds to Joyce's 'Dubliners'*, 17.
68 Ellmann, *James Joyce*, 250.

the Revival, Joyce's attitudes to Moore are the most complicated, swinging from admiration, in the case of *Evelyn Innes*, to mockery, in the case of *The Untilled Field*; Moore was the best-represented Irish writer in Joyce's Trieste library. This interest in Moore's work makes Ellmann's explanation of Joyce's allusive technique rather puzzling. 'The method', writes Ellmann, 'did not please Joyce very much because he considered it not imaginative enough, but it was the only way he could work.'[69]

Such an explanation hardly seems satisfactory for several reasons. First, the notion that Joyce – perhaps the most innovative writer in the English language – would go to the trouble of writing a story using a method he did not like or trust does not ring true. Secondly, Joyce did not see 'originality' as a necessary ingredient of great work. *Ulysses* and even more so *Finnegans Wake* become great cacophonies of competing texts and voices, from newspaper advertisements to music hall ditties to the Bible. In 'Ithaca', when Bloom describes his idea for an advertisement, he attempts to demonstrate that 'originality, though producing its own reward, does not invariably conduce to success' (*U* 800). And this was an outlook shared by Joyce as he makes clear in a letter to the composer George Antheil in 1931. 'I am quite content', he writes, when thinking of collaborating with the Frenchman on the writing of a libretto, 'to go down to posterity as a scissors and paste man for that seems to me a harsh but not unjust description.'[70] Thirdly, and most importantly for those trying to understand Joyce's use of allusion in *Dubliners*, subsequent critics have gone far beyond *Vain Fortune* as a source text for 'The Dead' and demonstrated that the story may be as full of competing chatter as the later novels. Far from being a technique that 'did not please' Joyce, then, it was when he wrote 'The Dead' in 1907, and remained for the rest of his life, the method of writing that he most favoured.

More convincing explanations of Joyce's early allusive method come from three later critics: Kelleher, Muldoon and Whelan. Kelleher has written of 'The Dead' that it 'is intricate and symbolistic beneath a surface of what seems calm, controlled narcissism – which may be why no interpretation of it has been wholly satisfactory to most students'.[71] Key to his reading of the story is a suggestion that it contains a series of references to the Old Irish saga, *Togail Bruidne Da Derga*. Maria Tymoczko, in her brilliant work of scholarship *The Irish 'Ulysses'* (1994), has given consider-

69 Ellmann, *James Joyce*, 250.
70 James Joyce to George Antheil (3 January 1931), in Joyce, *Letters*, ed. Stuart Gilbert (London: Faber and Faber, 1957), 297.
71 Kelleher, 'Irish History and Mythology', 40.

able weight to this theory and gone a great deal further than Kelleher in uncovering the importance of Irish mythology to Joyce as source material. Muldoon's *To Ireland, I* (2000) is a most ambitious attempt at reading the early Joyce as a writer peculiarly attached to allusive prose. Like the later Joyce, Muldoon has to come up with a neologism, 'conglomewriting', to describe the technique at play in 'The Dead'. Muldoon is heavily influenced by Kelleher, agreeing with the presence of *Togail Bruidne Da Derga* but going on to remark on its presence at a wider and a deeper level throughout the story. He then goes on to posit the existence of a whole host of other, more contemporary texts in 'The Dead'. Among the authors who he finds present with some degree of certainty are Samuel Ferguson, A. P. Graves, Standish O'Grady, J. M. Synge and Lady Gregory. He also tendentiously suggests Eibhlín Dubh Ní Chonaill's eighteenth-century lament, *Caoineadh Airt Uí Laoghaire*, Jeremiah Curtin's *Myths and Folklore of Ireland*, Alfred Nutt's *Studies on the Legend of the Holy Grail* (1888) and Osborn Bergin's *Fled Bricrenn: The Feast of Bricriu* (1899).

Finally, and most recently, Kevin Whelan muses on the literary sources for 'The Dead' and includes Thomas Moore's 'Oh, Ye Dead', Bret Harte's *Gabriel Conroy* and, somewhat more tentatively, James Clarence Mangan's 'Siberia'. He goes on to convincingly show that both George Moore's *A Drama in Muslin* (1886) and *Vain Fortune* (1892) as well as Sheridan Le Fanu's *All in the Dark* (1865) are there. Whelan links the snow of 'The Dead' to a Galway-based scene in *A Drama in Muslin* in which the character Alice Barton stares at the snow-covered landscape in despair; and in Le Fanu's novel he points to a direct link between the episode in 'The Dead' when Gretta stands on the stairs listening to 'The Lass of Aughrim' and a very similar moment in *All in the Dark*: 'She had quite vanished up the stairs and he still held the door handle in his fingers and stood looking up the vacant steps and, as it were, listening to distant music.'[72] As such, Whelan reads 'The Dead' as being 'structured around a matrix of symbolism'. 'Joyce's language', continues Whelan, 'was therefore intensely and consistently reverberative, an effect heightened by the constant imaginative absorption and reworking of literary precedents.'[73] In this conclusion, Whelan mirrors Ellmann's belief that Joyce's technique is akin to T. S. Eliot's allusive practices. The difference between the earlier and later critic is one of emphasis: Whelan sees the Joycean methodology in 'The Dead' as deliberate and effective, Ellmann as opportunistic and unsatisfactory. Whatever the effect, the allusiveness is there. What, then, was Joyce up to?

72 Quoted in Whelan, 'Memories of "The Dead"', 75.
73 Whelan, 'Memories of "The Dead"', 75.

Making Hares of Us All: Joyce's Motivations

Why does Joyce employ the allusive style in writing *Dubliners*? Certainly it is not, as Ellmann argued, that he could not think of a better approach – it is all far too deliberate and consistent for that. One very clear point of departure in trying to answer the question brings us back to a text that predates 'The Dead' and also several other of the stories that make up *Dubliners*: *Stephen Hero*. This abandoned novel has a youthful frankness in its discussion of aesthetic practice that is often absent in the more mature Joyce. While the novel it would eventually become, *A Portrait of the Artist as a Young Man*, sees Stephen defer to Thomas Aquinas for formulation of his theory of art, *Stephen Hero* is more concerned with the ongoing struggle between two critical schools, romanticism and classicism. And it is the latter outlook that wins out. Stephen, despite his own sense of separateness from the herd, rejects the romantic notion of poetic inspiration or of the individual organic genius and sees instead that, as Yeats was fond of quoting, art is art because it is not nature. Stephen, we are told, 'believed that every moment of inspiration must be paid for in advance. He was not convinced of the truth of the saying "The poet is born, not made" but he was quite sure of the truth of this at least: "The poem is made not born."' As a result of such thinking, the bohemian image of poet as hero, as exemplified by Byron, ought to be rejected: 'The burgher notion of the poet Byron in undress pouring out verses just as a city fountain pours out water seemed to him characteristic of most popular judgments on esthetic matters' (*SH* 37).

With the romantic temper brushed aside, Stephen goes on to provide a memorable definition of its classical opponent that tells us much about Joyce's technique, and about the writer who would, by the 1930s, he happy to call himself a scissors-and-paste man:

> But society is itself, he conceived, the complex body in which certain laws are involved and overwrapped and he therefore proclaimed as the realm of the poet the realm of these unalterable laws. Such a theory might easily have led its deviser to the acceptance of spiritual anarchy in literature had he not at the same time insisted on the classical style. A classical style, he said, is the syllogism of art, the only legitimate process from one world to another. Classicism is not the manner of any fixed age: it is a constant state of the artistic mind. It is a temper of security and satisfaction and patience. The romantic temper, so often and so grievously misinterpreted and not more by others than by its own, is an insecure, unsatisfied, impatient temper which sees no fit abode here for its ideals and chooses therefore to behold them under insensible figures. As a result of this choice it comes to disregard certain limitations. Its figures are blown to wild adventures,

lacking the gravity of solid bodies, and the mind that has conceived them ends by disowning them. The classical temper on the other hand, ever mindful of limitations, chooses rather to bend upon these present things and so to work upon them and fashion them that the quick intelligence may go beyond them to their meaning which is still unuttered. In this method the sane and joyful spirit issues forth and achieves imperishable perfection, nature assisting with her goodwill and thanks. (SH 82–3)

Stephen's rumination permits us to go at least some of the way towards understanding Joyce's penchant for allusion, his willingness to rework the work of others, even if that work seems at first unpromising. Rather than await the illusory Byronic moment, Joyce took the likes of Thomas Davis, William Rooney and George Moore and, as Stephen urged, began to 'work upon them and fashion them that the quick intelligence may go beyond them to their meaning'. As Ellmann writes in *The Consciousness of Joyce*, his subject 'felt more than most writers how interconnected literature is, how to press one button is to press them all'. Ellmann goes on to point to Joyce's possession of a volume likely to have sustained him in this outlook: 'In his library was Georges Polti's *Les Trente-six situations dramatiques*, in which hundreds of works, and some incidents of history and modern life, were conflated to show that all made do with three dozen basic plots.'[74]

While the classical temper wins what must be taken as a serious joust with the romantic, there is also an element of fun in Joyce's recycling. It might be argued, even, that what he is in part doing by drawing on the work of other writers is playing a sort of game with readers and critics alike, that he is, like A. P. Graves's Father O'Flynn, making hares of us all with his erudition and intelligence. He would not be the first nor the last writer to take this approach. Robert Frost, for one, was happy to hold his hands up to the charge and admit an element of fun in the allusive technique:

> A poet need make no apology
> Because his works are one anthology
> Of other poets' best creations
> Let him be nothing but quotations
> (That's not as cynic as it sounds)
> The game is one like Hare and Hounds
> To entertain the critic pack
> The poet has to leave a track
> Of torn up scraps of prior poets.[75]

74 Ellmann, *Consciousness of Joyce*, 48.
75 Robert Frost, *Collected Poems, Prose, and Plays*, ed. Richard Poirier and Mark Richardson (New York: Library of America, 1995), 542.

One is reminded here of Joyce's letter to Harriet Shaw Weaver written during the final furlongs of his composition of *Ulysses* in which he worries over his sanity, and describes his head as being 'full of pebbles and rubbish and broken matches and lots of glass picked up "most everywhere".[76]

Joyce liked gameplaying and he liked the idea of keeping us all guessing long after he was gone. So, as *Finnegans Wake* ends at the beginning and begins at the end and thus becomes a kind of machine for perpetual motion, so too in *Dubliners* Joyce may be attempting to create a book of books. It may be that some day we will all be reading *Dubliners* as we have become accustomed to reading *Ulysses* and *Finnegans Wake*, with the assistance of a set of annotations the size of a telephone book. 'Joyce was so indiscriminate in his use of allusion', writes one critic, 'so uninhibited by his audience's lack of knowledge, that much of his writing remains unintelligible, resisting our many attempts at exegesis.'[77] That critic's frustration in mind, one suspects that Joyce is enjoying a private joke in his very first published short story, 'The Sisters', as it appeared in the *Irish Homestead* in 1904 when he writes that it is 'often annoying the way people will blunder on what you have elaborately planned for'.[78] This phrase disappears from subsequent versions: again a matter of Joyce getting rid of the evidence?

Two final reasons for Joyce's allusiveness need consideration, and they are two directly opposing explanations – homage and attack. This chapter pointed earlier to Joyce's admiration for two of Yeats's mystical stories and considered John Paul Riquelme's theory that Yeats's tales of Red Hanrahan are alluded to in 'The Dead'. Riquelme argues that the allusion is there in order to covertly locate Joyce within the folktale tradition. While there's no doubt that Joyce admired aspects of Yeats, it is hard to go along with Riquelme here. The stories that make up *Dubliners*, after all, are as far from folktales as you could wish to read. The Yeats stories that Joyce openly enjoyed had their origins more in mysticism than in the folk past. And Joyce had elsewhere been quite openly hostile to any revivification of the past, this aspect of his worldview most openly, and most memorably, stated in 'Ireland, Island of Saints and Sages': 'Just as ancient Egypt is dead, so is ancient Ireland. Its dirge has been sung and the seal set upon its gravestone.'[79] There is no doubt that Joyce is fascinated with the past but

76 Joyce to Harriet Shaw Weaver (24 June 1921), in Joyce, *Letters*, ed. Gilbert, 167.

77 Claire A. Culleton, *Names and Naming in Joyce* (Madison, WI: University of Wisconsin Press, 1994), 38.

78 Stephen Daedalus [James Joyce], 'The Sisters', *Irish Homestead*, 13 August 1904. Reproduced in James Joyce, *Dubliners*, ed. John Kelly (New York: Alfred A. Knopf Everyman's Library, 1991), 267.

79 Joyce, 'Ireland, Island of Saints and Sages', 125.

he gravely doubts if there is an older Ireland that can be usefully revived. In this, he cuts against the dominant Irish literary aesthetic of his day, and so while Yeats, Rooney, Graves, Moore, Davis, Carbery and others can ghost in and out of his writing, it seems unlikely that he plays with their work in order to praise.

In fact, Joyce's use of other writers' work in 'The Dead' might usefully be contrasted with the use of 'The Dead' by subsequent generations of Irish artists. Such usage would make an interesting study in its own right, but to name but a few instances, one might look to Derek Mahon's poem 'The Snow Party', John McGahern's short story 'The Wine Breath', or, most clearly of all, Edna O'Brien's debut novel *The Country Girls* (1960), which contains the following very open allusion to her beloved Joyce:

> We drove along the Limerick road and while we were driving it began to snow. Softly the flakes fell. Softly and obliquely against the windscreen. It fell on the hedges and on the trees behind the hedges, and on the treeless fields in the distance, and slowly and quietly it changed the colour and the shape of things, until everything outside the motorcar had a mantle of white soft down.[80]

This is homage, straight and true, and not at all of the same order as Joyce's allusions to other texts. If praise and recognition is not Joyce's aim, then might he be after something more malicious?

Muldoon and Torchiana, though seeing quite different strands present in 'The Dead', are united in locating a common motivation on Joyce's part. The primary reason suggested by Muldoon for the creation of this strange Joycean collage is as 'a critique of late nineteenth-century Irish cultural nationalism'.[81] Donald Torchiana proffers a similar theory regarding Joyce's cut-and-paste methodology: 'The method, then, in part, has been to mock the literary ideals of the Revival and to show instead the paralysis of the imagination in Ireland.'[82] Joyce's antipathy to aspects of revivalism is well documented and plain for all to see. Two stories in *Dubliners*, 'A Little Cloud' and 'A Mother', are given over to lampooning different shades of the Revival, the English-language and Gaelic wings respectively. I have already discussed Joyce's rather cruel vivisection of Little Chandler as he dreams hopelessly of writing romantic poetry in the style of the 'Celtic Note'. Joyce would have been well aware that the use of this description for the poetry produced by Yeats and his school was resented by the revivalists; it was

---

80 Edna O'Brien, *The Country Girls* (1960) (London: Penguin Books, 1963), 99.
81 Muldoon, *To Ireland, I*, 50.
82 Torchiana, *Backgrounds for Joyce's 'Dubliners'*, 2–3.

a term used repeatedly by D. P. Moran to attack and belittle. Writing to Moran as editor of *The Leader* on its foundation in 1900, Yeats was clear on the matter: 'You have been misled, doubtless, by reading what some indiscreet friend or careless opponent has written, into supposing that I have ever used the phrases "Celtic note" and "Celtic Renaissance" except as a quotation from others.'[83]

In 'A Mother' the Gaelic Revival, of which Molly Ivors of 'The Dead' is a disciple, gets the same harsh treatment. The opening line of this story about an ambitious mother and a series of disappointing concerts staged by a revivalist society works as a nicely weighted sneer at the movement: 'Mr Holohan, assistant secretary of the *Eire Abu* Society, had been walking up and down Dublin for nearly a month, with his hands and pockets full of dirty pieces of paper, arranging about the series of concerts' (*D* 134). Kathleen Kearney, who we later discover is a friend of Molly Ivors, is hired to play piano accompaniment for the concerts. As usual, Joyce has not picked his names idly: the impresario and the piano player together would be 'Kathleen Holohan', a reference to *Cathleen Ni Houlihan*. Except that, while the Gregory/Yeats play was heroic and rousing, Mr Holohan is a small-time promoter with a lame leg, known to his friends as Hoppy, and Kathleen Kearney is the daughter of an upwardly mobile and mercenary bourgeois: 'When the Irish Revival began to be appreciable Mrs Kearney determined to take advantage of her daughter's name and brought an Irish teacher to the house' (*D* 135). The mother, by cashing in on her daughter's name, cashes in on Ireland itself – and this, in large part, is what Joyce felt the revivalists were up to.

There are several even clearer examples of Joyce's disparagement of the Revival beyond his fiction. 'The Day of the Rabblement', that remarkable precocious pamphlet published by Joyce in 1901, sees him rejecting the whole idea of literary coteries or cliques and declaring the need for the individual's artistic autonomy. 'The Holy Office' (1904), as discussed in the previous chapter, has him alluding to Yeats's 'To Ireland in the Coming Times' in order to mock the great man and his movement. In the same year we get a singular example of Joyce's vengeful and restless spirit in a letter to Stanislaus:

> For the love of the Lord Christ change my curse-o'-God state of affairs
> Give me for Christ' sake a pen and an ink-bottle and some peace of mind

---

83 W. B. Yeats to D. P. Moran (26 August 1900), in W. B. Yeats, *Uncollected Prose 2: Reviews, Articles and Other Miscellaneous Prose 1897–1939*, ed. John P. Frayne and Colton Johnson (New York: Columbia University Press, 1976), 241.

and then, by the crucified Jaysus, if I don't sharpen that little pen and dip
it into fermented ink and write tiny little sentences about the people who
betrayed me send me to hell. After all, there are many ways of betraying
people. It wasn't only the Galilean suffered that.[84]

He was true to his threat for the rest of his life, using the pen as a scalpel
with which to slice open the reputations of his contemporaries. In 1912
'Gas From a Burner' sees him rhyming verse with arse in disgust at the
debased products of revivalism. And all of this despite the fact that many
key revivalists, among them Lady Gregory, AE and W. B. Yeats, had gone
out of their way to help him.

---

84 James Joyce to Stanislaus Joyce (24 September 1905), in Joyce, *Letters*, vol. II, 110.

Conclusion:
Protestant Power and Plates of Peas

If Joyce's weapon was the sharpened pen, England's was, he wrote, a little blunter: 'her weapons were, and are, the battering-ram, the club and the noose'.[1] At the opening of the previous chapter I looked at one book held in Joyce's Trieste library and it seems apt to conclude with another, published in the year Joyce left with Nora for the Continent: Michael Davitt's *The Fall of Feudalism in Ireland*. In his preface to that book Davitt sums up what he feels has been the injurious nature of the relationship between England and Ireland:

> Historically put, England's rule of Ireland, down to 1879, has been a system-atic opposition to the five great underlying principles of civilized society, as these lived and had their being and expression in Celtic character: love of country, which is an exceptionally strong and affectionate sentiment in the Irish heart; a racial attachment to the domestic hearthstone and to family association with land, unequalled in the social temperament of any other people; a fervent and passionate loyalty to religious faith, unsurpassed by that of any Christian nation; and a national pride in learning which once made Ireland 'a country of schools and scholars,' with a wide European reputation.
>
> The social and spiritual qualities, recognized as virtues in other lands, have been held as crimes in Ireland during many centuries by English rulers. Patriotism was made to earn the penalty of the scaffold and the prison.[2]

I have tried to consider over the previous three chapters a number of ways in which Joyce, too, felt estranged from the systems of power prevalent in the Ireland of his times. That power came primarily in the form of the Roman Catholic Church and the British Empire. The latter source had manifested

---

1 Joyce, 'Ireland, Island of Saints and Sages', in Joyce, *Occasional, Critical, and Political Writing*, ed. Kevin Barry (Oxford: Oxford University Press, 2000), 119.
2 Michael Davitt, *The Fall of Feudalism in Ireland, or the Story of the Land League Revolution* (London and New York: Harper and Brothers, 1904), xv.

itself in Joyce's Ireland via the Protestant ascendancy, and that social order
in turn, led by people such as Lady Gregory and her husband, had given
birth to the Literary Revival. No matter how much the Revival tried to pull
him in, Joyce was never going to come to heel. He was of a different caste,
and he allowed the anxieties, the hopes and the ambitions of the power-
less to live among the pages of *Dubliners* in a variety of sometimes open,
sometimes veiled, ways.

In 1967 the Irish writer Niall Montgomery tried to sum up what he felt
was Joyce's achievement: 'he expressed our lives, he expressed the culture of
Ireland, he made the Irish Literary Revival look like a lot of old rope'.[3] There
is a note of gratitude there but also of a slightly unsettling triumphalism,
the final victory in a culture war, a debate about Irish authenticity, with
its roots in the nineteenth century and its conclusion still not clear. Two
years later, and coincident with the explosion of the Troubles in Northern
Ireland, a posthumous selection of Patrick Kavanagh's prose and correspondence raised the stakes of this debate to an openly sectarian pitch.
Protestants, he wrote, 'had invented Irish Literature as a sort of national
religion and they were shy about letting Catholic outsiders in on the jag'.[4]
Another Irish poet, and a great admirer of Kavanagh, is more circumspect
about the legacy of colonialism: 'We yield to our present', writes Eavan
Boland, 'but we choose our past. In a defeated country like Ireland we
choose it over and over again, relentlessly, obsessively.'[5]

Isabella Augusta Persse of Roxborough, later Lady Gregory of Coole,
frequently, and probably unfairly, bore the brunt of Joyce's frustrations.
'Roxborough Protestantism', wrote Yeats in *Dramatis Personae*, 'was on
the side of wealth and power.' But he was keen to demonstrate that Lady
Gregory had managed, in almost saintly fashion, to rise above the bigotries
and abuses associated with her class and background. Travel abroad had
allowed her, he wrote, to stay 'beyond the reach of the bitter struggle
between landlord and tenant of the late 'seventies and early 'eighties'.
Ultimately, he argued, she had maintained the love of the people of Coole
and Kiltartan by never losing 'her sense of feudal responsibility'. Thus
he finds an old Galway man willing to tell him that 'She has been like a

---

3 Niall Montgomery, 'A Context for Mr. Joyce's Work', in Maurice Harmon (ed.), *The Celtic Master: Contributions to the first James Joyce Symposium held in Dublin, 1967* (Dublin: Dolmen, 1969), 11.

4 Patrick Kavanagh, *Lapped Furrows*, ed. Peter Kavanagh (New York: Peter Kavanagh Hand Press, 1969), 46.

5 Eavan Boland, *Object Lessons: The Life of the Woman and the Poet in Our Time* (London: Vintage, 1996), 163.

serving-maid among us. She is plain and simple, like the Mother of God, and that was the greatest lady that ever lived.'[6]

When the historian James Charles Roy sought, at the close of the twentieth century, to research the history of the Persse family in Galway he was disappointed to find the family cemetery at Moyode overgrown and unkept. Commenting on this to a local man he got a sharp reply: 'They let our people die in ditches and rot unburied by the side of the lane. I'd bulldoze the place if it was my land.'[7] Whatever the historical accuracy of this statement, the feelings run deep. For the detached historian, sociologist, author or literary scholar the era of the Big House and of the ascendancy class may be rich in source material and hold a host of larger-than-life figures, intriguing documentation and curious *objets d'art*, but for those whose ancestors went cap in hand to pay rents to the small few of a different religion, accent and bearing, the memories of humiliation and subservience can still be acute. James Joyce, though never one of those to experience the gale days of rent collection, nonetheless felt deeply the strain of life in a conquered land, a member of that restless and yet paralysed majority who people the pages of *Dubliners*, ceaselessly circling, fingering dirty pieces of paper like Hoppy Holohan of 'A Mother' or, like Lenehan of 'Two Gallants', fumbling for the price of a plate of peas.

6 W. B. Yeats, *Autobiographies*, ed. William H. O'Donnell and Douglas N. Archibald (New York: Scribner, 1999), 295.
7 Quoted in James Charles Roy, *The Fields of Athenry: A Journey Through Irish History* (Boulder, CO: Westview Press, 2001), 230.

Select Bibliography

Works by James Joyce

Joyce, James, *A Portrait of the Artist as a Young Man* (1916) (Harmondsworth: Penguin Books, 1971).

—, *The Critical Writings*, ed. Ellsworth Mason and Richard Ellmann, fwd. Guy Davenport (1959) (Ithaca, NY: Cornell University Press, 1989).

—, *Dubliners: Text, Criticism and Notes*, ed. Robert Scholes and A. Walton Litz (1969) (Harmondsworth: Penguin Books, 1996).

—, *Dubliners*, int. John Kelly (1914) (New York: Alfred A. Knopf Everyman's Library, 1991).

—, *Dubliners*, ed. Terence Brown (Harmondsworth: Penguin Books, 1992).

—, *Dubliners*, ed. Jeri Johnson (Oxford: Oxford University Press, 2000).

—, *Dubliners: A Facsimile of Drafts and Manuscripts*, ed. Hans Walter Gabler (New York and London: Garland, 1978).

—, *Dubliners: A Facsimile of Proofs for the 1910 Edition*, ed. Michael Groden (New York and London: Garland, 1977).

—, *Dubliners: A Facsimile of Proofs for the 1914 Edition*, ed. Michael Groden (New York and London: Garland, 1977).

—, *Finnegans Wake* (1939) (Harmondsworth: Penguin Books, 1976).

—, *Letters*, vol. I, ed. Stuart Gilbert (London: Faber and Faber, 1957).

—, *Letters*, vols. II and III, ed. Richard Ellmann (London: Faber and Faber, 1966).

—, *Occasional, Critical, and Political Writing*, ed. Kevin Barry (Oxford: Oxford University Press, 2000).

—, *Selected Letters*, ed. Richard Ellmann (London: Faber and Faber, 1975).

—, *Stephen Hero: Part of the First Draft of 'A Portrait of the Artist as a Young Man'*, ed. Theodore Spencer; rev. edn with additional material John J. Slocum and Herbert Cahoon (1944) (London: Paladin, 1991).

—, *Ulysses*, ed. Declan Kiberd (1922) (Harmondsworth: Penguin Books, 2000).

Other Works

Adams, Robert M., *Surface and Symbol: The Consistency of James Joyce's 'Ulysses'* (1962) (New York: Oxford University Press, 1967).

An Craoibhín Aoibhinn [Douglas Hyde], *Righ Seumas*, trans. Lady Gregory (n.pl.: n.p., n.d. [1904]).

Anonymous, 'Interview with Mr. John Stanislas Joyce (1849–1931)', in Maria Jolas (ed.), *A James Joyce Yearbook* (Paris: Transition Press, 1949), 159–69.

Atherton, James, *The Books at the Wake: A Study of Literary Allusions in James Joyce's 'Finnegans Wake'* (London: Faber and Faber, 1959).

Attridge, Derek (ed.), *The Cambridge Companion to James Joyce* (Cambridge: Cambridge University Press, 1990).

—, and Marjorie Howes (eds), *Semicolonial Joyce* (Cambridge: Cambridge University Press, 2000).

Barnard, Alfred, *The Whisky Distilleries of the United Kingdom*, int. Richard Joynson (1887) (Edinburgh: Birlinn, 2003).

Barnes, Djuna, *Vagaries Malicieux: Two Stories* (New York: Frank Hallman, 1974).

Barry, Kevin, *The Dead* (Cork: Cork University Press, 2001)

Beck, Warren, *Joyce's 'Dubliners': Substance, Vision, and Art* (Durham, NC: Duke University Press, 1969).

Beckett, Samuel, et al., *Our Exagmination round his Factification for Incamination of Work in Progress* (1929) (London: Faber and Faber, 1972).

Begnal, Michael (ed.), *Joyce and the City: The Significance of Place* (Syracuse, NY: Syracuse University Press, 2002).

Beiner, Guy, *Remembering the Year of the French: Irish Folk History and Social Memory* (Madison, WI: University of Wisconsin Press, 2007).

Blake-Forster, Charles fFrench, *The Irish Chieftains; or, A Struggle for the Crown: with numerous notes and a copious appendix* (Dublin: McGlashan and Gill, 1872).

Blunt, Wilfred Scawen, *The Land War in Ireland* (London: Swift, 1912).

Bollettieri Bosinelli, Rosa M., and Harold F. Mosher (eds), *ReJoycing: New Readings of 'Dubliners'* (Lexington, KY: University Press of Kentucky, 1998).

Bowen, Zack, *Musical Allusions in the Works of James Joyce: Early Poetry Through Ulysses* (Albany, NY: State University of New York Press, 1974).

Brown, Francis (ed.), *Opinions and Perspectives from the New York Times Book Review* (Boston: Houghton Mifflin, 1964).

Brown, Terence, 'Introduction', in James Joyce, *Dubliners* (Harmondsworth: Penguin Books, 1992), vii–xlix.

Budgen, Frank, *Further Recollections of James Joyce* (London: Shenval Press, 1955).

—, *James Joyce and the Making of 'Ulysses' and other writings*, int. Clive Hart (Oxford: Oxford University Press, 1972).

Bulson, Eric, *The Cambridge Introduction to James Joyce* (Cambridge: Cambridge University Press, 2006).

Buxton, Rachel, *Robert Frost and Northern Irish Poetry* (Oxford: Clarendon Press, 2004)

Clery, Arthur, *Dublin Essays* (Dublin and London: Maunsel, 1919).

Colum, Mary and Padraic, *Our Friend James Joyce* (London: Gollancz, 1959).

Concannon, Mrs Thomas [Helena], *The Poor Clares in Ireland (a.d. 1629–a.d.1929)* (Dublin: M. H. Gill and Son, 1929).

Connolly, Cyril, *The Condemned Playground: Essays: 1927–1944* (London: Routledge, 1945).

—, *Previous Convictions* (London: Hamish Hamilton, 1963), 271.

Costello, Peter, *James Joyce: The Years of Growth 1882–1915* (London: Kyle Cathie, 1992).

Cullen, Paul, 'Last of Nun's Island whiskey for €146,000', *Irish Times*, 13 August, 2005, 6.

Culleton, Claire A., *Names and Naming in Joyce* (Madison WI: University of Wisconsin Press, 1994).

Curran, C. P., *James Joyce Remembered* (New York and London: Oxford University Press, 1968).

Davis, Thomas, *The Patriot Parliament of 1689*, ed. Charles Gavan Duffy (London: T. Fisher Unwin, 1893).

—, *Prose Writings*, ed. T. W. Rolleston (London: Walter Scott, n.d. [1890]).

Davitt, Michael, *The Fall of Feudalism in Ireland, or the Story of the Land League Revolution* (London and New York: Harper and Brothers, 1904).

Dudley-Edwards, Owen, 'Who was Mac An Cheannuidhe? A Mystery of the Birth of the Aisling', *North Munster Antiquarian Journal*, xxxiii (1991), 55–77.

Duffy, Charles Gavan, *A Bird's-Eye View of Irish History, enlarged and carefully revised* (Dublin: James Duffy and Sons, 1882).

—, et al., *The Spirit of the Nation*, int. John Kelly (1845) (Poole and Washington DC: Woodstock Books, 1998).

—, George Sigerson and Douglas Hyde, *The Revival of Irish Literature* (London: T. Fisher Unwin, 1894).

Dunford, Stephen, in collaboration with Guy Beiner, *In Humbert's Footsteps: Mayo 1798* (n. pl.: Fadó Books, 2006).

Egan, Patrick K., *The Parish of Ballinasloe: In History from the Earliest Times to the Present Century* (1960) (Galway: Kenny Bookshops and Art Galleries, 1994).

Eliot, T. S., *The Sacred Wood: Essays on Poetry and Criticism* (1920) (London: Methuen, 1960).

Ellmann, Richard, *James Joyce* (Oxford: Oxford University Press, 1959).

—, *James Joyce* (Oxford: Oxford University Press, rev. edn, 1982).

—, *The Consciousness of Joyce* (London: Faber and Faber, 1977).

—, *Yeats and Joyce* (Dublin: Dolmen, 1967).

Evans, B. Ifor, 'Who, it may be asked, was Finnegan?', *Manchester Guardian*, 12 May 1939.

Fairhall, James, *James Joyce and the Question of History* (Cambridge: Cambridge University Press, 1993).

Foster, John Wilson, *Fictions of the Irish Literary Revival: A Changeling Art* (Syracuse,

NY: Syracuse University Press; Dublin: Gill and Macmillan, 1987).

Foster, R. F., *W. B. Yeats: A Life, I: The Apprentice Mage, 1865–1914* (Oxford: Oxford University Press, 1997).

—, *W. B. Yeats: A Life, II: The Arch-Poet 1915–1939* (Oxford: Oxford University Press, 2003)

Frawley, Oona (ed.), *A New and Complex Sensation: Essays on Joyce's 'Dubliners'* (Dublin: Lilliput Press, 2004).

Frazier, Adrian, *George Moore, 1852–1933* (New Haven, CT: Yale University Press, 2000).

Frost, Robert, *Collected Poems, Prose, and Plays*, ed. Richard Poirier and Mark Richardson (New York: Library of America, 1995).

Garrett, Peter K. (ed.), *Twentieth-Century Interpretations of 'Dubliners'* (Englewood Cliffs, NJ: Prentice Hall, 1968).

Garvin, John, *James Joyce's Disunited Kingdom and the Irish Dimension* (Dublin: Gill and Macmillan, 1976).

Geckle, George L., 'The Dead Lass of Aughrim', *Éire-Ireland*, IX.3 (Fomhar 1974), 86–96.

Gibson, Andrew, *James Joyce* (London: Reaktion Books, 2006).

—, *Joyce's Revenge: History, Politics, and Aesthetics in Ulysses* (Oxford: Oxford University Press, 2002).

—, and Len Platt (eds), *Joyce, Ireland, Britain* (Gainesville, FL: University Press of Florida, 2006).

Gifford, Don, *Joyce Annotated: Notes for 'Dubliners' and 'A Portrait of the Artist as a Young Man'* (Berkeley, CA: University of California Press, 2nd edn, 1982).

—, with Robert J. Seidman, *'Ulysses' Annotated: Notes for James Joyce's Ulysses* (Berkeley, CA: University of California Press, 2nd edn, revised and enlarged, 1989).

Gilbert, John T., *A History of the City of Dublin*, int. F. E. Dixon, index compiled by Diarmuid Breathnach, 3 vols (1854–59) (Dublin: Gill and Macmillan, 1978).

Gilbert, John T. (ed.), *A Jacobite Narrative of the War in Ireland, 1688–1691*, int. J. G. Simms (1892) (Shannon: Irish University Press, 1971).

Gillespie, Michael Patrick, and Erik Bradford Stocker, *James Joyce's Trieste Library: A Catalogue of Materials at the Harry Ransom Humanities Research Center, The University of Texas at Austin* (University of Texas at Austin: Harry Ransom Humanities Research Center, 1986).

Givens, Seon (ed.), *James Joyce: Two Decades of Criticism* (New York: Vanguard Press, 2nd edn, 1963).

Gordon, John, *Joyce and Reality: The Empirical Strikes Back* (Syracuse, NY: Syracuse University Press, 2004).

Gorman, Herbert S., *James Joyce: His First Forty Years* (London: Geoffrey Bles, 1926).

Gregory, Lady Augusta, *Poets and Dreamers: Studies and Translations from the Irish* (Dublin: Hodges, Figgis; London: John Murray, 1903).

—, *Selected Writings*, ed. Lucy McDiarmid and Maureen Waters (London: Penguin Books, 1995).

—, *The White Cockade* (Dublin: Maunsel, 1905).

Griffith, Arthur, *The Resurrection of Hungary: A Parallel for Ireland* (Dublin: James Duffy, 1904).

Groden, Michael (gen. ed.), Hans Walter Gabler, David Hayman, A. Walton Litz, Danis Rose (asst. eds), *The James Joyce Archive* (New York and London: Garland, 1977–8).

Hardiman, James, *The History of the Town and County of the Town of Galway, from the earliest period to the present time, Embellished with several Engravings. To which is added, a copious appendix, containing the principal charters and other original documents* (Dublin: W. Folds and Sons, 1820).

Harmon, Maurice (ed.), *The Celtic Master: Contributions to the first James Joyce Symposium held in Dublin, 1967* (Dublin: Dolmen, 1969).

Hart, Clive (ed.), *James Joyce's 'Dubliners': Critical Essays* (London: Faber and Faber, 1969).

Heaney, Seamus, *Finders Keepers: Selected Prose 1971–2001* (London: Faber and Faber, 2002).

Hill, Judith, *Lady Gregory: An Irish Life* (Stroud: Sutton Publishing, 2005).

Hofheinz, Thomas C., *Joyce and the Invention of Irish History: 'Finnegans Wake' in Context* (Cambridge: Cambridge University Press, 1995).

Hough, Jennifer, 'Bottle of rare Galway whiskey to reach €145,000: Historic Nuns' Island bottle turns up in UK whiskey shop', *Galway Advertiser*, 11 August 2005, 1–2.

Hyde, Douglas, *Abhráin atá Leagtha ar an Reachtúire. Songs Ascribed to Raftery, being the fifth chapter of 'The Songs of Connacht'*, int. Dominic Daly (1903) (Shannon: Irish University Press, 1973).

—, *Abhráin Grádh Chúige Connacht or Love Songs of Connacht (Being the Fourth Chapter of the "Songs of Connacht")*, now for the first time Collected, Edited, and Translated, fourth edition (Baile Átha Cliath: Clóbhuailte le Gill & a Mhac; London: T. Fisher Unwin, 1905).

Igoe, Vivien, *James Joyce's Dublin Houses and Nora Barnacle's Galway* (Dublin: Wolfhound Press, 1997).

Irvine, John, *Uisce Beatha: The Evolution & Archives of the Irish Whiskey Distilling Industry* (n. pl.: Irish Distillers, 1985).

Jackson, John Wyse, and Peter Costello, *John Stanislaus Joyce: The Voluminous Life and Genius of James Joyce's Father* (London: Fourth Estate, 1998).

Jackson, John Wyse, and Bernard McGinley, *James Joyce's 'Dubliners': An Annotated Edition* (London: Sinclair-Stevenson, 1993).

Jeffares, A. Norman, *A Commentary on the Collected Poems of W. B. Yeats* (London: Macmillan, 1968).

Jenkins, William, *Sir William Gregory of Coole* (Gerrards Cross: Colin Smythe, 1986).

Jolas, Maria (ed.), *A James Joyce Yearbook* (Paris: Transition Press, 1949).

Joyce, P. W., *The Origin and History of Irish Names of Places*, first series (Dublin:

McGlashan and Gill; London: Simpkin, Marshall; Edinburgh: John Menzies, 1875).

Joyce, Stanislaus, *My Brother's Keeper: James Joyce's Early Years*, ed. Richard Ellmann, preface T. S. Eliot (1958) (Cambridge, MA: Da Capo Press, 2003).

—, *The Complete Dublin Diary of Stanislaus Joyce*, ed. George Healey (Ithaca, NY: Cornell University Press, 1971).

—, *Recollections of James Joyce by His Brother*, trans. Ellsworth Mason (New York: The James Joyce Society, 1950).

Kelleher, John V., *Selected Writings of John V. Kelleher on Ireland and Irish America*, ed. Charles Fanning (Carbondale, IL: Southern Illinois University Press, 2002).

Kelly, John, 'Introduction', in James Joyce, *Dubliners* (London: Everyman, 1991).

Kiberd, Declan, *Ulysses and Us: The Art of Everyday Living* (London: Faber and Faber, 2009).

Kinsella, Thomas, *The Dual Tradition: An Essay on Poetry and Politics in Ireland* (Manchester: Carcanet, 1995).

Lyons, F. S. L., *Culture and Anarchy in Ireland 1890–1939* (Oxford: Clarendon Press, 1979).

—, and R. A. J. Hawkins (eds), *Ireland under the Union: Varieties of Tension* (Oxford: Clarendon Press, 1980).

Lyons, Mary Cecilia, *Illustrated Incumbered Estates Ireland, 1850–1905*, fwd. Hon. Desmond Guinness (Whitegate, County Clare: Ballinakella Press, 1993).

McBride, Ian (ed.), *History and Memory in Modern Ireland* (Cambridge: Cambridge University Press, 2001).

McCourt, John, *The Years of Bloom: James Joyce in Trieste 1904–1920* (Dublin: Lilliput Press, 2000).

MacDermott, Martin (ed.), *The New Spirit of the Nation; or, ballads and songs by the writers of 'The Nation'. Containing songs and ballads published since 1845* (London: T. Fisher Unwin; Dublin: Sealy, Bryers and Walker; New York: P. J. Kenedy, 1894).

McGuire, E. B., *Irish Whiskey: A History of Distilling, the Spirit Trade and Excise Controls in Ireland* (Dublin: Gill and Macmillan; New York: Barnes and Noble Books, 1973).

McHugh, Roland, *Annotations to 'Finnegans Wake'* (Baltimore, MD: Johns Hopkins University Press, rev. edn, 1991).

MacManus, Anna [Ethna Carbery], *The Four Winds of Eirinn*, ed. Seumas MacManus (Dublin: M. H. Gill and Son, 1902).

Maddox, Brenda, *Nora: A Biography of Nora Joyce* (1988) (Harmondsworth: Penguin Books, 2000).

Malcolm, Elizabeth, *"Ireland Sober, Ireland Free": Drink and Temperance in Nineteenth-century Ireland* (Dublin: Gill and Macmillan, 1986).

—, 'Temperance and Irish Nationalism', in F. S. L. Lyons and R. A. J. Hawkins (eds), *Ireland under the Union: Varieties of Tension* (Oxford: Clarendon Press, 1980), 69–114.

Maley, Willy, 'Spectres of Joyce: Memory and Mourning in "The Dead"', in Frank Brinkhuis (ed.), *Memory, History, and Critique* (Cambridge, MA: MIT, 1996).

Manganiello, Dominic, *Joyce's Politics* (London: Routledge and Kegan Paul, 1980).

Maxwell, W. H., *History of the Irish Rebellion in 1798; with memoirs of the Union and Emmet's insurrection in 1803* (1845) (London: George Bell and Sons, 1891).

Moore, George, *Parnell and His Island*, int. Carla King (1887) (Dublin: University College Dublin Press, 2004).

Moran, D. P., *Tom O'Kelly* (Dublin: Cahill, James Duffy, 1905).

Moran, Gerard, and Gillespie, Raymond (ed.), *Galway, History and Society: Interdisciplinary Essays of the History of an Irish County* (Dublin: Geography Publications, 1996).

Morewood, Samuel, *An Essay on the Inventions and Customs of Both Ancients and Moderns in the use of Inebriating Liquors. Interspersed with Interesting Anecdotes, illustrative of the manners and habits of the principal nations of the world. With an historical view of the extent and practice of distillation, both as it relates to commerce and as a source of national income: comprising much curious information respecting the application and properties of several parts of the vegetable kingdom* (London: Longman, Hurst, Rees, Orme, Brown and Green, 1824).

—, *A Philosophical and Statistical History of the Inventions and Customs of Ancient and Modern Nations in the manufacture and use of Inebriating Liquors; with the Present Practice of Distillation in all its varieties: together with an extensive illustration of the consumption and effects of opium, and other stimulants used in the east, as substitutes for wine and spirits* (Dublin: William Curry, Jun., and William Carson; London: Longman, Orme, Brown, Green, and Longmans; Edinburgh: Fraser, 1838).

Muldoon, Paul, *To Ireland, I* (Oxford: Oxford University Press, 2000).

Murphy, Daniel J. (ed.), *Lady Gregory's Journals, Volume Two, Books Thirty to Forty-Four, 21 February 1925–9 May 1932* (Gerrards Cross: Colin Smythe, 1987).

Murphy, Richard, *The Battle of Aughrim and The God Who Eats Corn* (London: Faber and Faber, 1968).

Nolan, Emer, *James Joyce and Nationalism* (London and New York: Routledge, 1995).

O'Brien, Celsus (ed.), *Recollections of an Irish Poor Clare in the Seventeenth Century: Mother Mary Bonaventura Browne, Third Abbess of Galway 1647–1650* (Galway: Connacht Tribune, n. d. [1993]).

O'Brien, Flann, *The Dalkey Archive* (London: Macgibbon and Kee, 1964).

O'Brien, Sylvester (ed.), *Poor Clare Ter-Centenary Record 1629–1929* (Galway: Published by the Editor, 1929).

Ó Ciardha, Éamonn, *Ireland and the Jacobite Cause, 1685–1766: A Fatal Attachment* (Dublin: Four Courts Press, 2nd edn, 2004).

O'Connor, Frank, 'Work in Progress', in Robert Scholes and A. Walton Litz (eds), *Dubliners: Text, Criticism and Notes* (Harmondsworth: Penguin Books, 1996), 292–303.

O'Connor, Ulick (ed.), *The Joyce we Knew* (Cork: Mercier Press, 1967).

O'Dea, Michael, and Kevin Whelan (eds), *Nations and Nationalisms: France, Britain, Ireland and the eighteenth-century context* (Oxford: Voltaire Foundation, 1995).

O'Dowd, Peadar, *Old and New Galway* (Galway: Connacht Tribune and the Archaeological, Historical and Folklore Society, Regional Technical College, Galway, 1985).

O'Farrell, Patrick, *England's Irish Question: Anglo-Irish Relations 1534–1970* (London: Batsford, 1970).

O'Flaherty, Roderic, *A Chorographical Description of West or H-Iar Connaught*, ed. James Hardiman (Dublin: M. H. Gill/Irish Archaeological Society, 1846).

O'Kelly, P., *General History of the Rebellion of 1798 with many interesting occurrences of the two preceding years. Also a brief account of the insurrection in 1803* (Dublin: J. Downes, 1842).

O'Laoi, Padraic, *Nora Barnacle Joyce: A Portrait* (Galway: Kennys Bookshops and Art Galleries, 1982).

Ó Luanaigh, Dónal, 'Ireland and the Franco-Prussian War', *Éire-Ireland: A Journal of Irish Studies*, IX.1 (Earrach 1974), 3–13.

Owens, Cóilín, *James Joyce's Painful Case*, fwd. Sebastian D. G. Knowles (Gainesville, FL: University Press of Florida, 2008).

—, '"Clay" (2): The Myth of Irish Sovereignty', *James Joyce Quarterly*, 27.3 (Spring 1990), 603–14.

—, 'The Mystique of the West in Joyce's "The Dead"', *Irish University Review: A Journal of Irish Studies*, 22.1 (Spring/Summer 1992), 80–91.

Paseta, Senia, '1798 in 1898: The Politics of Commemoration', *Irish Review*, 22 (Summer 1998), 46–53.

Paulin, Tom, *Crusoe's Secret: The Aesthetics of Dissent* (London: Faber and Faber, 2005).

Pethica, James L., and James C. Roy (eds), *'To the Land of the Free from this Island of Slaves': Henry Stratford Persse's Letters from Galway to America, 1821–1832* (Cork: Cork University Press, 1998).

Pierce, David, *James Joyce's Ireland* (New Haven, CT: Yale University Press, 1992).

Pittock, Murray G. H., *Poetry and Jacobite Politics in Eighteenth-Century Britain and Ireland* (Cambridge: Cambridge University Press, 1994).

Platt, Len, *Joyce and the Anglo-Irish: A Study of Joyce and the Literary Revival* (Amsterdam and Atlanta, GA: Rodopi, 1998).

Pomfret, John E., *The Struggle for Land in Ireland 1800–1923* (Princeton, NJ: Princeton University Press, 1930).

Poole, Robert, '"Give Us Our Eleven Days!": Calendar Reform in Eighteenth-Century England', *Past and Present*, 149 (November 1995), 95–139.

Potts, Willard, *Joyce and the Two Irelands* (Austin, TX: University of Texas Press, 2000).

Power, Arthur, *Conversations with James Joyce*, fwd. David Norris (1974) (Dublin: Lilliput Press, 1999).

Riquelme, John Paul, *Teller and Tale in Joyce's Fiction: Oscillating Perspectives* (Baltimore, MD: Johns Hopkins University Press, 1983).

Rooney, William, *Poems and Ballads*, ed. Arthur Griffith, int. Patrick Bradley (Dublin: The United Irishman, M. H. Gill and Son, O'Donoghue, n.d. [1902]).

—, *Prose Writings* (Dublin and Waterford: M. H. Gill and Son, n. d. [1902]).

Roos, Bonnie, 'James Joyce's "The Dead" and Bret Harte's *Gabriel Conroy*: The Nature of the Feast', *The Yale Journal of Criticism*, 15.1 (Spring 2002), 99–126.

Roy, James Charles, *The Fields of Athenry: A Journey Through Irish History* (Boulder, CO: Westview Press, 2001).

Ryan, John (ed.), *A Bash in the Tunnel: James Joyce by the Irish* (Brighton: Clifton Books, 1970).

Ryan, John Clement, *Irish Whiskey* (Dublin: Eason and Son, 1992).

Scholes, Robert, and Litz, A. Walton (eds), *Dubliners: Text, Criticism and Notes* (1969) (Harmondsworth: Penguin Books, 1996).

Shields, Hugh, 'The History of *The Lass of Aughrim*', in Gerard Gillen and Harry White (eds), *Irish Musical Studies 1: Musicology in Ireland* (Dublin: Irish Academic Press, 1990), 58–73.

Simms, J. G., *Jacobite Ireland, 1685–91* (1969) (Dublin: Four Courts Press, 2000).

Spoo, Robert, *James Joyce and the Language of History: Dedalus's Nightmare* (New York: Oxford University Press, 1994).

Tindall, William York, *A Reader's Guide to 'Finnegans Wake'* (1969) (Syracuse, NY: Syracuse University Press, 1996).

Tobin, Seán (ed.), *Lady Gregory Autumn Gatherings: Reflections at Coole* (Galway: Lady Gregory Autumn Gathering, 2000).

Todhunter, John, *The Life of Patrick Sarsfield, Earl of Lucan, with a short narrative of the principal events of the Jacobite war in Ireland* (London: T. Fisher Unwin; Dublin: Sealy, Bryars and Walker, 1895).

Tóibín, Colm, *Lady Gregory's Toothbrush* (London: Picador, 2003).

Torchiana, Donald T., *Backgrounds for Joyce's 'Dubliners'* (Boston: Allen and Unwin, 1986).

Townsend, Brian, *The Lost Distilleries of Ireland*, fwd. John Clement Ryan (Glasgow: Neil Wilson Publishing, 1997).

Tymoczko, Maria, *The Irish 'Ulysses'* (Berkeley, CA: University of California Press, 1994).

Tynan, Katharine, *Ballads and Lyrics* (London: Kegan Paul, Trench, Trübner, 1891).

—, *Book of Irish History* (Dublin and Belfast: The Educational Company of Ireland, n.d.).

—, *Collected Poems* (London: Macmillan, 1930).

—, *Louise de la Vallière and other poems* (London: Kegan Paul, Trench, 1885).

—, *Twenty One Poems*, selected by W. B. Yeats (Dundrum: Dun Emer Press, 1907).

Tynan Hinkson, Katharine, *Cuckoo Songs* (London: Elkin Mathews and John Lane; Boston: Copeland and Day, 1894).

Vaughan, W. E., *Landlords and Tenants in Mid-Victorian Ireland* (Oxford: Clarendon Press, 1996).

Walsh, Edward, *Irish Popular Songs; with English metrical translations, and introductory remarks and notes* (Dublin: James McGlashan; London: William S. Orr, 1847).

—, and John Daly, *Reliques of Irish Jacobite Poetry; with biographical sketches of the authors, interlinear literary translations, and historical illustrative notes* (Dublin: Samuel J. Machen, 1844).

Walsh, Maurice, 'Whiskey', *The Bell*, 2.5 (August 1941), 17–26.

Watson, G. J., *Irish Identity and the Literary Revival: Synge, Yeats, Joyce and O'Casey* (Washington DC: Catholic University of America Press, 2nd edn, 1994).

Whelan, Kevin, 'The Memories of "The Dead"', *Yale Journal of Criticism*, 15.1 (2002), 59–97.

Whelan, Yvonne, 'Monuments, Power and Contested Space – the iconography of Sackville Street (O'Connell Street) before Independence (1922)', *Irish Geography*, 34.1 (2001), 11–33.

—, 'Written in Space and Stone: Aspects of the Iconography of Dublin after Independence', in Howard B. Clarke, Jacinta Prunty and Mark Hennessy (eds), *Surveying Ireland's Past: Multidisciplinary Essays in Honour of Anngret Simms* (Dublin: Geography Publications, 2004), 585–612.

Wilson, Edmund, *Axel's Castle: A Study in the Imaginative Literature of 1870–1930* (1931) (New York: Charles Scribner's Sons, 1950).

Witt, Marion, 'A Note on Joyce and Yeats', *Modern Language Notes*, 63 (November 1948), 552–3.

Yeats, W. B., *Autobiographies*, ed. William H. O'Donnell and Douglas N. Archibald (New York: Scribner, 1999).

—, *A Book of Irish Verse*, int. John Banville (1895) (London: Routledge, 2002).

—, *Cathleen Ni Hoolihan* (Dublin: A. H. Bullen, 1902).

—, *The Collected Letters, vol. I: 1865–1895*, ed. John Kelly and Eric Domville (Oxford: Oxford University Press, 1986).

—, *Essays and Introductions* (New York: The Macmillan Company, 1961).

—, *Ideas of Good and Evil* (1903) (Dublin: Maunsel, 2nd edn, 1905).

—, *The Letters*, ed. Allan Wade (London: Rupert Hart-Davis, 1954).

—, *Mythologies* (New York: The Macmillan Company, 1959).

—, *On the Boiler* (Dublin: Cuala Press, n.d. [1938]).

— (ed.), *Poems and Ballads of Young Ireland 1888* (Dublin: M. H. Gill and Son, 1888).

—, *The Poems*, ed. Daniel Albright (London: Everyman, 1994).

—, *The Tables of the Law and The Adoration of the Magi* (London: Elkin Mathews, Vigo Street, 1904).

—, *Uncollected Prose 2: Reviews, Articles and Other Miscellaneous Prose 1897–1939*, ed. John P. Frayne and Colton Johnson (New York: Columbia University Press, 1976).

Index